GENDER AND MIGRATION IN ITALY

Elisa Olivito's book is a multidimensional contribution to the constantly growing literature on gender and migration. It explores the complexities and controversies of the Italian migration context and policies of 'Open houses versus closed borders', where immigrant women, these 'forerunners' of Italian immigration, remain confined to domestic work.

Mirjana Morokvasic, ISP-CNRS-Université Paris Ouest, France

An amazing collection which sheds light on a multifaceted social reality that Italian observers too often ignore or approach with a gender-neutral gaze. Feminism, history, law and semiotics all contribute to unveil the universe of migrant women in Italy, at the same time offering an extraordinary picture of Italian society and institutional settings. A must-read!

Maria Rosaria Marella, University of Perugia, Italy

This stimulating and multi-voiced collection is an indispensable reader for scholars and students alike, in discursive fields as diverse as law, social sciences and gender studies. Passionately committed to uncovering and reinventing the themes of gender and migration, the authors measure the complex interplay between citizenship, access to power and resources and fundamental rights in the Italian context. This rich and multidisciplinary journey takes the reader to unfamiliar territories, using a whole range of directions to approach the subject. Be prepared to lose your way and find a new path to get back home!

Pascale Fournier, University of Ottawa, Canada

Law and Migration

Series Editor
Satvinder S. Juss, King's College London, UK

Migration and its subsets of refugee and asylum policy are rising up the policy agenda at national and international level. Current controversies underline the need for rational and informed debate of this widely misrepresented and little understood area.

Law and Migration contributes to this debate by establishing a monograph series to encourage discussion and help to inform policy in this area. The series provides a forum for leading new research principally from the Law and Legal Studies area but also from related social sciences. The series is broad in scope, covering a wide range of subjects and perspectives.

Other titles in this series:

Towards a Refugee Oriented Right of Asylum
Laura Westra, Satvinder Juss and Tullio Scovazzi
978-1-4724-5778-3

The Integration and Protection of Immigrants
Canadian and Scandinavian Critiques
Edited by Paul Van Aerschot and Patricia Daenzer
978-1-4724-3654-2

Asylum – A Right Denied
A Critical Analysis of European Asylum Policy
Helen O'Nions
978-1-4094-0409-5

Regional Approaches to the Protection of Asylum Seekers
An International Legal Perspective
Edited by Ademola Abass and Francesca Ippolito
978-1-4094-4297-4

Immigration, Integration and the Law
The Intersection of Domestic, EU and International Legal Regimes
Clíodhna Murphy
978-1-4094-6251-4

Gender and Migration in Italy

A Multilayered Perspective

Edited by

ELISA OLIVITO
University of Rome 'La Sapienza', Italy

Routledge
Taylor & Francis Group
LONDON AND NEW YORK

First published 2016 by Ashgate Publishing

2 Park Square, Milton Park, Abingdon, Oxfordshire OX14 4RN
52 Vanderbilt Avenue, New York, NY 10017

Routledge is an imprint of the Taylor & Francis Group, an informa business

First issued in paperback 2020

British Library Cataloguing in Publication Data
A catalogue record for this book is available from the British Library

The Library of Congress has cataloged the printed edition as follows:
Olivito, Elisa, author.
Gender and migration in Italy : a multilayered perspective / by Elisa Olivito.
pages cm -- (Law and migration)
Includes bibliographical references and index.
ISBN 978-1-4724-5575-8 (hardback)
1. Foreign workers--Legal status, laws, etc.--Italy. 2. Women migrant labor--Italy. I. Title.
KKH1328.A44O45 2015
304.80945--dc23

2015021231

ISBN 978-1-4724-5575-8 (hbk)
ISBN 978-0-367-59745-0 (pbk)

Contents

List of Figures *vii*
Notes on Contributors *ix*
Acknowledgements *xiii*

Introduction: Fortress Europe v. Compliant Italy? The Ambiguous Italian Policy towards Migrant Women 1
Elisa Olivito

PART I: MIGRANT WOMEN AND SOCIAL MOBILITY IN A HISTORICAL PERSPECTIVE

1 The 'Worker Nuns of Nigrizia': The Pious Mothers of *Nigrizia* between Italy and Africa during the Imperial Age (1872–1950) 21
Francesca Di Pasquale and Chiara Giorgi

2 Open Houses versus Closed Borders: Migrant Domestic Workers in Italy. A Gendered Perspective (1950s–2010s) 39
Raffaella Sarti

PART II: SELF-DETERMINATION, FAMILY AND WELFARE

3 The Third Movement: Family Life for a Fee 63
Silvia Niccolai

4 Autonomy and Self-Realization of Migrant Women: Constitutional Aspects 77
Laura Ronchetti

5 The Case of Healthcare and Social Services for Migrant Women: Between Anti-Discrimination and Anti-Subordination 97
Anna Lorenzetti

6 Migration and (Legal) Irritants: Italian Family Law and Gender Equality 119
Elisa Olivito

PART III: CULTURE, PATRIARCHY AND RELIGION

7 Gender and Culturally Motivated Crimes:
The Italian Perspective 143
Valentina Masarone

8 From Culture to Patriarchy: Recent Changes in
Judicial Reasoning and in Normative Classifications of
Multicultural Conflicts 161
Ilenia Ruggiu

9 Gender and Religious Symbols in the European Public Sphere:
Unveiling the Paradoxes of Italian Toleration 177
Susanna Mancini

PART IV: CITIZENSHIP AND SECOND-GENERATION MIGRANT WOMEN

10 Second-Generation Migrant Women and the Acquisition of
Italian Citizenship 195
Elena Paparella

11 Translating Cultural Identities, Permeating Boundaries:
Autobiographical and Testimonial Narratives of
Second-Generation Immigrant Women 215
Cristina Greco

Index *231*

List of Figures

2.1 Domestic workers registered with Inps, Italy 1991–2013 41
2.2 Housewives and economically active women, Italy 1951–2001 46
2.3 Life expectancy at birth, Italy 1961–2011 47
2.4 Foreign carers and domestic workers enrolled with Inps according to their origin (percentages) 1991–2012 50

Notes on Contributors

Francesca Di Pasquale is a post-doctoral researcher at NIOD, Institute for War and Genocide Studies (Amsterdam) within the 'Four Centuries of Labour Camps' project. Her research analyses the emergence of labour camps in Italy and its former colonies from Italian unification to the Second World War. From 2008 to 2011, she was tasked with leading a scientific project aimed at the recovery and enhancement of the Libyan Historical Archive at the Centre of National Archives and Historical Studies (Tripoli, Libya).

Chiara Giorgi is Assistant Professor at the Department of Political Science, University of Genoa, where she teaches History of Political Institutions. She has been a visiting professor at the University of Connecticut and is a member of the board of the journal *Parole Chiave* (Carocci), a member of the scientific committee of Società per gli studi di Storia delle Istituzioni, a member of the board of the journal *Le Carte e la Storia* (Il Mulino) and a member of the history section of Fondazione Lelio e Lisli Basso (Rome). Her research interests are colonialism administration and the civil service of Italian colonialism, the Italian welfare state in a historical perspective, the history of socialism and the history of women and gender.

Cristina Greco holds a PhD in Communication earned at the University of Rome 'La Sapienza'. She is a member of the research group in semiotics, supervised by Isabella Pezzini; within this group, she takes a special interest in studies on the graphic novel, urban art and cultural memory. She is currently conducting a research effort on behalf of an Italian trade union about intercultural spaces and the autobiographical and testimonial narration of immigrants in Italy.

Anna Lorenzetti is a Research Fellow in Constitutional Law and a temporary lecturer in Gender Analysis and Anti-discrimination Law at the University of Bergamo (Law Department). She holds a PhD in European Public and Tax Law from the University of Bergamo. Her research interests are European anti-discrimination law and equality, gender and the law, LGBTI rights and social rights. She has published extensively in those areas, including the volume *Diritti in Transito* on the legal condition of transgender people. She is a member of the Research Centre Politesse Politics and Theories of Sexuality at the University of Verona and a member of the editorial board of *Diritto Pubblico comparato ed europeo* and of articolo29.it.

Susanna Mancini (PhD, European University Institute) is Professor of Law at the University of Bologna School of Law and an adjunct professor at the Paul H. Nitze School of Advanced International Studies at Johns Hopkins University. She has served as visiting professor at the Central European University (Budapest), the Cardozo School of Law (NYC), the Fordham School of Law (NYC), the Interdisciplinary Center (Israel) and the University of Toulouse. She has written widely on comparative constitutional law, and specifically on law and religion, federalism and secession, multiculturalism, minority rights, citizenship, reproductive rights, and gender and the law. Her latest publication is *Constitutional Secularism in an Age of Religious Revival* (co-edited with M. Rosenfeld) (Oxford University Press, 2014).

Valentina Masarone (PhD, University of Naples) is Associate Professor of Criminal Law and a member of the teaching committee at the Department of Law, University of Naples 'Federico II'. She spent several research periods at the Institut für die gesamten Strafrechtwissenschaften at Ludwig Maximilian University of Munich (Germany) and is a member of the editorial staff of the legal review *Critica del diritto*. She holds a course for undergraduate students in European and International Criminal Law at the Department of Law, University of Naples 'Federico II'.

Silvia Niccolai is Full Professor of Constitutional Law and former Jean Monnet Chair of European Law (2006–2011) at the University of Cagliari, Italy. Her research focuses on equality and anti-discrimination. With Ilenia Ruggiu, she edited *Dignity in Change: Exploring the Constitutional Potential of EU Gender and Anti-Discrimination Law* (Epap, Fiesole, 2010). She also authored, with A. Stewart and C. Hoskyns, *Disability Discrimination by Association. A Case of the Double Yes?* (in *Social & Legal Studies*, 2/2011).

Elisa Olivito (PhD, University of Perugia) is Associate Professor of Public Law at the University of Rome 'La Sapienza' Faculty of Law, where she teaches Constitutional Justice. She has been a visiting researcher at the University of Toronto Faculty of Law, at Harvard Law School and at the Universidad del Cuyo of Mendoza (Argentina). A former editor-in-chief of the Italian Constitutional Association online review www.rivistaic.it, she is a member of the editorial staff of *Democrazia e diritto* and of the online review www.costituzionalismo.it. She has written on affirmative action policy and gender issues, migration and multiculturalism, secularism and religious symbols, legal fictions, environmental rights and participatory democracy, housing rights.

Elena Paparella (PhD, University of Rome 'La Sapienza') is Assistant Professor in Public Law at the Faculty of Economics, University of Rome 'La Sapienza', where she teaches Public Law, Public Law and Economics, Constitutional Law of Economics and Environment, and Advanced Law and Economics. She was a visiting scholar at the Max-Planck-Institut für ausländisches öffentliches Recht und Völkerrecht in Heidelberg. She has written on labour, constitutional law, social rights, immigration and second-generation rights, the right to education for disabled people, the economic-financial crisis in the Eurozone, and the role of the European Central Bank.

Laura Ronchetti is a Researcher in Constitutional Law at the Institute for the Study of Regionalism, Federalism and Self-Government (National Research Council-CNR, Rome). She is leading the research group of the CNR Migration Project (2009–2014). She is member of the Italian National Contact Point of the European Migration Network (2014–2015). She has also carried out research on political, sexual and reproductive rights and on multiculturalism. She has being visiting scholar at the following universities: the Indiana University School of Law (Bloomington, USA), Columbia Law School (New York, USA) and Humboldt-Universität (Berlin, Germany). She also worked at the Department for Equal Opportunities of the Italian Government (1996–2001) and participated at the UN's 'Beijing + 5' Assembly in New York in 2000.

Ilenia Ruggiu, PhD, is Associate Professor at the Department of Jurisprudence, University of Cagliari, where she teaches Constitutional Law and is Director of the master's degree programme on 'The Multilevel Governance'. Her research interests are federalism, multiculturalism, legal anthropology, comparative method and gender studies. She is currently working on a book on "Patriarchy and the Law". She has being visiting scholar in several European and North-American Universities including California-Berkeley, Southern California, Georgetown, Victoria BC, Glasgow, Edinburgh, Seville. Her more recent publication is: 'Is begging a Roma cultural practice? Answers from the Italian law and Anthropology', forthcoming in *Romani Studies* (June, 2016).

Raffaella Sarti teaches Early Modern History and Gender History at the University of Urbino, Italy, and has worked in Paris, Vienna, Bologna and Murcia. Her main research field is the history of domestic service and care work. She was a promoter of the Servant Project, funded by the European Commission. She collaborates with ACLI-COLF, the leading Italian organization of domestic workers. She is the author of about 100 publications in several languages on domestic service and care work, slavery in the Mediterranean, marriage and celibacy, the family and material culture, graffiti and wall writings, and gender and the nation. Her publications in English include *Europe at Home. Family and Material Culture 1500–1800* (New Haven, London: Yale University Press, 2002), *Proceedings of the Servant Project* (ed.) with I. Schopp and S. Pasleau (Liège: Éditions de l'Université de Liège, 2005), *Men in a Woman's Job: Male Domestic Workers, International Migration and the Globalization of Care*, special issue of Men and Masculinities (2010) (ed.) with F. Scrinzi.

Acknowledgements

As editor, my thanks go first to my colleagues who took part in this publication, both for their enthusiastic support and for their contributions.

This book is part of the research project *Migration and cultural claims in the Italian experience: migrant women in multicultural encounters*, financed by Università di Roma 'La Sapienza' with organizational support from Dipartimento di Scienze giuridiche at the Faculty of Law. I thus thank the University and the Department for their support.

I would also like to thank Professor Satvinder S. Juss (King's College London, School of Law, UK) for having believed in the publishing project right from the start and for having included it in *Law and Migration*, the Ashgate book series he directs.

Special thanks are extended to Alison Kirk (Publisher for Law and Legal Studies at Ashgate Publishing), who supported and attentively followed the book from the very beginning.

Lastly, I would like to express my gratitude to Professors Gaetano Azzariti and Giorgio Repetto for having followed the book's publication with their valuable thoughts and suggestions.

Introduction
Fortress Europe v. Compliant Italy? The Ambiguous Italian Policy towards Migrant Women

Elisa Olivito

Italian Trends in Migration Law and Policies

Migratory flows to Europe have brought about considerable changes in the affected countries. Endless doctrinal discussions have thus ensued on the reception and integration strategies each of these countries has adopted and on the 'models' of regulation and immigration policy that may be inferred from national experiences. However, this race to find sound analysis tools has often led to facile oversimplifications, and the experiences of legal systems which do not lend themselves well to simplistic categorization have often been neglected. This attitude has resulted, for example, in the scant – or stereotyped – attention given to the Italian setting and in the consequent difficulty of grasping some of its most important traits. And yet, Italy offers a particularly interesting point of view, from which one may observe not only the particular way that migration has changed (or intensified) some features of the country, but also how the problems it has given rise to have been intertwined with those of gender relations.

The unique nature of the Italian migratory context may be understood first by considering both the type of immigration that has affected the country and the consequent measures adopted by the Government.[1] From both standpoints a variety of distinctive elements, certainly of use for better-grasping the book's theme and structure, may be glimpsed.

Over the past 40 years, Italy has seen a major trend reversal as it has been transformed from a country of emigration into one of immigration (Castles, de Haas

1 According to a report of the Organisation for Economic Co-operation and Development (OECD) commissioned by CNEL (Consiglio nazionale dell'Economia e del Lavoro – National Council for Economics and Labour), in comparison with other countries, Italy's situation is unique from many standpoints: the volume and features of the immigrant population; the frequency of flows; the system of residence permits and regularization procedures; the employment rates; the qualifications and skills of immigrants and their children; and the integration policies and their implementation on national territory (OECD, 2014).

and Miller, 2014: 113). In cultural, economic and social terms, this has resulted in major changes in Italian society, requiring public institutions to provide an appropriate response to the transformations taking place. Over the years, the phenomenon has taken on the characteristics of the so-called 'Mediterranean immigration model', distinguished from longer-standing immigration towards other European countries given the special social, economic and demographic features of the countries of southern Europe (Germani, 2001). Migration towards Italy actually began to take on importance only in the early 1970s, at a time when other European countries were gradually starting to close their borders and large-scale legal immigration thus had to cope with increasingly restrictive regulations (Colombo and Sciortino, 2004: 53). For Italy, this meant an inextricable intertwining of economics, irregular work and irregular (or 'clandestine') immigration (Mingione and Quassoli, 2000), aggravated both by the initial lack of migration laws and policies and by the continued reliance on forms of *ex post* regularization of migrants already present in the country (Pugliese, 2011). They chiefly entered the sectors of seasonal farm work and services, with migrant women in particular being absorbed by the Italian family's growing demand for domestic and care services. Therefore, the arrival of women with their own independent migration plan was another unique element on the Italian migration landscape, taking shape at a time when the welfare system and gender relations were headed towards a slow but inexorable process of change (King and Zontini, 2000).

Nevertheless, only in the second half of the 1980s – and as a consequence of more intensified and complex waves of migration – did Italian lawmakers begin to adopt provisions in this area, in a steady crescendo of repressive and derogatory measures and with a view more to the problems of public security than to the migrants' needs and living conditions. Moreover, the first actions took place only when it had become clear that the *Belpaese* was now the destination of an immigration highly diversified in its geographical origin and socio-demographic features, which thought of Italy not only as a country of transit towards northern Europe, but as one of stable residence as well. Despite this, the initial approach to the phenomenon was entirely partial and fragmentary and was dealt with by the approval of a law (Law no. 943/1986, known as the 'Foschi Law') that concentrated only on certain aspects. Law no. 943/1986 chose a focus based strictly on labour law, resting upon three elements: a) granting rights only to 'non-EU' workers legally residing in the territory (article 1); b) the prior encounter between domestic labour demand and foreign labour supply, 'upon ascertaining the lack of Italian and EU workers' (article 8); c) the regularization, through amnesty, of non-EU nationals (irregularly employed or seeking employment) who, by no later than three months after the law entered force, had demonstrated that, on the date of the law's promulgation, they had been residing in Italy or were living there on any grounds (article 16).[2] Moreover, Law no. 943 appropriated a terminology

2 The first regularization was ordered by two Circulars from the Ministry of Labour on 2 March and 9 September 1982.

already established in common speech, in which the expression *extracomunitari* referred to migrants originating from countries outside the European Economic Community (Schierup, Hansen and Castles, 2006: 164).

The first attempt at systemically regulating the issue came a few years later with Law no. 39/1990 (the 'Martelli Law'), which, following a further increase in the migratory flow towards Italy, converted a new amnesty provision into law (Decree Law no. 416/1989). On that occasion, migrants were given some fundamental rights and the laws on granting political asylum were changed. Moreover, the entry and stay of non-EU nationals were more comprehensively regulated, with the establishment of entry visas for reasons other than work (such as, for example, tourism, study, medical care and religion) and the introduction of administrative measures for undocumented migrants (that is, expulsion and escort to the border). An even more important new feature was the planning of incoming flows for reasons of work; indeed, the number of entries of legal immigrants was established every year by inter-ministerial decree, based on the needs of the national economy, the financial resources for receiving the immigrants and the presence of non-EU workers on the territory. Lastly, in line with prior provisions, Law no. 39/1990 also introduced an amnesty for non-EU nationals already present in Italy, ordering the regularization of whoever could confirm having entered Italy prior to 31 December 1989 (and thus regardless of whether or not there was an existing labour relationship). However, this amnesty – like the ones that followed it – was availed of only minimally by foreign nationals who had entered Italian territory legally but whose residence permits had since expired. Instead, regularization applications were submitted mostly by those foreign nationals who, thanks precisely to the amnesty, had managed to obtain their first residence permit (UNAR, 2013: 127 ff). This set off a vicious circle of stopgap measures, demand for irregular work and illegal immigration.

The Martelli Law soon showed numerous shortcomings and there were several attempts to introduce more restrictive immigration legislation. After a series of additional regularization provisions[3] and some judgments of the Constitutional Court in the matter of migrants' rights, that law was in the end replaced by Law no. 40/1998 (the 'Turco-Napolitano Law'), later incorporated into Legislative Decree no. 286/1998 ('Consolidated Act of Provisions concerning immigration and the condition of third country nationals').[4] Given impetus also by the European Union's progressively expanding purview in the matter of visas, asylum and immigration, these measures finally introduced a systematic framework, containing provisions on entry and stay, refoulement, the right to family unity and social rights. This marked the definitive acknowledgement of the structural (yet rapidly changing)

3 Particularly significant was Decree Law no. 489/1995 ('Dini Decree'), which, however, lapsed because, after a series of reiterations, it was not converted into law. The legal effects arising from the regularization were then safeguarded with Law no. 617/1996.

4 Approval of the Consolidation Act was then followed by yet another regularization, ordered with the Decree of the President of the Council of Ministers of 16 October 1998.

nature of the migration phenomenon and the consequent awareness of the need to prepare ordinary yet flexible planning instruments. The new legislation was aimed at pursuing the following goals: limiting and regulating entries, first of all through the three-year planning of entry flows for work and the establishment of yearly entry quotas;[5] combating illegal immigration, also through more restrictive and repressive laws regarding the expulsion and refoulement of irregular migrants;[6] preparing instruments for the integration and inclusion of (regular) migrants through the recognition of rights and duties, access to social services and the educational system, and the promotion of interculturality (*interculturalità*).[7]

The containment of immigration and, above all, the binary logic of regular/irregular immigration, were later confirmed and further aggravated by Law no. 189/2002 (the 'Bossi-Fini Law'), which emended the Consolidation Act of 1998. In particular, this measure's approval fully confirmed the three paradoxes of Italian migration policies.

> The first is the relative continuity of immigration policies, regardless of changes of government, and despite the fact that attitudes to immigration are a characteristic feature and a source of bitter conflict between the competing coalitions … . The second paradox is that the main difference between centre-left and centre-right in Italy relates far more to proclaimed strategies and values than to legislation; hence hardcore concepts of immigration and core beliefs are not reflected in the area of operational aspects and policies, which are normally considered more malleable and changeable … . The third paradox, connected with the first two, is that in both the governing coalitions – centre-left and centre-right – there is a discrepancy between public rhetoric and public action regarding illegal immigration. Although policy paradigms diverge, at least in the case of the major parties in the two political alliances, they agree on one point: they condemn clandestine and illegal immigration, and both coalitions have adopted special measures to combat it. However, centre-left governments introduced, and

5 The previous system, in which the entry of non-EU workers depended on the non-availability of other Italian or foreign workers already entered on the lists of jobseekers, was essentially abandoned.

6 In particular, Law no. 40/1998 introduced the detention of migrants awaiting expulsion in centres for temporary permanence and assistance (*Centri di permanenza temporanea e di assistenza* – CPTA), later renamed in 2008 centres for the identification and expulsion of migrants (*Centri di identificazione e di espulsione* – CIE). See Bascherini, 2012: 2.

7 From the standpoint of the migrants' 'integration', Italy has also aimed to depart from the so-called 'integration models' adopted in other European legal systems and often reductively referred to as the 'assimilationist model' (France), the 'multiculturalist model' (United Kingdom, Canada) and the ethnic-national model (Germany): see Bertossi and Duyvendak, 2012. However, as the chapters of this volume will show, Italy's choice of a hybrid integration 'model' is not without obvious contradictions and attitudes that are often pluralistic solely in utilitarian terms.

> centre-right governments have maintained, a basic welfare system (comprising most public health and education services) for undocumented immigrants, and both have introduced mass regularisation schemes. In particular, the largest regularisation ever performed in Europe was approved by the second Berlusconi government. (Zincone, 2006: 347–8)

Albeit in relative continuity with earlier legislative measures, the Bossi-Fini Law nevertheless brought the result of harshening the measures on the expulsion of foreign nationals and their detention in special detention centres, while on the other hand strengthening the linkage between entering/staying in the territory and carrying out/maintaining a working activity. From the former standpoint, entry quotas were lowered, particularly for states reluctant to cooperate in the struggle against illegal immigration (or to readmit their citizens subject to repatriation), and the period of the foreign national's detention in those centres was extended. As regards labour immigration, the possibility of regular entry for this reason was considerably limited and hampered. Issuance of the residence permit was first of all subject to the signing of a 'residence contract' between the employer and the non-EU national, with the employer taking on responsibility for the worker's accommodation as well as for paying the expenses for his or her re-entry in the country of origin upon the contract's expiry. To establish an employment relationship, a perverse mechanism was introduced (*chiamata nominativa o numerica*, or 'name and number hiring'), allowing foreign nationals to obtain entry visas provided that, prior to their departure, there was an employer committed to hiring them.[8] Moreover, for foreign nationals losing their jobs, the period of registration in the lists of jobseekers (and their stay in Italian territory) was reduced from one year to six months,[9] while authorization for the entry of new foreign workers once again required prior verification of the non-availability of other Italian or EU workers. On this occasion as well, the overall harshening of immigration laws was accompanied by another amnesty, reserved first for workers employed in the domestic and care sector (article 33, Law no. 189/2002) and then extended to dependent workers involved in other kinds of subordinate employment.[10]

---

8 Moreover, the actual encounter between foreign labour supply and demand was made even more difficult by the abolition of what was termed *sponsorizzazione* (sponsorship). Article 23 of the Consolidation Act of 1998 had in fact established that an Italian citizen or a regularly resident alien could sponsor the entry of a foreign national to allow him or her to enter the labour market. The applicant had to demonstrate being able to ensure the foreigner's housing, livelihood and healthcare for the entire duration of the stay. The entry authorization then allowed the foreign national, upon inclusion in the lists of jobseekers, to obtain a yearly residence permit for the purpose of entry into the labour market.

9 Art. 4, paragraph 30, of Law no. 92/2012 has now restored the former term (one year).

10 The operating range regularization was expanded by Decree Law no. 195/2002, converted with amendments into Law no. 192/2002.

Subsequently, as the position of regular migrants grew gradually more precarious, and above all as irregular migrants were criminalized, the years 2008 and 2009 saw the adoption of the so-called 'security packages' – a formula indicating a series of repressive measures taken by the fourth Berlusconi government in pursuit of the protection of public security and the 'struggle against clandestinity' (illegal entry and residence). Through a symbolic and propagandistic use of criminal law, Law no. 125/2008 – included in the first package[11] – introduced into the criminal code the so-called 'aggravating circumstance of clandestinity', according to which crimes committed by foreign nationals irregularly present in Italy would to be subject to punishment increased by up to one third in comparison with the same crime committed by an Italian citizen or by a regularly resident alien. In the second security package, Law no. 94/2009 introduced the 'crime of clandestinity' – the crime of illegal entry and residence in the state's territory – as well as that of refusal to comply with a removal order issued for illegal entry into national territory.[12] In addition to an overall harshening of the detention and expulsion measures, Law no. 94/2009 lengthened the period of legal residence needed to apply for Italian citizenship, in the case of marriage with an Italian citizen, from six months to two years.[13] Moreover, in the matter of integration, an Italian language test had to be passed in order to be issued an EU long-term residence permit and, when submitting the residence permit application, it became mandatory to sign an 'Integration Agreement' based on a system of credits: loss of all the credit points was to result in revocation of the residence permit and expulsion.

However, the public security wave in Italian migration policies did not keep two new amnesty measures – one in 2009 and the other in 2012 – from being introduced. Thus, the trend in Italian migration policies – on the one hand narrowing the channels of regular entry by intermittently regulating migration

11 This was the conversion into law, with amendments, of Decree Law no. 92/2008, containing urgent measures on public security.

12 In this regard, it bears mentioning, however, that the Constitutional Court declared the aggravating circumstance of clandestinity unconstitutional (judgment no. 249/2010), while dismissing the question of the constitutionality of the crime of clandestinity, holding that it was a matter of choice falling within the sphere of legislative discretion (judgment no. 250/2010). On the other hand, the provision establishing the crime of failure to comply with the removal order was first declared unconstitutional by the Constitutional Court, in the part where it did not order the conduct to be punished only in the absence of justification (judgment no. 359/2010); then, after a judgment by the Court of Justice (*El Dridi* judgment, C-61/11/PPU, 28 April 2011), it was amended, with punishment by detention being replaced by a fine. Lastly, Law no. 67/2014 delegated the Government to transform into an administrative offence the crime of illegal entry into national territory.

13 The law had also established, for foreign nationals intending to marry in Italy, the obligation of presenting to the civil registrar, in addition to the approval issued by the competent authority in their own country, 'a document attesting to the regularity of their stay' (article 1, paragraph 15). However, the Constitutional Court, with judgment no. 245/2011, declared the provision unconstitutional.

flows, while on the other hand resorting to *ex post* proceedings for migrants that had entered the country illegally – was further consolidated. Entirely unique was the regularization ordered with Decree Law no. 78/2009,[14] because it was reserved solely for workers employed in the domestic labour and care sector. At a time when the economic crisis had already begun, the decision was in fact taken to open a small window solely for those workers who responded to the country's productive, employment and welfare needs. The year 2012 then saw the introduction of Legislative Decree no. 109 which, in implementing Directive 2009/52/EC (Minimum standards on sanctions and measures against employers of illegally staying third-country nationals) with a transitional provision, allowed employers to regularize the position of non-EU nationals without valid residence permits (or with expired permits), employed full-time for at least three months or as domestic workers with a commitment of no less than 20 hours a week (article 5).

Italian Gender Relationships and the (Ambivalent) Control of Female Migration

Although brief, the analysis of Italian policies and legislation in the matter of immigration is an essential step for comprehending the special ways in which the Italian migratory landscape is intertwined with gender issues. Over the years, Italy has adopted a decidedly ambiguous approach towards women's immigration, affected strongly by significant changes in gender relations. Similarly to other southern European countries, it was the arrival of many migrant women which turned Italy from a country of emigration to one of immigration. Already in the early 1970s, the strictly male migratory flows originating from North Africa were joined by women from the Philippines, Cape Verde and South America (Favaro and Tognetti Bordogna, 1991). Over the years, the female presence grew constantly as a result of family reunification processes (Tognetti Bordogna, 2004: 164 ff). Moreover, there are several reasons why women's immigration has been so fragmentary, in terms both of geographical origin and of migration plan: this has depended in part on the economic, socio-cultural and demographic features of the migrant women's countries of origin. But to a great degree it has stemmed from transformations in Italian society, anomalies in the domestic labour market and more general trends in transnational migration processes (King and Andall, 1999: 144). For this reason, although two types of women's immigration – one following the male component and the other independent – may also be seen for Italy, it is essential to avoid facile simplifications, because '[i]ndividual situations are frequently more complex than this' (King and Zontini, 2000: 37).

As is known, after several years of little attention paid to the features and problems of women's migration, starting in the 1980s some pioneering works gave rise to 'gender and migration studies'. In particular, the leading researches

14 Converted with amendments by Law no. 102/2009.

by Annie Phizacklea (1983) and Mirjana Morokvasic (1984) lifted the veil on the importance of the 'gender' factor in migration processes, opening the way for increasingly numerous and often multidisciplinary contributions on the issue. The various elements capable of casting light on how and to what degree gender affects migratory phenomena, as well as on the problems impacting migrant women most directly, have thus become the subject of analysis. In particular, to assess how gender and migration are intertwined, influencing the host country's socioeconomic and structural dynamics, consideration was made of the reasons behind women's decisions to emigrate and their choice of country of destination, their ways of entering the labour market and their social mobility, the possibility of forming and reconstituting family relationships and, lastly, the processes of integration or of cultural/social resistance (among many studies, Kofman, Phizacklea, Raghuram and Sales, 2000; Anthias and Lazaridis, 2000; Anthias, Kontos and Morokvasic-Muller, 2013; Oso and Ribas-Mateos, 2013).

The Italian landscape occupies a special position in this new attention to the relationship between gender and migration, and a quick glance at some data is enough to understand why. According to data from the Italian national institute of statistics (Istat – Istituto nazionale di statistica) as of 1 January 2015, the percentage of foreign women residing in Italy exceeds 52 per cent of the total of foreigner nationals (Istat, 2015a), while the number of births to foreign women has progressively increased (Istat, 2014c).[15] Based on the data on expired and unrenewed residence permits, a greater trend for migrant women to remain in Italy and undertake stabilization processes has been found (UNAR, 2013: 157). Moreover, as of 1 January 2014, women holding long-term residence permits represent about 50 per cent of the total (Istat, 2014a), although the acquisition of this permit is often due to having joined a family member residing in Italy for some time. As for acquiring Italian citizenship, for migrant women marriage is still the most prevalent mode of access: acquisitions on this ground account for more than 46.8 per cent of the total for the female population and 11.2 per cent for men. On the other hand, as regards geographical mobility, while men show greater mobility than women in the case of migrants from India, Albania and Morocco,

15 The situation is rapidly evolving, however, and the fertility of migrant women varies depending on the reasons for entry into Italy. According to Istat data, the migrants 'that made their entry or that "emerged" following regularization, in the 10 years thereafter carried out most of their reproduction plans in our country, thus making an important contribution to the increased fertility for the period. Although remaining at fertility levels decidedly higher than those of Italian women (2.37 and 1.29 births per woman respectively in 2012), the average number of children per woman among foreign nationals is also rapidly declining and their contribution to the population's overall fertility is progressively falling … The case of immigrant women with migration plans chiefly for reasons of work is different. These women's fertility in Italy is generally low. This is the case, for example, with Ukrainian, Moldavian, Philippine and Ecuadorean women, who have high employment rates, mainly in services to families' (Istat, 2014c: 144). See also Istat, 2015c: 205. Istat documents are available at http://www.Istat.it/en/.

the situation is reversed from those from Ukraine, Ecuador, Peru, and Moldova. In this regard, it is also important to stress that the greatest tendency towards mobility among women is recorded for those nationalities that most often see migrations of female breadwinners (Istat, 2014a).

As mentioned, the figures and features of women's immigration in Italy are at any rate highly correlated with the trends in the domestic market, consequent transformations in gender relations and more general changes in Italian society. Indeed, women's employment rates – although lagging far behind and in percentages lower than those in other European countries – have gradually increased, especially since the mid-1990s; and, after the recent economic and financial crisis, the number of female jobseekers has seen constant growth (Istat, 2013: 110–15).[16] However, these changes have been offset by the endemic difficulties of Italian women in reconciling work and family (due also to an uneven distribution of care activities between men and women), the ageing of the Italian population and the inadequacy of welfare benefits, especially in the fields of assistance to the elderly and childcare services (Del Boca, 2002).

All these elements contributed to the emergence, for migrant women, of a labour demand restricted largely to the segment of domestic and care work. Moreover, although the employment rate of foreigners is continuing to grow thanks above all to the female component, migrant women are doubly disadvantaged, with the drawbacks of being women coming in addition to those derived from being foreigners. They have greater difficulties reconciling work and care activity, due also to a lack of networks of family and friends, which considerably impacts their participation in work (Caritas/Migrantes, 2014: 132–51).[17] Moreover, conditions – sex, age, educational level and working position, role in the family and sector of employment – being equal, foreign women are nine times more likely than Italian women to find unqualified employment. Lastly, added to this disadvantage are

16 The current increase in the supply of women's labour is also the result of new family strategies for coping with the economic constraints triggered by the crisis. However, some traits of Italian female employment are confirmed: the employment of women in professions for which the required degree is lower than that possessed, occupational segregation (prevalently in the sectors of trade and services), the greater presence of non-standard work and a strong salary disparity (Istat, 2014b: 124 ff; Istat, 2015b: 149 ff).

17 According to Istat data, the employment rate of foreign women is on average higher than that of Italian women, but that of foreign mothers between 25 and 44 years of age is 14 percentage points lower (Istat, 2013: 107). Moreover, foreign mothers between 15 and 49 years of age have an employment rate far lower not only than Italian mothers, but also than foreign women living alone or in couples without children. However, employment rates show considerable differences between the various communities, due also to cultural factors or to the specific features of the migration plan: for Albanian women, for example, the rate falls to 34.5 per cent, and even to 21.0 per cent for Moroccan and Indian women. Only Philippine women show a rather high employment rate (75.6 per cent), but still an 11.2 percentage point decline from 2008 (Istat, 2014b: 126).

wages that differ considerably both from those of male migrants and from those of Italian workers, male or female (Istat, 2013: 108–9; Istat, 2015b: 180 and 194).

Some ambiguities in Italian migration policy, despite continuity with the broader European perspective, thus fit within this framework. Generally speaking, after an initial phase of 'lawless tolerance' of immigration, Italy has also slowly begun to go down the 'Fortress Europe' path. With the signing of the Maastricht Treaty, Europe's direction in immigration soon became clear.

> The opening up of Europe with the removal of barriers to the mobility of capital, commodities, and labour within the EC will also close off possibilities for those of non-European origin, both citizens and residents of EC states and those living outside its borders. This exclusion applies in very concrete terms: as border controls are brought down between EC states, they are being replaced by greatly strengthened external border controls, and by increased internal surveillance.
>
> …
>
> All migrants face increasing restrictions. These restrictions recently have been applied as well to the last group of states that are considered to be the weak line of defence against invasions of illegal immigrants, such as Italy … and Spain … (Kofman and Sales, 1992: 29, 31)

Moreover, in parallel with the adoption of restrictive migration policies, the Italian landscape in women's immigration has assumed traits that have already taken shape in other European countries: migrant women's employment in jobs beneath their skill-level and qualifications, very low wages, frequent exposure to health and safety risks, widespread presence in informal sectors of the economy and frequently unstable labour relationships. Added to this is the circumstance that, similarly to what has taken place in other settings, the 'blame the victim paradigm' has made inroads into Italian public discourse and scientific debate as well: 'it has been assumed that migrant women's culture of origin, their lack of preparation for modern, urban societies and work are responsible for their situation and lack of choices' (Morokvasic, 1991: 71).

However, despite certain similarities, the Italian experience in the matter of women's migration has retained some particular features, corresponding to lawmakers' highly ambivalent attitude over the years. While on the one hand Parliament has progressively restricted the channels for entering and staying in Italy (both for work and for family reunification), on the other it has left some openings which, by the way in which they were shaped, have been occupied chiefly by migrant women. Particular reference is made here to the 'preferential lanes' created solely for domestic and care work over the years, first through ministry circulars and then with the aforementioned amnesty of 2009. However, although these provisions created a privileged channel of entry for migrant women, they have also resulted in their regimentation within opportunistic schemes of labour regulation and of promotion of 'private' welfare (Bascherini and Niccolai, 2010: 501 ff).

While on the one hand the *ad hoc* amnesties may appear to be an anomalous, albeit carefully circumscribed, deviation from the defensive stance of 'Fortress Europe', on the other this has all resulted in a dubious operation of selecting female migrant workers and categorizing them within predefined social and gender relationships. Initially, due to protectionism, the opening to immigrant domestic workers was conditional upon verifying the absolute lack of supply by Italian women, often discarded because they came at a higher cost (Andall, 2000). Moreover, the first actions in this sense had provided 'that foreign female domestic workers could be hired only under full-time contracts; and that they could have only one contract, upon the expiration or termination of which they were mandatorily required to return to their country of origin, and could not return to Italy for a period of three years' (Colombo, 2003: 323–4). What's more, a circular from the Ministry of Labour[18] had allowed new entries of non-EU female domestic workers provided that they were introduced exclusively under live-in arrangements and, for two years, they could neither change sector nor, *de facto*, employer. The condition that domestic work be performed for only one employer was also included in the 2009 amnesty, thus demonstrating a failure to sufficiently consider the particular features of the domestic work performed by migrant women, who are often engaged in several different labour relationships (Bascherini and Niccolai, 2010: 519–20).

At any rate, so ambivalent a control over migrant women, also given its significance as a dispositive of biopolitics, strongly conditioned public discourse, as it tended to offer a dual representation of migrant women, nullifying the complexity of their experiences (Vicarelli, 1994: 7). Migrant women were seen (and 'disciplined') either only as workers or only as women following someone else's migration plan; a hierarchy was thus imposed on how their multiple identities were represented (Andall, 2000: 19). The aforementioned measures show, for example, how migrant women were pushed into live-in labour relationships, with the intent (and effect) of discouraging them from reuniting with other family members and from creating and caring for their own families.

Mirroring this, through the regulation of family reunification, an ambiguous form of control over migrant women was implemented, helping to form and perpetuate certain stereotypes. In fact, the restriction of the right to family reunification to the nuclear family alone, and the progressive harshening of the economic, housing and working conditions required to apply for it,[19] had the perverse effect of strengthening and even promoting the image of migrant

18 Ministry of Labour, circular no. 156/1991.

19 Currently, foreign nationals requesting reunification (admitted only for certain family members) must first of all be holders of residence permits for subordinate employment or for autonomous work for a duration of no less than one year. They must also demonstrate having a minimum yearly income and housing in compliance with hygienic

women as vulnerable subjects, because they are dependent on others. These are actually requirements that, similarly to what has occurred in other legal systems, 'exemplify the construction of family norms and the role of the state in shaping gender relations, in particular in setting the conditions of marriage and social reproduction, and sustaining female dependency' (Kofman, 1999: 279). Indeed, by embodying two principles – the 'male bread-winner principle' and the 'marriage principle' (Lutz, 1997: 105) – currently under pressure in Italy as well, the reunification requirements create the conditions for making migrant women dependent upon the legal status and the economic situation of their respective husbands or children (Pezzini, 2010: 210).

Aims and Structure of this Book

In examining the relationship between gender and migration in Italy, the book adopts a dual perspective. On the one hand, the attempt has been made to observe the special features of the Italian migration context, underscoring its links with the country's historical, social and cultural patterns; on the other, the choice was made to focus attention on specific issues, to cast light on how Italian doctrine approaches the themes of gender and migration. Therefore, the chapters of the volume, while discussing problems broadly debated in the international literature, deal with them from the viewpoint of 'Italian theory'. The objective, then, is a dual one: raising questions about the difficulties encountered by migrant women residing in Italy, while at the same time understanding whether and how doctrinal and judicial perspectives adopted elsewhere have found fertile terrain in the Italian setting. To weave the two levels of analysis together, a multidisciplinary approach capable of shedding light on the different attitudes in Italian scholarship appeared useful.

Part I includes two historical chapters which, albeit from different viewpoints, examine the social mobility of migrant women. Francesca Di Pasquale and Chiara Giorgi deal with the subject from a perspective in some ways opposite that of immigration to Italy, casting an unusual gaze on the links between colonial, postcolonial and gender issues (Chapter 1). The authors investigate the experience of the 'Comboni Missionary Sisters' – the order founded by Daniele Comboni in 1872 – and the role they played in the missionary project for the evangelization of Africa. Di Pasquale and Giorgi discuss in particular the mobility that the women (Italian and African alike) in the order had between the 1940s and 1950s: consecration allowed them to cross geographical and cultural boundaries between Africa and Europe. It was therefore a unique experience of 'gendered migration' and of ambiguous questioning of hierarchical race and gender structures. The main figures in this were both Italian women (the Comboni sisters), called to Africa

---

and sanitary as well as with residential suitability requirements (article 29, Legislative Decree no. 286/1998).

to provide their contribution to the evangelization process, and African women, involved from the start in a missionary project that was in some ways visionary but in others not immune to strong gender stereotypes.

Raffaella Sarti, on the other hand, analyses the issue of the mobility of migrant women from the standpoint of their widespread presence in the domestic labour and care sector (Chapter 2). Through a historical analysis of the phenomenon, and aided by statistical data, the author illustrates the reasons that led to the exponentially growing demand for domestic labour in Italy and the prevalent employment of migrant women in this sector. On the one hand, this fact helps to explain some particular features of the Italian migratory setting; on the other, it allows us to shed light on the conflict between the progressive closing of the borders and the Italian governments' indulgence of a certain immigration, including illegal immigration, provided that it was for care work. Joining a highly fruitful debate on this issue, the chapter sees the intertwinement between gender, domestic labour and migration issues as a starting point for comprehending the cultural, economic and social encounters or clashes experienced by migrant women within the domestic sphere.

The relationship between domestic work and women's immigration is also dealt with in the chapter by Silvia Niccolai (Chapter 3), which opens Part II of the book on self-fulfilment, family and welfare. The author overturns the recurring criticism raised against salaried domestic work, which holds the widespread employment of migrant women in this sector to be proof of the uneven distribution of housework between men and women, and therefore of the failure of Western feminism. The chapter counters this reconstruction with a different interpretation: the women and men who rely on the work of migrant women because they do not have the time to dedicate to their own families and household chores are actually as much victims of the capitalist assumptions of the global economy as the domestic workers are. They are trapped in a new and contradictory 'Third Movement' (in Polanyi's sense): from one standpoint, the gears of capitalist production have managed to invade the domestic sphere, making it the object of economic transactions; from another standpoint, there is no lack of spaces for providing this sphere with re-signification and value.

Laura Ronchetti (Chapter 4) also writes in terms of re-signification, dealing with the relationship between gender and migration from the constitutionalist perspective of migrant women's autonomy and self-fulfilment. Through a cross-reading of the Italian constitution, constitutional and European case-law on migrants' rights and the obstacles specifically encountered by women, the chapter highlights the Constitution's transformational potential in terms of a principle of anti-subalternity and anti-subordination. In consideration of the kaleidoscopic nature of migrant women's identities and the multiple barriers to their self-fulfilment, the author promotes a reinterpretation of the constitutional text that allows women's specific discriminations to be dealt with and a new idea of 'constitutional citizenship' distinct from 'national citizenship' to be constructed. This different notion of citizenship is founded upon the possibility of the migrants' actual participation in common life and upon their attainment of certain fundamental rights.

The multiple discriminations experienced by migrant women are also examined by Anna Lorenzetti (Chapter 5), who deals with this issue from the standpoint of the difficulties in accessing healthcare services and welfare benefits. In this regard, the chapter provides some statistical and regulatory data that show the multiple social, cultural and economic barriers migrant women come up against in accessing these benefits. Some obstacles are conveyed and reinforced first of all by Italian legislation, where it differentiates the level of benefits guaranteed for migrant women based upon whether or not they are staying in Italy regularly. On the other hand, other forms of discrimination derive from those regional laws that further restrict the channels for accessing benefits. This results in creating greater difficulties precisely for those women at greatest disadvantage in enjoying adequate medical care: irregular migrant women and Roma women. Moreover, to highlight the negative repercussions on migrant women of a gender-neutral approach, the chapter intersects analysis of Italian legislation on healthcare services and social benefits with European anti-discrimination law on access to the supply of goods and services.

Part II closes with remarks by Elisa Olivito (Chapter 6) on how immigration has affected Italian family law and the idea of gender equality enshrined in it. Through examination of Italian case-law and legislation on polygyny, repudiation and family reunification, the chapter highlights how the formation/reunification of migrants' families on national territory has laid bare some preconceptions in the guarantee of equality between spouses. Indeed, the pre-assumption of the nuclear, monogamous family as a model risks working to the detriment of migrant women, whose actual needs are often sacrificed in the name of a counterproductive and formalistic egalitarian principle. The chapter attempts to point out that, precisely in the field of family law, solutions which are more aware of the interests actually in play may be imagined. These would be an alternative both to rejecting outright the claims for accommodating other family models and to upholding them uncritically. The risk that is otherwise run is that of underestimating the strategic positions that migrant women take in order to have their needs met and their ability to navigate between multiple legal and cultural contexts.

Part III is dedicated to the relationship between gender, migrations and religious/cultural diversity. The issue is dealt with by Valentina Masarone from the standpoint of Italian criminal law (Chapter 7). The doctrinal debate on the impact that cultural factors may have on determining the crime and, consequently, the punishment has had echoes in Italy, too. In this regard, as an alternative to a clear choice between an assimilationist and a multiculturalist model, the author reinterprets this problem in light of constitutional principles and the Italian debate on the function of criminal law and punishment. In this perspective, an examination is thus offered of the legal doctrines regarding 'culturally motivated crimes' and on how the approaches of the scholarship may impact migrant women. To identify the relationships between the legal constructions of these crimes and the position of migrant women, special attention is devoted to how Italian lawmakers have introduced the crime of 'female genital mutilation' into the criminal code. From the standpoint of the crime, aggravating circumstances and punishment, the new article of the criminal code appears actually to operate more on the symbolic level than as a concrete and effective deterrent.

The relationship between law and culturally determined behaviours is also investigated by Ilenia Ruggiu (Chapter 8), who raises some questions on the understanding in patriarchal terms of practices usually associated with minority groups. For some time, 'gender-sensitive' arguments have been introduced into the debate on multiculturalism and minority rights, in order to highlight that multiculturalist accommodations sometimes risk negatively impacting women's rights. From this perspective, the author, relying on judgments and laws regarding cultural practices, observes how, in the normative classification of certain behaviours, a transition from a cultural to a patriarchal argument is taking place. It is then a matter of understanding whether that transition yields legal consequences and whether this new way of categorizing multicultural problems is persuasive and effective, especially in terms of the ability to impact the underlying power relationships. The chapter underscores the risk of underestimating the cultural dimension of practices and, at the same time, of adopting an abstract notion of patriarchy.

Reference to the subject of patriarchy is also a recurring theme in the doctrinal debates concerning the use of religious symbols in public spaces. Susanna Mancini (Chapter 9) examines this issue, highlighting how 'patriarchal prejudice' is often associated with the condition of Muslim migrant women and their desire to continue wearing headscarves in host countries. The representation of these women as victims of a culture that is 'other', patriarchal and contrary to gender equality is a frequently recurring one in European case-law; at the same time, it is one of the reasons adopted for introducing the legislative prohibition against wearing this symbol in public places. In this regard, the author underscores that the attitude of lawmakers and of Italian judges to the headscarf may at first sight appear to be one of greater opening, as there are no laws prohibiting the possibility of wearing it in public places or judgments against women wearing the burqa. However, upon more careful examination, this opening is in part conditioned upon the privileged position accorded to the symbols of the Catholic religion and in part a sign of a failure to question Italy's own patriarchal preconceptions and models of cultural domination.

Part IV concentrates on citizenship and on the condition of second-generation migrants. In particular, Elena Paparella (Chapter 10) relates some problematic aspects of Italian citizenship law to the legal status of immigrants' children. The need to update this law has been debated for a number of years, as it is no longer adequate for the needs of a society highly changed by strong migratory flows. From this perspective, the chapter shows how second-generation immigrants, once they are adults, fall into a sort of legal limbo that deprives them of some fundamental rights. Nevertheless, the author underscores how young second-generation migrants, born and/or raised in Italy, have developed interesting forms of association and political activism, through which they promote a different and more inclusive idea of citizenship. These participation experiences are not without contributions by second-generation migrant women, showing both their unique position and the specific nature of the issues that are raised.

The special condition of second-generation migrant women is also the subject of the chapter by Cristina Greco (Chapter 11), who deals with it from the different standpoint of the dynamics of constructing and reconstructing both individual and collective identities. Through the autobiographical narratives of second-generation migrant women, Greco investigates how they create their own paths of personal subjectivity and re-position themselves with respect to their culture of origin as well as to that of the country where they were raised. By putting into play identity processes that represent both continuity with and a break from tradition, second-generation migrant women embody an idea of dual citizenship that goes beyond geographical and cultural boundaries. The author particularly examines the bond between identity and difference that migrant women bear, and the contaminations they introduce into 'Italian culture' and the cultures of the migrants' communities. In this context, their own narratives become instruments for questioning the model of femininity derived from the culture of origin and that of destination.

References

Andall, J. (2000). *Gender, Migration and Domestic Service: The Politics of Black Women in Italy*. Burlington: Ashgate.

Anthias, F. and Lazaridis, G. (eds) (2000). *Gender and Migration in Southern Europe: Women on the Move*. Oxford: Berg.

Anthias, F., Kontos, M. and Morokvasic-Muller, M. (eds) (2013). *Paradoxes of Integration: Female Migrants in Europe*. London: Springer.

Bascherini, G. (2012). A proposito delle più recenti riforme in materia di trattenimento dello straniero nei centri di identificazione ed espulsione. *Rivista Aic*, 1, 1–15. Available at http://www.rivistaaic.it.

Bascherini, G. and Niccolai, S. (2010). Regolarizzare Mary Poppins. Lavoro nello spazio domestico e qualità della cittadinanza. *Rivista del diritto della sicurezza sociale*, 10(3), 499–533.

Bertossi, C. and Duyvendak, J.W. (2012). National models of immigrant integration: The costs for comparative research. *Comparative European Politics*, 10, 237–47.

Caritas/Migrantes (2014). *XXIII Rapporto immigrazione 2013. Tra crisi e diritti umani*. Todi: Tau.

Castles, S., de Haas, H. and Miller, M.J. (2014). *The Age of Migration: International Population Movements in the Modern World*, 5th edn. New York: Palgrave Macmillan.

Colombo, A. (2003). Razza, genere, classe. Le tre dimensioni del lavoro domestico in Italia. *Polis*, 317–42.

Colombo, A. and Sciortino, G. (2004). Italian immigration: The origins, nature and evolution of Italy's migratory systems. *Journal of Modern Italian Studies*, 9(1), 49–70.

Del Boca, D. (2002). *Low Fertility and Labour Force Participation of Italian Women: Evidence and Interpretations*. OECD Labour Market and Social Policy Occasional Papers, No. 61, OECD Publishing. Available at http://dx.doi.org/10.1787/263482758546.

Favaro, G. and Tognetti Bordogna, M. (1991). *Donne dal mondo. Strategie migratorie al femminile*. Milano: Guerini e Associati.

Germani, A. (2001). Immigrazione: il modello mediterraneo. *Affari sociali internazionali*, 29, 107–16.

Istat (2013). *Rapporto annuale 2013 – La situazione del Paese*. 3. *Il mercato del lavoro*. Roma: Istat.

Istat (2014a). *Cittadini non comunitari regolarmente soggiornanti – Anni 2013–2014*. Roma: Istat.

Istat (2014b). *Rapporto annuale 2014 – La situazione del Paese*. 3. *Il mercato del lavoro nei cinque anni della crisi: dinamiche e divari*. Roma: Istat.

Istat (2014c). *Rapporto annuale 2014 – La situazione del Paese*. 4. *Tendenze demografiche e trasformazioni sociali: nuove sfide per il sistema di welfare*. Roma: Istat.

Istat (2015a). *La popolazione straniera residente per età e sesso al 1° gennaio 2015*. Roma: Istat.

Istat (2015b). *Rapporto annuale 2015 – La situazione del Paese*. 4. *Mercato del lavoro: soggetti, imprese e territori*. Roma: Istat.

Istat (2015c). *Rapporto annuale 2015 – La situazione del Paese*. 5. *La varietà dei territori: condizioni di vita e aspetti sociali*. Roma: Istat.

King, R. and Andall, J. (1999). The geography and economic sociology of recent immigration to Italy. *Modern Italy*, 4(2), 135–58.

King, R. and Zontini, E. (2000). The role of gender in the South European immigration model. *Revista de sociologia*, 60(1), 35–52. Available at http://www.raco.cat/index.php/papers/article/viewFile/25564/25398.

Kofman, E. (1999). Female 'birds of passage' a decade later: Gender and immigration in the European Union. *International Migration Review*, 33(2), 269–99.

Kofman, E. and Sales, R. (1992). Towards Fortress Europe? *Women's Studies Inf. Forum*, 15(1), 29–39.

Kofman, E., Phizacklea, A., Raghuram, P. and Sales, R. (2000). *Gender and International Migration in Europe: Employment, Welfare and Politics*. London: Routledge.

Lutz, H. (1997). The limits of European-ness: Immigrant women in Fortress Europe. *Feminist Review*, 57, 93–111.

Mingione, E. and Quassoli, F. (2000). The participation of immigrants in the underground economy in Italy. In King, R., Lazaridis, G. and Tsardanidis, C. (eds) *Eldorado or Fortress? Migration in Southern Europe*, 27–56. London: Macmillan.

Morokvasic, M. (1984). Birds of passage are also women. *International Migration Review*, 18(4), 886–907.

Morokvasic, M. (1991). Fortress Europe and migrant women. *Feminist Review*, 39, 69–84.

OECD (2014). *Jobs for Immigrants* (vol. 4) *Labour Market Integration in Italy*. OECD Publishing. Available at http://dx.doi.org/10.1787/9789264214712-en.

Oso, L. and Ribas-Mateos, R. (eds) (2013). *The International Handbook on Gender, Migration and Transnationalism: Global and Development Perspectives, Series: International Handbooks on Gender*. Cheltenham and Northampton: Edward Elgar.

Pezzini, B. (2010). *Una questione che interroga l'uguaglianza: i diritti sociali del non-cittadino*. In *Lo statuto costituzionale del non cittadino*, 163–228. Napoli: Jovene.

Phizacklea, A. (ed.) (1983). *One Way Ticket: Migration and Female Labour*. London: Routledge and Kegan Paul.

Pugliese, E. (2011). The Mediterranean model of immigration. *Academicus*, 3, 96–107.

Schierup, C.-U., Hansen, P. and Castles, S. (2006). *Migration, Citizenship, and the European Welfare State: A European Dilemma*. Oxford: Oxford University Press.

Tognetti Bordogna, M. (2004). Lavoro e immigrazione femminile una realtà in mutamento. In Delle Donne, M. and Melotti, U. (eds) *Immigrazione in Europa. Strategie di inclusione-esclusione*, 147–76. Roma: Ediesse.

UNAR (2013). *Immigrazione: dossier statistico 2013. Dalle discriminazioni ai diritti*. Centro Studi e Ricerche IDOS. Roma: Idos.

Vicarelli, G. (ed.) (1994). *Le mani invisibili. La vita e il lavoro delle donne immigrate*. Roma: Ediesse.

Zincone, G. (2006). The making of policies: Immigration and immigrants in Italy. *Journal of Ethnic and Migration Studies*, 32(3), 347–75.

PART I:
Migrant Women and Social Mobility in a Historical Perspective

Chapter 1

The 'Worker Nuns of Nigrizia': The Pious Mothers of *Nigrizia* between Italy and Africa during the Imperial Age (1872–1950)

Francesca Di Pasquale and Chiara Giorgi[1]

Introduction

From 1872, when the Comboni women's institution was established, and all throughout the period of the European colonial occupations of Africa, the 'Pious Mothers of Nigrizia', that is, the nuns of the religious order founded by Daniele Comboni, were key players of the missionary project for the African evangelization.[2] According to the ambitious and, at the same time, extremely pragmatic Comboni view, women played a key role for the conversion of *Nigrizia*,[3] fuelled by the belief that, unlike priests, nuns could fit into African society, penetrating the core of native families.

Throughout the late nineteenth and early twentieth centuries, within the entangled history of missions in Africa that combined evangelization with 'civilization' – imperialism with the hierarchization of race and gender – the

---

1 This chapter is the result of the fruitful exchange and the shared work of both the authors. However, Section 1, *'True Women' for Africa. The nuns in Daniele Comboni's missionary project*, was mainly written by Francesca Di Pasquale, while Section 2, *The Pious Mothers of Nigrizia in the Horn of Africa*, was mainly written by Chiara Giorgi.

The study is the first analysis of the history of the Pious Mothers of Nigrizia, with particular reference to their mobility. It should be underlined that the historical archive of the Comboni Missionary Sisters is still under archival processing. Access was limited to only some records, provided by Sister Mariateresa Girola, who is in charge of the archive. For this invaluable help and, more generally, for the very stimulating exchange of ideas, we wish to thank Sister Mariateresa Girola and Sister Maria Vidale.

2 See Romanato (2003: 259) and Vidale (2012).

3 According to the *Dizionario universale della lingua italiana*, by Carlo A. Vanzon, published in 1836, *Nigrizia* was the vast African area which included many regions like *Bambara*, *Tumbuctu*, *Congo*, *Niffe*, *Funda*, *Bornù*, *Mandara*, *Darfur*, *Cordofan*, and many others. It bordered the Sahara to the north, the south of Egypt (*Nubia*) to the east, Guinea to the south and Senegal and Gambia on the west. See Vanzon (1836: 179). Actually, for Comboni, *Nigrizia* was synonymous of Africa.

history of the Comboni mission displayed very distinctive features.[4] We can consider, for example, the primitive form of 'inculturation' that Comboni, in the light of the previous and mainly ruinous missionary experiences, tried to implement to spread the Catholic creed among natives (Romanato, 2003: 296). The centrality of the 'Worker Nuns of Nigrizia'[5] in Comboni's plan was certainly one of the most significant features of his project. 'Created' by Comboni for the primary aim of devoting their lives entirely to the conversion of *Nigrizia*, starting in the second half of the nineteenth century, dozens of women, mainly from Italy, began journeying to Africa. In turn, some African women were involved in the missionary project from its beginning, according to the guiding principle of the *Piano per la rigenerazione dell'Africa* (Plan for the regeneration of Africa) by Comboni, which is 'saving Africa with Africa'.[6]

The history of the 'Pious Mothers of Nigrizia' represents a fruitful perspective from which to analyse female mobility during the imperial age, and our chapter looks into their history through this specific point of view. More precisely, here we use the word mobility, on the one hand, referring to its spatial meaning, that is, to the history of migrations and exchanges between Europe and Africa, which characterized the history of the Pious Mothers. Their history was transnational indeed, not uniquely for the history of women on the move between Italy and Africa. Daniele Comboni was born in the Austro-Hungarian Lombardy-Venetia, and the Habsburg Empire was his main political and social point of reference. The Comboni mission raised funds and obtained political support mainly in that territory. Therefore, the European boundaries were the first to be crossed.

On the other hand, we aim to explore if and how the Comboni missionary activities triggered social mobility in both Italian and African nuns alike. In Comboni's letters, the woman's role is exalted, even astonishingly so. However, through a deeper analysis, other features also come to light, in particular his view of women. If at first it may seem far-sighted, at the same time it also included some discriminatory features. Notwithstanding the preeminent position that Comboni assigned to nuns in terms of African evangelization, on the whole in many respects it subverted the role of women, as established by European bourgeois imaginary in the second half of the nineteenth century.

As mentioned above, the Comboni female congregation admitted African women to the mission from its onset. Fortunata Quascè, from Sudan, was the first African woman in the Comboni mission to take her nun's vows. She experienced all the tribulations characterizing the history of the first decades of the Comboni

4 Within the extensive literature on missionaries, Italian colonialism and religion in Africa, see in particular: Betti (1996); Borruso (1988, 1989); Ceci (2007); Chelati Dirar (2002 and 2003); Fonzi (1988 and 1996); Franzinelli (1992); and Prudhomme (2007). For the Comboni mission, see Romanato (2003).

5 'Suore operaie della Nigrizia': Vidale (2012: 78).

6 In Italian: 'Salvare l'Africa con l'Africa'. After the first edition in 1864, the *Piano* was re-edited in 1871. See Comboni (1991: 840–52).

sisters in Africa, not least of which, the captivity by Mahdi 'rebels' during the Dervish revolt in Sudan (1882–86).[7] During the colonial age, on the other hand, the mode of relating to African women seemed to change in accordance with the political imperatives of the Italian government and, in particular, to native African politics. Indeed, in colonial Eritrea, not until July 1939 did the first six young Eritrean women take their vows as 'Pious Sisters of Nigrizia'. They represented the first group of 'native novice women' (*novizie indigene*).[8] In 1942, four other Eritrean women also took their vows. In May 1946, six native nuns (including one of mixed 'race') joined the congregation. In the following years, the number of Eritrean women aspiring to join the mission constantly increased.

In sum, the Combonian sisters' experience was at the centre of multiple dynamics concerning not only the question of women's mobility between Italy and Africa and within Africa itself, but also more general themes like gender relations and the conflicts this sparked, including with those opposing missionary nuns and priests, the men who embodied colonial power and the ecclesiastical hierarchy. After Comboni's death, the difficulty of securing any formal recognition of the congregation's autonomy – which existed *de facto* across Europe and Africa – was principally due to the various kinds of resistance put up by their male counterparts. The various representatives of the male counterparts, including their highest-ranking leaders, seem to have been rather alarmed by the autonomy that a female congregation brought to the expansion of its activity beyond the central African mission initially planned for it. The fear also concerned the foundation of other European bases helping it to recruit and train personnel ready to join its African missions.

In many regards, this history requires the deployment 'in the field' of an analysis depsychologising and resocialising – as Judith Butler put it – the role of the *Nigrizia* nuns in the plan conceived by Daniele Comboni. The subjectivity of the women working in the service of this project (whether Italians or Africans) should thus be analysed in light of numerous factors and protagonists – convinced as we are that this is an important chapter in the history of gender, the history of Africa and, at the same time, the history of Italian colonialism.

'True Women' for Africa: The Nuns in Daniele Comboni's Missionary Project

In terms of the results attained, that is, the number of 'outposts' and of Africans involved, and for the intensity of its penetration, the Comboni mission certainly

7 For the history of Fortunata Quascè see Vidale (2005).

8 The ceremony had solemn and impressive tones. In February 1938, the first six candidates to join the mission officially started their trial period, under the blessing of Pope Pious XI. See the record n. 5963, VI/H10/2/v2, Asmara, Casa Comboni, 7 October 1939, on the occasion of the *Festa del S. Rosario*, held in the historical archive of the Comboni Missionary Sisters.

achieved much more than previous missionary experiences had in the Curacy of Central Africa.[9]

Daniele Comboni first travelled to Africa in 1857 with five other missionaries of the Verona Religious Institute, founded by the priest Nicola Mazza, where Comboni himself entered the seminary. In the following decade, he travelled widely throughout Africa, as his assignment, bestowed onto him by Father Mazza, was the liberation of enslaved boys and girls. He also travelled throughout Europe as well, particularly in Germany; here he established contacts with the 'Society of Cologne', the humanitarian institute which became one of the main sources of funding for the Comboni missionary activities. In 1867 he wrote the first edition of the *Piano per la rigenerazione dell'Africa* ('Plan for the Regeneration of Africa'), which was his project, but also his manifesto for the mission in Africa. In his plan, Daniele Comboni sought to work for Africa, availing himself of men and women capable of dealing with the massive African environmental barriers and to interact with African 'otherness' in a way that also proved fruitful for the evangelization project. To this end, he envisaged establishing intermediate outposts, which were later founded in Egypt, in order to allow the missionaries to gradually come into contact with the African climate and culture. The continent would have been converted and 'civilized' by Africans themselves; the training of native clergy and the integration of African people into the missionary project was aimed at fully penetrating the continent. Following the proposal advanced by *Propaganda Fide*,[10] in 1872 Pope Pious IX appointed Comboni Pro-Vicar Apostolic of Central Africa. Five years later he became bishop (Romanato, 2003: 248–70).

In many respects, women were the keystone of the Comboni missionary plan: 'A Sister of Charity in central Africa is worth three priests in Europe and this century of persecution of the Church … is the century of the catholic woman'.[11] According to Comboni, his mission was successful, whereas previous ones had been less so, because of the frontline involvement of the 'omnipotent ministry of the woman bringing the Gospel and of the Sister of Charity, who is a shield, power, and a guarantee of the Missionary's ministry'.[12] The 'Pious Mothers of

9 On the missions in Africa before Comboni, see Romanato (2003: 25–189). The Curacy of Central Africa was established by *Propaganda Fide* in 1846. Through the curacy, the Holy See aimed at the evangelization of the whole continent. Actually, until the period of activity of Comboni, it had operated only in the territories of present-day Sudan: Romanato (2003: 50–60).

10 *Propaganda Fide* was the ecclesiastic institution, founded in 1622, which had jurisdiction over all the territories peopled by 'infidels', that is over the missions, aiming at the evangelization of non-Christian and non-Catholic people.

11 In Italian: 'La Suora di Carità nell'Africa Centrale fa come tre preti in Europa e questo secolo di persecuzione contro la Chiesa …, è il secolo della donna cattolica'. See the letter to the mother superior of the Sisters of St Joseph, 30 July 1877, in Vidale (2012: 77).

12 In Italian: 'onnipotente ministero della donna del Vangelo, e della Suora di carità, che è lo scudo, la forza, e la garanzia del ministero del Missionario'. See the letter to Mother Maria Annunziata Coseghi in Gebel Nuba, 24 July 1878, in Comboni (1991: 1515).

Nigrizia' order was established in 1872, even before the Comboni Fathers order, because nuns were the key to the evangelization of Africa.[13] In 1877, five years after the Pious Mothers were founded, the first five missionary sisters arrived in Africa; they were 'the vanguard of the new Institution whose mission is to foster its apostolic activities in the many regions of central Africa'.[14]

In his view, women were not exalted by their spirituality or purity, but, instead for very concrete features, starting with their physical resilience to the African climate, which, according to Comboni, was greater in European women than in men.[15] Comboni sought nuns who were like 'soldiers',[16] ready to sacrifice themselves and even die for Africa: 'cannon fodder'[17] for the evangelization of *Nigrizia*, according to the crude definition of the Vicar Apostolic. They had to be 'saints', but without bigotry, because in Africa it is necessary to instead be tolerant.[18] After all, Comboni was not predominantly a mystic or a theorist, but an extremely pragmatic man. Throughout his missionary activity he combined very innovative features with others which were a legacy of the traditionalist culture, based on a 'granitic faith' that was not at all undermined by the Age of Enlightenment (Romanato, 2003: 8, 367).

In the *Piano*, the position of women originated from a utilitarian view of their contribution to the mission, rather than aiming at women's liberation or at the subversion of the gender dynamics that defined women's roles in nineteenth-century Europe. Comboni sought 'instruments' for the conversion of *Nigrizia* and looked for 'true women', that is, first of all educated but also 'trustworthy,

13 Maria Bollezzoli, who came from the Ursuline Sisters, was the first mother superior. Before the institution of the Pious Mothers, Comboni had worked in Africa with the nuns belonging to the French order of St Joseph of the Apparition. Comboni decided to institute the congregation in Verona to rally nuns for *Nigrizia* because of the scarce number of sisters made available by the French order for the African mission. For the foundation of the congregation see Vidale (2012).

14 In Italian: 'l'avanguardia della nuova Istituzione destinata a riprendere la sua azione apostolica nelle numerose contrade dell'Africa Centrale'. The first five missionary sisters in Africa were Sister Teresa Grigolini and Sister Marietta Caspi from the diocese of Verona, Sister Maria Giuseppa and Sister Concetta Corsi from the diocese of Trani, and Sister Vittoria Paganini from the diocese of Padua. See the letter to Jean Francois Des Gares, 17 May 1878 in Comboni (1991: 1484) and Vidale (2012: 85–110).

15 The reference to the physical resilience of the 'European woman' is found in the first edition of the *Piano*: 'Sunto del nuovo disegno della Società dei sacri cuori di Gesù e Maria per la conversione della Nigrizia proposto alla S. Congregazione di Prof. da Fide da D. Daniele Comboni dell'Ist.o Mazza 1864', in Comboni (1991: 240).

16 See the letter to Mother Emile Julien from the Saint Joseph Order, Cairo, 15 December 1872, in Comboni (1991: 941).

17 In Italian: 'Carne da macello'. See the letter to Jean François Des Garets, 19 June 1879, in Comboni (1991: 1608).

18 In Italian: 'ma non col collo storto, perché in Africa bisogna averlo dritto'. From the letter to Father Giuseppe Sembianti, 12 February 1881, in Comboni (1991: 1834).

handsome and judicious'[19] women, and, if possible, with a handsome dowry. The woman with all of these qualities was the ideal candidate for the entrance enrolment in the Pious Mothers, even if she were an illegitimate child, who were usually not admitted to the mission: as Comboni explained 'every rule is subject to exceptions ... because suckers do not go to heaven', expressing frankly the pragmatism mentioned above.[20] On the other hand, admittance to the mission was forbidden for the 'lowly female servants': those who 'came to escape starvation', because 'Africa will not be converted by the household help from Verona'.[21]

According to Comboni, the presence in Africa of the Pious Mothers was an instrument for the 'civilization' of the 'barbaric' populations and the 'infidels', and this idea originated, first of all, from his view of the condition of 'ignominy' of the African women, in particular for those living among Islamic populations, where they were regarded 'only as a domestic tool, an instrument of immorality'.[22] Taking into account the subjection of women, but also the practice of slavery, Comboni's view of Islam was not exempt from intolerance, denoting disregard and rejection of the populations which embraced Muslim faith. On the whole, if, on the one hand his judgment of African populations was seemingly advanced, on the other hand it resulted from an extremely stern culture according to which the territories of 'infidels' were marked by backwardness and immorality, whereas conversion to Christianity meant civilization. After all, in the European colonial culture, women's conditions among natives were one of the main cultural markers indicating the gap between colonists and colonized and between 'barbarity' and 'civilization' (Levine, 2004; Sorgoni, 2000).

Nine years after founding the Pious Mothers, four Comboni Sisters missionaries' outposts were already operating in Africa, and specifically in Kharthoum, el-Obeid, Gebel Delen and Malbes. The latter was a Christian village established by Comboni missionaries, modelled after the Jesuits' *Reducciones* in South America and populated by families trained by the mission to live in a Christian way.[23] The presence of the nuns in this village, which was the most 'advanced' and, at the same time, violent experiment with African populations by Comboni missions, further demonstrates Comboni's absolute faith in the

19 In Italian: 'serie, buone, di giudizio'. See the letter to Father Giuseppe Sembianti, 12 February 1881, in Comboni (1991: 1825).

20 In Italian: 'ogni regola patisce le sue eccezioni ... perché i menchioni [sic] non vanno in paradiso'. From the letter to Father Giuseppe Sembianti, 20 April 1881, in Comboni (1991: 1888).

21 In Italian: "furono tutte servacce che venivano per cavarsi la fame'; 'Colle serve di Verona non si converte l'Africa'. From the letter to Germano Tomellieri, 24 April 1872, in Comboni (1991: 900).

22 In Italian: 'Solamente come un arnese di casa, come uno strumento di immoralità', in the *Rapporto sulla azione apostolica del Vicariato dell'Africa centrale*, 1877, sent to Pia Opera della Santa Infanzia di Parigi, in Comboni (1991: 1338).

23 Romanato (2003: 322) rightly reports on the process of 'de-Africanization' characterizing this experience.

evangelizing capabilities of the Pious Mothers.[24] His project to evangelize Africa through women originated from his understanding that only women could fully penetrate African society, through their female African counterpart, and, thus, instil the first seeds for conversion. In his *Piano*, the *Corpo delle giovanette negre* ('Corps of the young black women') was made up of female preceptors, to educate in the Catholic religion 'the dissolute female African society', of 'expert teachers and family women, which have to promote female education in reading, writing, arithmetic, spinning, sewing, weaving, taking care of the sick, as well as practicing all the more practical female skills for central *Nigrizia*'.[25] Finally, among those not pursuing marriage, the 'Virgins of Charity' would have been selected to constitute 'the most distinguished phalanx of the women's Corps whose mission it would be to … practice the ministry of catholic women among the *Nigrizia* tribes'.[26] The first involvement of African women commenced in 1867, when fourteen women coming from the 'white river' arrived in Europe on the occasion of the redemption of some slaves, 'having been educated in all the female skills', and which Comboni assigned to 'educate the black girls in Egypt and to move to their native land in order to disseminate among those tribes the advantages and the benefits of civilization which they have received from the European culture'.[27]

Among these was Fortunata Quascè, who was the first 'Virgin of Charity' of the Comboni mission. Fortunata arrived in Verona in 1853 with a group of boys and girls redeemed from slavery at the Cairo market by the mission of Father Mazza. Actually, among other things, redemption implicated the eradication of these 'black' youths from their native cultural, social context and environment, with the effect that most died an untimely death in Europe due to the problems of adapting to the new environment. The young women trained in religious institutes were compelled by circumstance to become nuns, as they had no other opportunity for social integration (Romanato, 2003: 214). Of course, this general framework does not provide the whole picture of the African Pious Mothers, as the history of Fortunata Quascè shows in many respects: as she wrote in a letter to Comboni, she chose the religious life with conviction and joy (Vidale, 2005: 82–5). At the same time, what she experienced in Africa and, in particular, her captivity during

24 From the letter to the father of the missionary, sent from Malbes, 24 April 1881, in Comboni (1991: 1892).

25 In Italian: 'degradata femminil società africana'; 'abili maestre e donne di famiglia, le quali dovranno promuovere l'istruzione femminile in leggere, scrivere, far conti, filare, cucire, tessere, assistere agli infermi, ed esercitare tutte le arti donnesche più utili ai paesi della Nigrizia Centrale', in *Plan for the Regeneration of Africa*, in Comboni (1991: 238–9).

26 In Italian: 'istruite in tutte le arti femminili'; 'la più eletta falange del Corpo femminile destinata … ad esercitare il ministero della donna cattolica fra le tribù della Nigrizia', in *Plan for the Regeneration of Africa*, in Comboni (1991: 238–9).

27 In Italian: 'istruire in Egitto le piccole morette e a spostarsi nel loro paese natale al fine di comunicare a quelle tribù i vantaggi e i benefici della civilizzazione che esse hanno ricevuto dalla civiltà europea'. See the letter to De Lamenie De Brienne, 22 August 1867, in Comboni (1991: 417).

the Mahdi revolt, also demonstrates that missionary penetration into Africa in the nineteenth and twentieth centuries was characterized by violent religious clashes. The first African women were primarily trained to convert *Nigrizia* and to uproot Islam in African territories, which, at the time of these missions of the apostolic curacy, was rapidly spreading. According to testimonials from nuns, it seems that the brutality of the Mahdi 'rebels' towards Comboni missionaries sisters and, in particular, the 'black' nun in order to force her to forswear Catholicism and reconvert to her native religion, had the same origin, that is, the struggle between two monotheisms (Vidale, 2005: 109). Anyway, the life of Fortunata Quascè was an important piece of the history of the Pious Mothers and testifies to the 'worldiness, to the Africanity' which connoted the origins of this women's missionary institute (Vidale, 2005: 9).

On the whole, the Comboni sisters who had served in Africa during the first decade of the congregation's history had to ride out unspeakable hardships, adapt themselves to complicated and very unstable circumstances, and face many adversities, not least captivity during the Mahdi revolt. Some missionary outposts were set up by the nuns without no outside support. After Comboni's death in 1881, the nuns experienced a troubled period, mainly because of the opposition by the Jesuits, who, at that time, were in charge of the training for Comboni priesthood. The dispute was resolved thanks to the firmness of Maria Bollezzoli, mother superior of the Pious Mothers, but also to the support of the bishop of Verona, Luigi di Canossa, and of the first Comboni male missionaries who had worked with the nuns in Africa. In particular, Luigi di Canossa was the first supporter of Comboni and was familiar with the Pious Mothers congregation since its constitution (Vidale, 2013: 75–95). In order to weaken the female congregation, some priests resorted to conjectures on the supposed weak 'morality' of some sisters. This attempt to denigrate the nuns was consistent with the gender view of nineteenth-century imperial Europe, which considered women, by their very nature, to be constantly liable to slip back into immorality.[28]

All things considered, the missionary experience gave them a preeminent position, inconceivable for the time in late nineteenth-century Europe, and overturned the view of the 'holy and pious' woman. Even though the memoirs and more recent historical reconstructions by the Pious Mothers bear out this same pious view, the events after Comboni's death show that these first female apostles for *Nigrizia* were well-aware of having conquered a new role in the missionaries scenario and, furthermore, had no intention of forfeiting it.

28 Vidale (2013: 167–8). Furthermore, in 1898, Monsignor Roveggio, new Vicar Apostolic, removed Francesca Dalmasso from the position of mother provincial superior for Africa, because she was regarded hardly 'submissive'. See Vidale (2013: 209–10).

The Pious Mothers of *Nigrizia* in the Horn of Africa

In 1952–53, the number of pupils at Comboni College was the highest of any of the 32 schools controlled by the various religious orders ('several of which were sections of the School run by the Italian state in Eritrea').[29] Even more importantly for our purposes, the attendees at the *Sacra Famiglia/Santa Famiglia* (an educational arm of the Comboni congregation considered the institution that gave greatest expression to the missionaries' efforts) were of similarly large numbers. How was this possible? And what role did the Comboni nuns have in educational matters, which they considered – according to their own accounts – their main field of intervention?[30]

The Pious Mothers of Nigrizia's first arrival in the Italian colonies dates back to 1914, when Costanza Caldara (then General Superior to the Comboni congregation) sent six nuns to Eritrea on the instigation of Luigi Bonomi, a collaborator of the Comboni missionaries in Sudan and former prisoner of the Mahdi's. After a remarkable journey, the Comboni sisters arrived in Massawa in December 1914, with the Italian government's full agreement and with the goal of offering assistance at the Regina Elena colonial hospital in Asmara (where Bonomi was the chaplain). This first phase in the Pious Mothers of Nigrizia's presence – which we could, moreover, frame in terms of a period of women's mobility in Italian missionary efforts (whether from Italy or Egypt) – was entirely occupied by this welfare work (mostly nursing care) and characterized by numerous tensions resulting from friction with Italian military and medical personnel.[31] Up until 1927, the Pious Mothers of Nigrizia worked in the Regina Elena hospital; then, on the express say-so of the colonial government, they also extended their nursing activities to Massawa's Umberto I hospital (where the first community was formed); and soon afterward they took to the educational field, in the Vittorio Emanuele III state school.

This school was also the Italian government's wish and on the orders of Governor Jacopo Gasperini, it was dedicated to the education of Eritreans only. It was situated in the Amba Galliano area.[32] Of note, here, is that the Comboni nuns assumed a decisive role on account of other religious orders' reticence over engaging in the field of education, as well as the colonial government's lack of interventionism in this regard. As we know, already by the beginning of the era of

29 Puglisi (1953: 145–8). In the Comboni College there were 550 students; in Sant'Anna there were 450 students and in the *Sacra Famiglia* there were 420.

30 Chelati Dirar (2002: 149–88; 2003: 391–410).

31 In Eritrea the 'Pious Mothers of Nigrizia' had been preceded by the Daughters of St Anne (1895) which came after the Sisters of Charity, coadjutors of the fathers 'Lazarists'. The first superior in Eritrea was Pia Marani.

32 In 1929, the missionaries' residential community was moved to the new complex built by the Italian government near to the school where they were working. On Italian educational policy in Eritrea see Palma (2007: 211–38); Negash (1987: 78).

the apostolic prefecture, the missionaries had a sort of mandate covering all aspects of public education. This was a result of the Eritrean colony's lack of resources and more generally of the government's own awareness that the Catholic missionaries were useful for helping to spread Italian culture (moreover, they were useful to encourage both a 'social and cultural Italianisation of the colonial territory' and the 'production of colonial subjects'). The Catholic missionaries also consolidated the colonial authority, in particular due to the linguistic and ethnographic knowledge they had accumulated over their years 'on the ground'. Without doubt, this – strategically important – supply-teaching role had the support not only of the Vicar Apostolic (Celestino Cattaneo, Camillo Carrara's successor), but also of the colonial authorities themselves (as personified in the new Fascist governor Corrado Zoli). It also provided, indirectly, the basis for the growth of their leading role in education and, in some aspects, confirmed the usefulness and effectiveness of women's involvement in the work of evangelization in Africa, as Comboni himself had foreseen in his own time. As for the question of adequately preparing the Comboni nuns for their teaching activity, the first women involved – in some cases called up from missions in Egypt – were the most educated and those with most experience of teaching elsewhere; in time, other nuns followed and these latter had teaching diplomas and had previously worked in state primary schools. Small schools were also set up in other localities, mostly for Eritreans. For example, in Dekhemhare the Comboni nuns obtained the military authorities' permission to open a labour school for 'indigenous girls', but also, soon afterwards, a (separate) nursery school for Italians' sons. In Senafe, from 1938 until the outbreak of the war, the already legally recognized school for Eritreans was entrusted to the Pious Mothers. Near Cheren, at the cathedral of Chidane Mehret, the Comboni nuns were given control of teaching and management functions at the Catholic girls' school created by the first Eritrean Catholic bishop of Oriental rite.

With Italy's invasion of Ethiopia, the Comboni nuns mostly turned from teaching activities to nursing care at various military hospitals, though they did maintain some presence at a few small parish schools, most of them frequented by Eritreans. In this same period, the Comboni nuns – whose numbers had grown on account of the General Superior's urgent demands on the 'contingent' present in Egypt – collaborated with the military chaplains and began to undertake their first own parish work, together with the Capuchins. Yet only in 1937 did their first missionary work begin in some areas of Eritrea, when the Comboni nuns were assigned the apostolic prefecture of Gondar and when Pietro Villa was appointed apostolic prefect. The Mothers of Nigrizia, accompanying the Comboni fathers, thus began their own missionary work in Adigrat in the apostolic prefecture of Tigrai, and soon afterwards (1939) in Gondar (in the *Casa del fanciullo*, 'kids' house'). At the same time, as educational and welfare work expanded, Asmara saw the first training of young Eritrean women in the so-called religious life. At the end of the conflict, with the Vittorio Emanuele III school returning to its educational activity (having been used as a military hospital) the Italian government decided to donate its new annexes to the Pious Mothers of Nigrizia. These were converted into a boarding school for Italian children and would have been the headquarters of the *Istituto Santa Famiglia*. One of the annexes was devoted to a girls' school, 'training' them in what was considered specifically women's work. A telling sign of the Italian government's support was the positive judgment passed by Andrea Festa – director of education in Eritrea – ordering a display of this work to be shown at the Naples *Oltremare* exhibition.[33]

We ought to note that the girls' schools, like those for boys, prepared what the missionaries themselves called 'a fertile terrain for religious vocations'. In the same period, the nuns regained control of what was the first nucleus of the future *Casa Comboni*. In subsequent years it became a shelter for all those who found themselves in difficulties and, with the opening of the orphanage, a space for encounters between Italian nuns and Eritrean women – and girls. Opening in 1932 as the *Pia Opera Daniele Comboni* (not without opposition) it was requisitioned by the air force on the eve of the Ethiopian war. Only in 1938 was it handed back to the Mothers of Nigrizia, principally devoted to sheltering single mothers with children and subsequently the wholly Fascist project called *Protezione della Giovane* ('Protecting Young Women'). It was also here that the indigenous novitiate began, starting with Eritrean girls who wanted to become nuns, most of whom had first been taken in as orphans: 'Such it was that the first six of them aspiring to the religious life were chosen'.[34] In July 1939 the first African novices were joined by a group of Italian novices from Verona, with the goal of 'building up the indigenous novitiate'. Thus, 1939 was the year when the authorities gave the green light to the Novitiate for National and Indigenous Women (this also being the 25th anniversary of the first Italian missionaries' arrival in Eritrea). In 1940 the Italian nuns working in the Apostolic Vicariate of Eritrea were some 130 in number, spread across various villages and for the most part dedicated to hospital and educational activities (in state schools).

At the time the Second World War broke out, various communities of Comboni nuns were created in several different parts of Eritrea, within the terms of the educational and healthcare activities authorized or encouraged by the Italian government. However, the war also marked the beginning of the Pious Mothers' departure from their missionary posts (and indeed many of the missions themselves came to an end) and, at the same time, it was decided that *Casa Comboni* was a shelter for refugees and the missionaries themselves.

Throughout the length of the conflict, the Pious Mothers played a significant role in the wider context of the Catholic church's welfare efforts 'devoted to the needs of the newly-impoverished' and seeking to alleviate 'the oppressive situation of the Italian community' (Guazzini, 2008: 66–7) whom they offered

33 Despite being aware that the schools that aspired to the highest teaching standards had been those belonging to the Swedish mission, closed in 1932. See Trevaskis (1960: 33)

34 'Suore missionarie comboniane' (undated: 21).

spaces for socializing.[35] With the closing down of all the state schools in Asmara (due to bombings) the *Istituto Santa Famiglia* became the new main centre for the private tuition of Italian and 'mixed-race' boys and girls.[36] The *Istituto* was respected – or rather, authorized and legalized – even by the occupiers, thanks to an agreement between the Italian school authorities and the top officials of the British administration. As we read in a report from the historical archive of the Comboni Missionary Sisters, the Vicar Apostolic himself indicated in a visit to the *Istituto Santa Famiglia* (a few days after the British arrived) what very particular rules to follow: 'these are sad days, he said, but we must not lose hope: if we stick to our religious role and avoid interfering in politics, they will leave us in peace. They gave me their word'.[37]

Thus the fall of the Italian colonial government and the onset of the new British administration did not change the nature of the Comboni nuns' educational and welfare activities. This happened despite the initial blow interrupting the expansion of missionary activities in the most remote parts of Ethiopia, and their expulsion from teaching in public schools for the local population. Indeed, the missionaries who had just previously been carrying out aid work helping refugees would soon return to such a role, helping prisoners, escapees and the displaced.

> In Dekhemhare, to take one example from the missionary records, on 3 September 1941 three sisters set up a nursery at the "Casa del Bimbo" and the other 15 Pious Mothers who had provided their services at the military hospital, after having had to comply with the military high command's order to head collectively for Asmara, were now able to return there. They then provided various parochial and educational services for the local population and the roughly 8,000 Italians.[38]

While in some places the British administration took the control of the schools for indigenous pupils out of the Italian missionaries' hands, and many schools were now put to some other use, the missionaries, who were tolerated by the British, in many cases did manage to remain in their posts. They were often given the responsibility of assisting the village populations 'morally and materially', above all where there was a large number of women (i.e. war widows). In this

---

35 About the British Military Administration see Trevaskis (1960), Negash (1997), Lucchetti (2012).

36 Not by chance did it set up classes from the first grade of elementary school to the fifth grade of *ginnasio*.

37 'Suore missionarie comboniane' (n.d.: 34). In Italian: 'A Decamerè, per riportare un esempio tratto dalla cronaca missionaria, tre sorella il 3 settembre del 41 avevano iniziato un loro asilo presso la "Casa del Bimbo" e le altre 15 Pie Madri che avevano prestato il loro servizio presso l'ospedale militare dopo aver dovuto adempiere l'ordine militare superiore di partire collettivamente per Asmara vi avevano potuto far ritorno. Esse allora si prestarono per svariate opere parrocchiali ed educative in favore della popolazione locale e dei circa 8000 italiani'.

38 'Suore missionarie comboniane' (publication untitled).

same period, on the personal initiative of General Superior Carla Troenzi – who had been in Asmara ever since the war broke out – the first Eritrean novices to be invested in 1939 were admitted to the order as Pious Sisters of Nigrizia (with a consecration that could be renewed each year). The years following 1943 were the period in which the Comboni nuns' educational activity reached its height: they were active in numerous elementary and middle schools.[39] They were particularly active in Asmara, not only in their teaching 'on the Italian model', but also through their presence at English and Tigrinya schools working under the framework established by the new authorities.

Casa Comboni's own main activity was the Eritrean girls' school (this also providing English- and Tigrinya-language classes) and indeed it served as the female branch of the Comboni College (founded in 1947). At the beginning of the 1950s the *Istituto Santa Famiglia* (later *Sacra Famiglia*) – which from 1946 moved to a new building as a college or school – was further extended, becoming – as Puglisi's early accounts show – 'one of the most important educational centres' belonging to the Congregation of the Pious Mothers of Nigrizia. This period also saw the birth of a teacher-training institute and a language school specifically devoted to girls of non-Italian nationality; these, too, were managed by the Comboni nuns and both of them recognized by the colonial government. Outside Asmara, some missionaries continued to be active visiting the villages – as they had always done, moving between the missions set up in various locations – also providing healthcare for the ill, services for children and in some cases working on the upkeep of churches. On the other hand, their evangelization effort required them to move around, penetrating into the most difficult areas (Senafe, for example, where there was also a strong Muslim and Coptic-schismatic element).

Meanwhile – still in the early 1950s – faced with the alternative of setting up a local congregation built around the Pious Sisters of Nigrizia, consecrated in 1942, or bringing them into the Pious Mothers, they chose the latter option. Thus they fully accomplished the long process (beginning in 1939) that ultimately did see Eritrean women joining the Comboni congregation.

Conclusions

The most important questions emerging from this history without doubt concern the Comboni nuns' interactions with the colonial power and, more generally, with the Italian and British colonial administrations.[40] At the same time, they

39 As well as continuing to be present, without any significant break, at the Regina Elena hospital in Asmara and the Umberto I hospital in Massawa, to which we could add their welfare work in the women's prisons.

40 The relation 'between colonialism and missions' is the question of greatest interest when it comes to the European Christians' second colonisation of Africa in the second half of the nineteenth century. See Calchi Novati (2011: 295).

also concern their relations with the male ecclesiastical hierarchy, above all in the first period of this experience (the second half of the nineteenth century). The central feature of the Combonian nuns' relations with the Fascist and then British authorities – in a situation of never-directly-expressed conflict – was the female Catholic missionaries' ceaseless defence of their own autonomy. And there certainly were moments of tension with the Italian authorities and indeed with the British authorities.

However, this tension was often concealed, indirectly surfacing from direct accounts and particular acts, and it was managed – but also ignored – by the women missionaries for the sake of guaranteeing the survival of their welfare and educational activities. Thus they sought to 'take advantage' of the role historically attributed to women, which was also indirectly recognized in their own case: the field of care and the sphere of social reproduction. Moreover, the teaching they supplied (in the context of state schools' lack of resources) but above all the intermediary role they embodied in their relations with the local societies played in their favour as they sought to conserve a certain margin of autonomy. More generally, the missionaries intensified their presence in Eritrea (and Ethiopia) during the colonial occupation era, becoming ever more active in 'creating centres of community life' and 'taking on a leading role in Eritrean life'. They benefited from the colonial authorities' encouragement of Catholicism in terms of the creation of new missionary schools, the management of existing ones, and the strengthening of Italian propaganda (beginning with Salvago Raggi's governorship and continuing under Fascism).[41]

The formation of a local clergy was also of great importance to the overall picture from the very origins of the missions' history.[42] It was believed that this would help the evangelization process by bringing the populations closer to Catholic values and making their conversion easier. Above all, the Combonian missionaries encouraged the development of an African clergy (one of Comboni's own first objectives) as well as African nuns, according to the idea that they could 'plant' Christianity in African reality and the basic postulate that evangelization in Africa had to be the work and the responsibility of Africans themselves.[43] The Comboni nuns are placed in this context, which provides a policy of compromise with the Italian government. Particularly significant in this regard was the great importance the Comboni plan ascribed to the centrality of Africa and its potential and, in turn, to women. Not by chance were the first religious schools for girls in the Horn of Africa established with the help of the Congregation of the Pious Mothers of Nigrizia, and the first Eritrean nuns – coming long after their first appearance in the Egyptian and Sudanese contexts and incomparably later than the Eritrean priests – were the Pious Sisters of *Nigrizia*.

41 Taddia (1986: 170).

42 Conscious 'of the importance of the training of Eritrean prelates, the Apostolic Vicariate's policy vigorously encouraged their development'. See Taddia (1986: 174–5).

43 See Calchi Novati and Valsecchi (2005: 162).

Finally, also of interest in this experience is the great importance of the theme of 'moving', as missionaries journeyed from Italy to Africa, between African cities (Cairo, Khartoum, Asmara), between different parts of Eritrea itself, and between one mission and another. If, indeed, the phenomenon of mobility was of considerable importance to the history of colonial administrators for the purposes of a 'far-reaching and secure control over territory and the colonized populations',[44] so too could we advance similar considerations with regard to the Catholic missions.

This is all the more true when we look at Comboni's own plan: 'saving Africa with Africa' meant entering into direct contact with the local populations, and, above all, with women. It meant 'penetrating' (this word being something of a commonplace in missionary accounts and testimonies) into populations who were distant and inaccessible – not only in a geographical sense. That is, it meant finding the key to access another world – to know it, get closer to it and bring it toward a shared set of objectives – and for Comboni, women seemed to offer this key.

In short, we could say that using women (the Comboni nuns) to evangelize among African women and to evangelize in Africa more generally was a particular experience both in the history of European Catholic missions in Africa and in the subjectivation experienced by Italian women migrants to Africa as well as African women themselves, with all its light and shade.

References

Betti, C. (1996). Le missioni religiose. *Fonti e problemi della politica coloniale italiana*, vol. I., 702–27. Roma: Ministero per i beni culturali e ambientali. Ufficio centrale per i beni archivistici.

Borruso, P. (1988). I missionari cattolici italiani nella 'colonia eritrea', 1922–1936. *Analisi storica*, 6, 35–58.

Borruso, P. (1989). Le missioni cattoliche italiane nella politica imperiale del fascismo (1936–40). *Africa*, 1, 50–78.

Calchi Novati, G.P. and Valsecchi, P. (2005). *Africa: la storia ritrovata. Dalle prime forme politiche alle indipendenze nazionali*. Rome: Carocci.

Calchi Novati, G.P. (2011). *L'Africa d'Italia. Una storia coloniale e postcoloniale*. Rome: Carocci.

Ceci, L. (2007). *Il vessillo e la croce. Colonialismo, missioni cattoliche e islam in Somalia (1903–1924)*. Rome: Carocci.

Chelati Dirar, U. (2002). Collaborazione e conflitti: Michele da Carbonara e l'organizzazione della Prefettura Apostolica dell'Eritrea (1894/1910). *Quaderni storici*, 109(1), 149–88.

44 Giorgi (2012: 229). In Italian: 'un controllo ramificato e sicuro sul territorio e sulle popolazioni colonizzate'.

Chelati Dirar, U. (2003). Church and State Relations in Colonial Eritrea: Missionaries and the Development of Colonial Strategies, 1869–1911. *Journal of Modern Italian Studies*, 8, 391–410.

Comboni, D. (1991). *Gli scritti*. Bologna: EMI.

Di Pasquale, F. (2015). Civilizzare le civilizzatrici. Insegnanti italiane nello spazio mediterraneo fra Ottocento e Novecento. In Deplano, V. and Pes, A. (eds) *Quel che resta dell'impero. La cultura coloniale degli italiani*, 169–89. Milan: Mimesis.

Fonzi, F. (1988). Mondo cattolico, missioni e colonialismo italiano. *Clio*, 1, 17–53.

Fonzi, F. (1996). La Chiesa cattolica e la politica coloniale. *Fonti e problemi della politica coloniale italiana*, I, 438–63. Roma: Ministero per i beni culturali e ambientali. Ufficio centrale per i beni archivistici.

Franzinelli, M. (1992). Il clero e le colonie: i cappellani militari in Africa Orientale. *Rivista di storia contemporanea*, 4, 558–98.

Giorgi, C. (2012). *Soggetti e politiche della mobilità coloniale*, in Rosoni, I. and Chelati Dirar, U. (eds) *Votare con i piedi. La mobilità degli individui nell'Africa orientale italiana*, 199–229. Macerata: Eum.

Guazzini, F. (2008). *De-fascistizzare l'Eritrea e il vissuto dei vinti, 1941–1945*, in Carcangiu, B.M. and Tekeste Negash (eds), *L'Africa orientale italiana nel dibattito storico contemporaneo*, Roma: Carocci, Roma

Levine, P. (ed.) (2004) *Gender and Empire*. Oxford/New York: Oxford University Press.

Lucchetti, N. (2012). *Italiani d'Eritrea: 1941–1951 una storia politica*. Rome: Aracne.

Negash, T. (1987). *Italian Colonialism in Eritrea, 1882–1941: Policies, Praxis, and Impact*. Uppsala: Uppsala University.

Negash, T. (1997). *Eritrea and Ethiopia, the Federal Experience*. Uppsala: Nordista Afrikainstitutet.

Palma, S. (2007). *Educare alla subalternità. Prassi e politiche scolastiche nella colonia Eritrea*, in Carcangiu, B.M. and Negash, T. (eds) *L'Africa orientale italiana nel dibattito storico contemporaneo*. Rome: Carocci.

Prudhomme, C. (2007). *Missioni cristiane e colonialismo*. Milan: Jaca Book.

Puglisi, G. (1953). La scuola in Eritrea ieri e oggi. *Africa*, 8/5, 145–48.

Romanato, G. (2003). *L'Africa nera fra Cristianesimo e Islam. L'esperienza di Daniele Comboni (1831–1881)*. Milano: Corbaccio.

Sorgoni, B. (2000). Donne in colonia: definizione giuridica per un immaginario di genere. *Studi Piacentini*, 28, 203–15.

Suore missionarie comboniane, *75 anni di storia (1914–1989)* (n.d.).

Taddia, I. (1986). *L'Eritrea-colonia 1890–1952: paesaggi, strutture, uomini del colonialismo*, Milano: Franco Angeli.

Trevaskis, G.K.N. (1960). *Eritrea: A Colony in Transition, 1941–1952*. London: Oxford University Press.

Vanzon, C.A. (1836). *Dizionario universale della lingua italiana*. Livorno: Stamperia di Paolo Vannini.

Vidale, M. (2005). Salvare l'Africa con l'Africa: Fortunata Quascè, la prima pia madre della Nigrizia africana. *Archivio Madri Nigrizia*, 9.
Vidale, M. (2012). La congregazione delle Pie Madri della Nigrizia. Origini e fondazione (1867–1881). *Archivio Madri Nigrizia*, 20(S/1).
Vidale, M. (2013). La congregazione delle Pie Madri della Nigrizia. Dalla morte del fondatore al primo Capitolo generale (1881–1898). *Archivio Madri Nigrizia*, 22(S/2).

Chapter 2

Open Houses versus Closed Borders: Migrant Domestic Workers in Italy. A Gendered Perspective (1950s–2010s)[1]

Raffaella Sarti

Introduction

This chapter analyses the growing numbers of international migrant domestic workers employed by Italian families, explaining why the Italian case is noteworthy even to scholars not especially interested in Italy. It will explain the reasons for this growing presence and will provide readers with data on the numbers and nationalities of the women and men working in this sector.

The main focus of the chapter will be on the contradiction between the efforts made by the Italian authorities to control the national frontiers and thus prevent undesired immigration, and the care needs of Italian families. While one's house is often conceived of as a close space of intimacy, in the last decades it has actually (and paradoxically) been for a large numbers of Italians the main arena of encounters with foreigners.

Unexpected Scenes

The third millennium started, in Italy, with scenes that only a few years earlier nobody would have expected. On 22 November 2001, a surprising sit-in took place in Rome outside the Chamber of Deputies. Several thousand elderly people protested vociferously. Their slogans were: 'Do not prevent migrant workers from helping us to live!' and 'I need you!' (referring to migrant domestic workers). In the following months, other sit-ins took place in other Italian cities. Many of the elderly ladies and gentlemen who protested were accompanied by their migrant carers. At that time the Italian Parliament was discussing a restrictive bill on immigration that excluded an amnesty for irregular migrants working in Italy. Italy had then a right-wing government which emphasized both the fight against 'clandestine' immigration and the need to send irregular immigrants back home (Sarti, 2008a).

1 English revision by Clelia Boscolo, University of Birmingham.

Italy was (and is) rapidly ageing:[2] in the early 2000s, it was the country with the highest percentage of elderly people in the world.[3] Both families and public welfare were facing increasing difficulties in caring for the elderly and many families had (and have) resorted to private carers.[4]

It was calculated that if irregular carers were expelled, at least 150,000 elderly people would be left without their carers (Sarti, 2010: 96). This was one of the reasons why many people were worried. The protests by the elderly and other actors on the Italian political scene (in part fighting for the migrants' rights, in part interested in having a low-cost workforce) were successful: the approved version of the law was different from the proposed one (Law no. 189/2002, the so-called 'Bossi-Fini' Law). Although still very rigid, it allowed for the regularization of undocumented domestic workers already working in Italy. Shortly afterwards, the regularization of dependant workers, too, was allowed. The need for private carers had been the battering-ram used to breach the wall against regularization. Politicians who wanted to strengthen the Italian borders and send undocumented migrants back home were forced to officially recognize that the doors of the Italian homes – the 'sacred' intimacy of the private sphere – had been opened to undocumented foreigners. Part of public opinion described undocumented migrants (or even all migrants) as unwanted intruders; in fact, such discourse never stopped, but the new opportunity for undocumented carers, domestic and dependent workers to be regularized made it obvious that the supposedly unwanted migrants (or at least an important number of them) were actually very useful to many Italians and even welcomed by them (Sarti, 2008a).

As many as 700,000 individuals applied for regularization. Applications by people who declared themselves to be domestic workers were more than 340,000; about 316,000 were accepted. This was huge: before regularization, domestic workers (both Italian and foreigners) registered with the National Institute for Social Insurance (Inps) numbered about 250,000.[5] In previous years, the total figure had fluctuated between 200,000 and 260,000, but the percentage of foreigners had grown rapidly: 5.6 per cent between 1972–1982, more than a fifth (20.5 per cent) in 1992 and half of the total by 1996 (Sarti, 2004: 18, table 1); after regularization, they reached three-quarters of the total (75 per cent in 2003). In the following

2 The ageing index was 38.9 in 1961, 127.1 in 2001 and 148.6 in 2012; see Istat (2001: 4; 2002: 32; 2014a: 150).

3 In 2001 and 2002, 19 per cent of the Italian population was aged 65 or over. In 2013, the country with the largest elderly population was Japan (25 per cent), followed by Italy and Germany (both 21 per cent); see The World Bank (2014).

4 Employing irregular migrants was an offence punishable by 3–12 months' imprisonment.

5 Both Italian and foreign domestic workers must be registered with Inps; irregular migrants cannot register and can only work in the 'black' economy. Registered domestic workers were 256,539 in 2000 and 261,425 in 2001 (Sarti, 2008a: 178). Inps data is regularly updated, so there may be small differences with the figures reported in my previous essays.

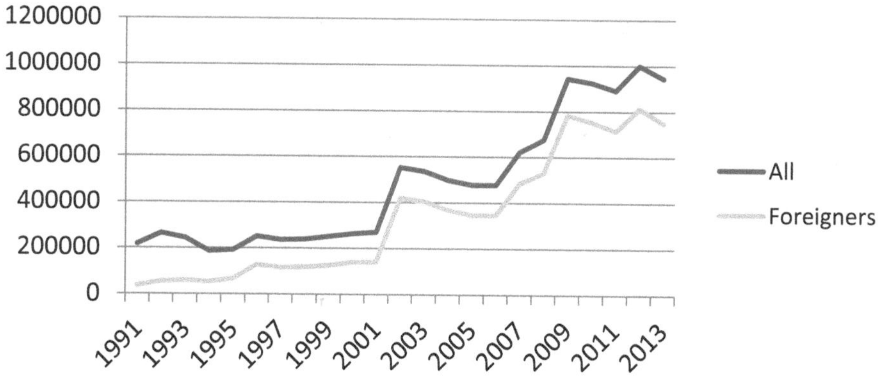

Figure 2.1 Domestic workers registered with Inps, Italy 1991–2013
Source: Inps databank.

decade, their number increased further, though with some fluctuation: in 2012 – when registered domestic workers reached almost 1 million (999,901) – foreigners were 81.3 per cent of the total: 812,761 individuals, 174.474 men (21.5 per cent) and as many as 638.287 women (78.5 per cent).[6]

In addition to registered domestic workers, many unregistered workers still exist and operate in the black economy: probably another half-a-million, both migrants and Italians (Pasquinelli, 2013: 42, 47). Thus, in Italy (a country with 60 million inhabitants), there may be, today, more than 1 million foreigners working as *colf* and *badanti*, i.e. as domestic workers and private carers. Their arrival has contributed, within a few decades, to transforming Italy from a (mainly) sending country into a (mainly) receiving one (Sarti, 2008b: 87), even though, because of the recent economic crisis, Italians are increasingly emigrating (Istat, 2014b).

The Role of Italy within a Booming Research Field

Domestic work has been analysed by historians at least since the nineteenth century. Between the late nineteenth and the early twentieth centuries, it was also analysed by sociologists and social scientists, but later on it was neglected by them, often because they believed it would disappear – after a phase of expansion and feminization – thanks to economic and social progress, modernization and/or industrialization. Significantly, the few who studied it often considered it as an indicator of the degree of modernity reached by a country. Especially since the 1990s, however, noting the growing presence of (international) migrant domestic workers in many different contexts, they have shown increasing attention to this

6 http://www.inps.it/webidentity/banchedatistatistiche/domestici/index01.jsp? Accessed 2 December 2014.

phenomenon, which blatantly contradicted well-rooted interpretative schemes. In the last few years, their interest has been booming (Sarti, 2014).

Interpretations of the growing flows of migrant domestic workers are diverse. Often, however, they have been considered a consequence of the growing economic and demographic imbalances between the global North and the global South, and/or between Western Europe and the former socialist countries of Eastern Europe. The increasing demand (and supply) of services in the globalized labour market is also interpreted as one of the reasons of the feminization of both migration flows and survival strategies.[7] According to Saskia Sassen (1991; 2002), the formation of the so-called 'global cities' has created a growing demand for services and manual workers. At the same time, in a world where millions of people experience poverty, unemployment and poor state help, entire nations become increasingly dependent on feminized survival networks such as those linked to the migration of (mainly female) domestic workers and the remittances they send home. Rhacel Parreñas (2001; 2005) has analysed the development of global care chains within the growing international division of reproductive labour and its commodification, denouncing the negative consequences that the export of care-work from poor to rich countries has on the poorer nations, especially on the individuals who mainly need to be cared for, such as the children left behind by the migrant domestic workers themselves, even though these women are sometimes successful in overcoming the problems caused by their transnational motherhood.

Italy has played an important role within this booming research field, having been analysed within some of the most influential books on the issue, namely Andall's (2000), Anderson's (2000) and Parreñas's (2001). Actually, some Italians had noted the growing presence of foreign domestics at an early stage and had looked into it.[8] Yet, with only a few exceptions, such as Campani's essays (1989; 1993), the publication of their research did not have international impact, probably because it was normally written in Italian. Furthermore, most of it was in the form of short essays rather than books, and these were in part produced not by academics but by researchers linked to the domestic workers themselves, particularly the Catholic association of domestic workers Acli-Colf, which commissioned studies aimed at understanding social change and elaborating policies (Turrini, 1977; Alemani and Fasoli, 1994; Alemani, 2010). Though interesting both on a political and a scientific level, these publications were of no great consequence in Italian academia either. The poor attention towards the conditions of domestic workers by most Italian intellectuals was indeed a by-product of their marginal position. Over time, however, research increasingly focused on (migrant) domestic workers employed in Italy. Especially by the 2000s–2010s, some of the studies reached an

7 According to Lutz (2008: 3), 'growing demand for labour power in the domestic work sector has contributed to the feminization of migration more than any other area of work'. For a useful review essay see Vianello (2013).

8 Turrini (1977: 34); Crippa (1979); Sacconi (1984); Campani (1989); Favaro and Tognetti Bordogna (1991); Alemani and Fasoli (1994); Vicarelli (1994); Ambrosini (1998).

international audience, thus contributing to making the Italian case an important one (Sarti, 2014: 302–3).

An Interesting Case: Modernization Efforts

A Western country that experienced rapid modernization and economic growth after the Second World War, Italy was an ideal case to test the impact of these transformations on domestic work. According to the forecasts that circulated in the 1950s, 1960s, and 1970s, domestic service was destined to change radically and even to disappear (Sarti, 2014). These ideas were also shared by the few Italian intellectuals who, in that period, analysed domestic workers. In 1953, the working conditions of domestics appeared, to Gianluigi Degli Esposti (1953: 55–9), backward, slave-like, and 'pre-liberal'. Yet he believed that the changing social life, growing female industrial employment and mechanization of many services, including domestic ones, would make the very figure of the maid, except those serving idle ladies, anachronistic. Degli Esposti had been prompted to write his article by the approval of a law which extended compulsory illness insurance to domestic workers.[9] The 1950s saw the approval of important laws regulating paid domestic work, which in the first half of the twentieth century had been excluded from almost any legislation aimed at protecting work.[10] Maternity protection (1950)[11] and thirteenth-month salary (1953)[12] were introduced, and in 1958 the first (and, up until now, the only) Italian comprehensive law on domestic work was approved (Law no. 339/1958) (Sarti, 2010). Since this law granted domestic workers some rights,[13] many employers protested. While replying to a reader who had sent him a letter complaining about the new law, the editor of the popular magazine *Epoca*, Enzo Biagi, invited masters and mistresses to be patient and to treat their domestic workers, whom he assimilated to 'the last of the Mohicans', compassionately. He, too, believed that domestics were nearing extinction.[14]

Things were indeed changing rapidly, even though, if glancing at statistical data, this was not apparent: according to census data, female domestic workers

9 Law no. 53/1952.

10 Domestic workers had been excluded from the protection given to working minors and women; maternity protection; limitation of working hours; collective wage agreements; the subjection of jurisdiction, in the case of dispute, to work tribunals established by the authorities; and protection in case of involuntary unemployment. They only benefited from compulsory insurance against invalidity, old age (1923) and tuberculosis (1927). The Italian Civil Code of 1942 (articles 2240–46) had introduced some rights, such as paid holidays, but had not extended to domestic workers many rights granted to other categories; see Sarti (2010: 36–9).

11 Law no. 860/1950.

12 Law no. 940/1953.

13 The law, however, did not eliminate discrimination against them.

14 *Epoca*, No. 398, 18 May 1958; Sarti (2014: 286, Figure 1).

in 1951 were 7.4 per cent of economically active women and nearly the same percentage in 1961 (7.3 per cent) (Sarti, 2004: 35; Figure 2.2). Yet the percentage of live-in domestics was decreasing dramatically: in 1951 they were 74 per cent of people employed in the sector and only 41 per cent in 1961 (Colombo, 2005). Live-out charwomen, often working for several families, were replacing live-in maids. Some groups of domestic workers were fighting not only to improve their working conditions but also to reshape their social identity. Interestingly, in the 1960s, in order to define themselves, the domestics in the Italian Association of Christian Workers (Acli) introduced a new term – *colf*[15] – to replace the traditional and stigmatizing ones. They were successful: *colf* has become very common (e.g. Turri, 2010: 175). They were also struggling to be entitled to collective bargaining. In 1969, the Italian Constitutional Court eventually declared illegitimate the part of article 2068 of the Civil Code that excluded collective bargaining in the domestic sector.[16] In 1974, the first national collective contract was eventually signed. In that period, some groups of domestic workers, such as Acli-Colf, became increasingly involved in the workers' movement. They tried to create a new type of domestic worker, no longer working only for private families but also (and possibly mainly) for public services, thanks to new forms of public home-care and assistance designed to reduce hospitalization and institutionalization. They also tried to encourage the formation of new cooperative companies among domestic workers (Turri, 2010: 179–82; Sarti, 2010: 110–11). In the same period, a communist woman (Vittoria Lotti), wishing to offer services and care not only to middle- and upper-class families but also to lower-class ones, created a cooperative company, the Cadiai (1974), to develop home-care for the sick, the elderly and children (Sarti, 2010: 111–12). Though many domestic workers still denounced stigmatization and backward working conditions (Turrini, 1977), the domestic sector was experiencing important changes. At the same time, it was shrinking: in 1951, the Italian census recorded 378,000 domestic workers, in 1971 only 220,000. 'Women servants no longer exist and the young believe that it is right not to have any', the well-known Italian writer Natalia Ginzburg wrote in 1969 (Ginzburg, 1969).

An Insufficient Change: Old Solutions for (Relatively) New Problems

At that time, Italy was still a country left every year by thousands of emigrants. Yet something was changing: since the early 1970s, immigrants had begun to be more numerous than emigrants (Einaudi, 2007: 55–6). The demand for domestic work played an important role in stimulating the growing immigration. In 1968–69

15 Abbreviation of *collaboratrice familiare*, i.e. a person who collaborates with a family. Although introduced to give a new dignity to domestic workers, this term was actually ambiguous: *collaboratore* is like a helper, not the same as *lavoratore* [worker].

16 Corte costituzionale, judgment no. 68/1969.

the Constitutional Court had established that domestic workers employed for less than four hours a day had the same rights as the others, and in 1971, illness insurance was extended to them.[17] This meant that employers had to pay social security contributions for them, too (Sarti, 2010: 70–71). The idea that social security contributions should not be paid for foreign domestic workers circulated until at least 1972, when the Labour Ministry made clear that it was wrong.[18] Moreover, while there was a demand for live-in domestic workers, Italian women were increasing unwilling to work as live-ins. Both of these reasons boosted the demand for foreign domestics, who had begun to arrive in the early 1960s (Andall, 2000: 113–19).

The first to arrive had been a few women from Spain, but soon growing numbers of African women started to enter Italy as immigrants, especially from Eritrea. While, according to a common stereotype, migrant workers are generally young, single men, the forerunners of work-immigration to Italy were largely women destined to work as domestics in the private sphere (Einaudi, 2007: 84–7). In a context where less-asymmetric labour relationships where slowly spreading and domestic work was actually experiencing some modernization, many middle- and upper-class Italians resorted to networks rooted in the recent-but-rapidly-forgotten colonial past to continue to be served more or less as usual.[19] They would soon also exploit other networks that were not *strictu sensu* colonial but also implied a clear hierarchy between a centre and several peripheries around the world, i.e. the Catholic networks which had their core in Italy and Rome as the See of the Papacy. These networks were especially important for the booming arrival of domestic workers from the Philippines (the word *Filippina* was to become synonymous with domestic worker),[20] but would also be important for those arriving from other (mainly Catholic) countries, particularly Latin America.

In this period, Italy was also witnessing important changes in family law that made the legal framework of Italian family life less patriarchal and authoritarian: divorce was introduced (1970) and the authority of the head of the family became officially shared by both spouses (1975). Thanks to a strong feminist movement, abortion was permitted (1978). While some feminists tried to change the subordinate female position within the family, advocating (unsuccessfully) a salary to housewives, others fought to get paid employment outside the home, sometimes even showing a kind of contempt towards housewifery and domestic chores (Gissi, forthcoming). Scholars still debate whether, before the 1970s, female participation rates in the workforce really were as low as shown by official statistics, often

---

17 Decree of the President of the Republic no. 140/1971; Corte costituzionale, judgments no. 101/1986, no. 16/1969 and no. 114/1969.

18 Labour Ministry, Circ. 37/106/III, 30 December 1972, quoted by Andall (2000: 120).

19 On black domestic workers, see Andall (2000) and Marchetti (2011, 2014).

20 On Filipino domestic workers, see Del Rio (1979); Korsieporn (1990); Parreñas (2001); Magat (2004, 2007); Banfi (2008); Basa and De la Rosa (2007).

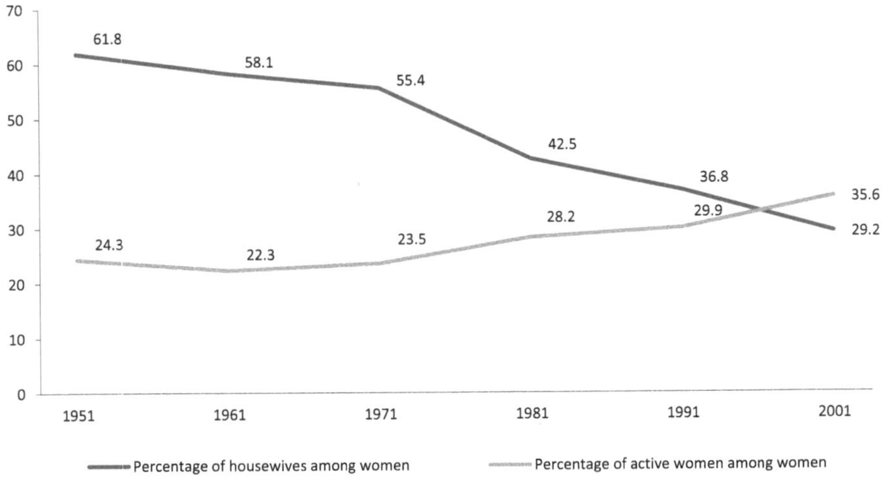

Figure 2.2 Housewives and economically active women, Italy 1951–2001
Source: Istat, Population Censuses, 1881–2001.
Note: For the definition of economically active population (*popolazione attiva*) in the 1951 and 1961 censuses, see Vitali (1970: 326–7). The data of 1961–91 are about the 'economically active population in employment status', which coincides with the category of *popolazione attiva* of previous censuses. In 2001, this category was replaced by that of *forze di lavoro* ('labour force'), which differs from the previous one because it also includes people looking for their first job; however, a comparable category can be calculated. The age groups considered are those on which the classifications of the economically active population are based in the different censuses. The data refer to the resident population. The percentage of active women differs from the activity rate as defined by Istat, i.e. the ratio between people belonging to the labour force and population aged 15 and over. The term *casalinghe* ('housewives'), appears in Italian censuses as late as 1961; in 1951 (and earlier) the category is called 'attendants to domestic care-work' or 'attendants to the care of their homes'.

arguing that working women were actually much more numerous but remained statistically invisible because they performed precarious and unregistered work (Badino, 2008: 23–62). However, according to official data, female employment rates have been growing since the 1960s (Figure 2.2) and it is pretty certain that the number of employed women increased, though quite possibly by not as much as shown by official statistics.

To keep things going, domestic chores and care-work should have been distributed in a new way between men and women, private families and public services. Yet this happened only to a limited degree. While women entered the extra-domestic labour market, men never entered the sphere of domestic work to the same extent. Furthermore, the Italian authorities never stopped thinking of Italian families as the main providers of care. As a consequence, they never

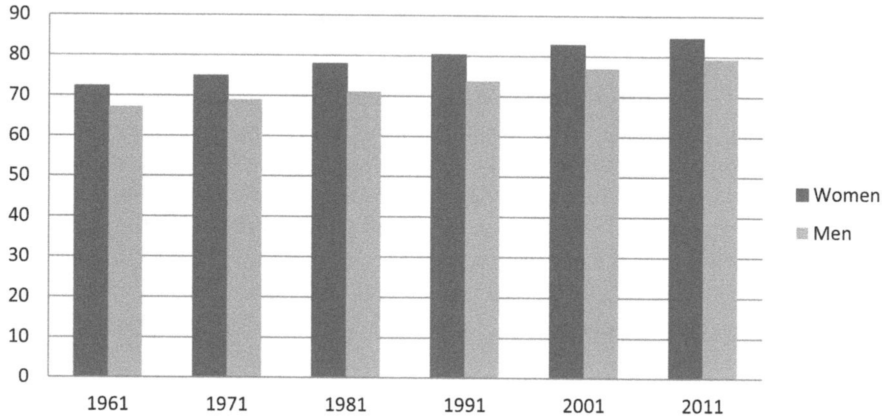

Figure 2.3 Life expectancy at birth, Italy 1961–2011
Source: Istat (2011: 5); Istat (2014: 17).

developed a strong public welfare, despite some change over time.[21] Italian families, and especially women, adopted several strategies to cope with these imbalances, sometimes rather painful, such as dramatically reducing their fertility rates, to the point that for a few years Italy had the lowest fertility ever experienced by humankind.[22] Yet, because of an increasingly ageing population, the need for care remained high, or even increased.

Another strategy was to resort to paid domestic work: significantly, since the 1980s, hiring a domestic worker had no longer been considered the privilege of affluent families aiming to free idle housewives from the drudgery of housework and allow them to enjoy leisure. Rather, it had increasingly been presented as a necessity for overburdened women struggling to cope with work both within and outside their home (Turrini, 1977: 48; Sacconi, 1984: 41; Alemani and Castelletti, 1994: 32; Eurispes, 2002: 2). Efforts to transform both work and the family had led to a contradictory outcome. There had been important changes which affected the women's role both within and outside the family. Yet the gender division of tasks within the family had not radically changed. Nor had the provision of public services grown as would have been necessary. Thus, growing numbers of families resorted to a solution – hiring a domestic worker or a carer (even live-in) – that only a few years earlier many would have considered destined to vanish, even though most middle- and upper-class families had actually never stopped enjoying some paid help.

21 E.g. Esping Andersen (1990); Saraceno (1994); Bimbi (1999); Sarti (2005: 263–271); De Marchi and Sarti (2010).

22 The so-called 'lowest low fertility' cannot be explained with one cause only; see Dalla Zuanna and Micheli (2004); Billari (2008).

In Italy, cleaning ladies and charwomen used to be lower-class Italian women, often internal migrants from the countryside and/or from the poorer areas of the country (Turrini, 1977: 32–4). Many of them, usually married women with children, were not willing to work as live-ins. On their part, young, unmarried Italian girls were increasingly unwilling to work and live under the same roof as their employers. Thus, if Italian families increasingly resorted to live-in domestic workers and caregivers, it was because there was a new supply of people willing to take on those roles, i.e. the international migrants, whose numbers were growing. On this scene, Italian migration policies were not neutral, even though they were not able to reach their goals (at least the official ones).

Migration Policies

For a long time, Italian migration policies focused on emigration. As for immigration, until 1986, Italian laws were conceived to control the presence of a few foreigners (refugees, businessmen, renters, tourists), not to regulate the immigration of (many) workers and their families (Einaudi, 2007: 33). During Fascism, police regulation was strengthened to prevent the arrival of people considered a threat to public order or without means of subsistence, to make expulsion easier if such undesired strangers happened to be in the country, and to control the mobility of foreigners within the national borders. There were no particular rules to regulate the inflow of foreign workers who, actually, for a long time were only a few. Hiring a foreigner was permitted; the employer was obliged to communicate to the police the start and end of the employment relationship, the job performed by the worker, and other information.

From 1963 onwards, however, several circulars tried to regulate the inflow of foreigners.[23] They were mainly aimed at limiting competition with Italian workers, thus showing a self-perception of Italy as a country where work was scarce and had to be protected. These circulars devoted special attention to paid domestic work: they introduced procedures to make sure that social security contributions were paid for foreign domestics, too (1972), established that recruiting domestic workers from abroad be possible only after verifying that there weren't any Italians willing to take on the job (1973), tried to fight illegal recruitment agencies (1975; 1979) and allowed, in 1979, a regularization of undocumented domestic workers: many other regularizations would follow. Importantly, the 1979 circular condemned foreign domestic workers to be more dependent on their employer than Italian ones. It was indeed the employer who was entitled to apply to renew the yearly authorization to work in Italy for the domestic worker. Only in a few cases could the domestic worker break the contract and move to another employer. Furthermore, foreign domestic workers were allowed to work only as live-ins. Thus, the Italian authorities themselves prompted a segmentation of the labour

23 Circ. 51/22/IV, 4 December 1963.

market, contributing to creating a cleavage between Italian live-out domestic workers and live-in migrant ones forced into a more 'backward' work relationship.[24]

The procedure foreseen by the circulars was inadequate to regulate the growing inflow of foreigners and, in 1982, the Italian authorities banned immigration to work. Yet domestic workers in this case, too, were treated differently from other workers, since they were partially excluded from the ban. In 1986, a law on immigration was eventually approved (Law no. 943/1986, the so-called 'Foschi Law'). It included special rules for domestic workers who were eventually allowed to work as live-outs and for more than one employer (Sarti, 2010: 85–6). But, shortly afterwards, the release of new work permits for domestic workers was suspended. A new law was approved (Law no. 39/1990, the so-called 'Martelli Law') both because the procedure to get work permits was too complex and the international scene was changing after the fall of the Berlin Wall in 1989. As the previous ones had, it allowed the regularization of the irregular workers present in Italy; this regularization, however, was much more successful than the previous ones, leading to regularize about 218,000 immigrants (Sarti, 2010: 87–8).

Even though the law established that the Italian authorities should set every year the number and types of immigrants who would be accepted, for a long time this was not systematically done. Only workers arriving from abroad through nominative calls were permitted to work in Italy, provided that they would not take a job that could be taken by Italians or by foreigners residing in Italy. Despite the provisions of the new law, the Italian Labour Ministry surprisingly confirmed the ban for domestic workers, yet this caused several reactions and the recruitment of foreign domestic workers was eventually allowed. Moreover, the obligation to check whether there were Italians who could take on the job before hiring foreigners was abolished. Again, however, foreign domestic workers were only allowed to work full-time for one employer, who had to provide them with housing. In the following years, a high percentage of the work permits were issued to domestic workers, to the point that the authorities introduced, once again, the obligation to check whether Italians or resident immigrants were willing to take on the job before hiring foreigners, an obligation that generally was not fulfilled (Sarti, 2010: 89–92).

The efforts made by the Italian authorities to control immigration were unsuccessful, and there were huge numbers of foreign workers who arrived without any documents or were over-stayers after arriving with a tourist permit. In the following years, the authorities thus allowed another regularization (246,000 people in 1995–96) and approved a new law (Law no. 40/1998, the so-called 'Turco-Napolitano Law'), also made necessary because of the new international context created by the Schengen Agreement. This was a comprehensive law

24 Labour Ministry, Circ. 37/106/III, 30 December 1972 and Circ. 38/107/III, 25 June 1973; Foreign Ministry, Circ. 22, 8 May 1973; Labour Ministry, Circ. 7/122/II, 21 July 1975; Circ. 8026, 21 May 1979 and Circ. 140/90/79, 7 December 1979; see Andall (2000: 119–24); Einaudi (2007: 107); Sarti (2010: 79–84) and Gjergji (2013).

regulating every aspect of immigration; some Italians hold it as too severe, others as too liberal. Additionally, many families considered the minimum income that, according to the new law, an employer must have in order to hire a foreigner too high (Einaudi, 2007: 259). In this context, the right-wing government started to discuss yet another law designed to make immigration more difficult and the expulsion of irregular immigrants easier. It was this proposed law that provoked the reactions which eventually led to the huge regularization of 2002 mentioned in the first pages of this chapter (another regularization of about 217,000 people had taken place after the law of 1998) (Sarti, 2010: 95–9).

In the next years, the annual plans (*decreti flussi*) allocated growing percentages of the work permits available to immigrants from outside the EU to domestic workers (18.8 per cent in 2005; 70.2 per cent in 2008; see Piperno, 2010: 342). Moreover, the maximum numbers were often changed in order to accept more applicants than initially set (this choice was also justified by the need for care and domestic work). Finally, the borders of the European Union were broadened to include Poland, the Czech Republic, Slovakia, Hungary, Slovenia, Lithuania, Latvia, Estonia, Cyprus and Malta in 2004, and Romania and Bulgaria in 2007 (Sarti, 2010: 99–102). This contributed to a growing presence of eastern European carers and domestic workers (Figure 2.4).

While increasing flows of immigrants arrived to Italy (with domestic workers still representing an important share), part of the public opinion and of the policy makers, fearing the alleged 'invasion' by foreigners, showed growing concern. In 2009, being an undocumented migrant became a criminal offence (Law no.

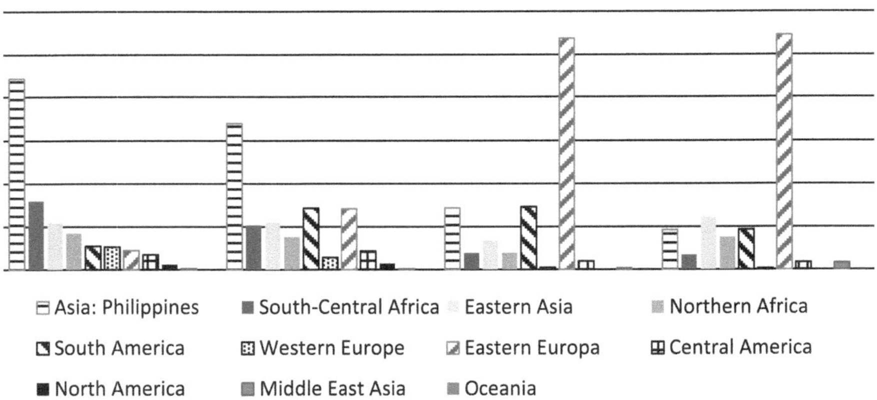

Figure 2.4 Foreign carers and domestic workers enrolled with Inps according to their origin (percentages) 1991–2012

Source: Inps databank.

94/2009).[25] Significantly, however, the Defence Minister Ignazio La Russa immediately calmed worried families employing undocumented migrants, explaining that there would not be any witch hunting of 'clandestine' domestic workers. At the same time, yet another regularization, reserved only for carers and domestic workers, was approved (with almost 300,000 applications) (Sarti, 2010: 102–3). Nor was this the last one, because another one – accompanied by the introduction of harsher punishments for employers hiring undocumented migrants – took place in 2012, and 86 per cent of the 134,000 applications were presented by carers and domestic workers (Stuppini, 2013: 183–4).

Closed Borders versus Open Houses? A Gendered Perspective

Italian migration policies have tried to control the borders and regulate the inflow of foreigners. Yet they have proved unable to prevent (irregular) migration that actually met the demand by Italians, especially by Italian families in need of help. This need has contributed to attracting migrants. The large supply of people willing to work as domestics and carers has, in turn, prompted new demand.[26]

Resorting to a charwoman is a choice that has to do with traditional status issues and class lifestyles, as well as with limited redistribution of domestic chores between men and women, a problem particularly serious for (middle- and upper-class) working women (Näre, 2013). In a sense, these women were and are able to take on roles once foreclosed to the female sex by way of leaving traditional domestic tasks to other women, both lower-class nationals and foreigners, even highly educated ones (Luciano, 1994; Andall, 2000). The reasons for hiring babysitters may be similar, but they also have to do with their being able or unable to count on the help of other family members, especially grandparents. As for resorting to carers for the elderly, it has become commonplace even with the working class (Näre, 2013).[27]

This is possible because the Italian welfare system supports people mainly through monetary transfers (such as pensions) that may be used to hire carers. A paradoxical consequence is that public provisions were and are used to pay not only regular migrants, but also the irregular ones whom the Italian migration policies officially tried and try to keep out of the Italian borders (De Marchi and Sarti, 2010).

Women and their roles were and are at the very core of this huge phenomenon: they have been both the 'causes' and the protagonists of it. Female migrant domestic workers were the forerunners of work-migration to Italy (Campani, 1989; Andall, 2000; Einaudi, 2007). The efforts made by the Italian domestic

25 On 2 April 2014 it became again an administrative offence.

26 Sarti (2010); van Hooren (2010); Ambrosini (2013). According to Williams (2012) there is growing convergence across Europe in the employment of migrant care labour.

27 For a comparative analysis of demand, see Triandafyllidou and Marchetti (2015).

workers to improve their working conditions (e.g. by refusing live-in positions, conquering social protection, etc.) made it more difficult and/or more expensive for a family to hire domestics, thus indirectly contributed to directing employers towards (forcibly) more-subservient and less-expensive foreigners. If families were increasingly looking for domestic workers, this was to a large extent because they needed to support and partially replace Italian women in the domestic sphere. At the same time, the arrival of many women willing to work as domestics and carers at relatively low costs encouraged people to resort to them. The large supply created new demand. In a sense, the growing recourse to foreign domestic workers has started as a conservative reaction to the democratizing efforts made by some of the Italian domestic workers and (feminist) Italian women. The former struggled to improve their working conditions and to have a new role within society, the latter to democratize the family and to conquer new roles outside the home. This might have implied a radical change of both the gendered roles within the domestic sphere and the domestic sphere itself within Italian society. Italian society as a whole has shown to be unprepared to 'take seriously' all these new instances aiming at greater class and gender equality, and to pursue such a radical change. Women themselves have often contributed to smoothing the potentially highly de-stabilizing consequences of the new aspirations of many of them by accepting the double burden of work inside and outside the home and by looking for private solutions (such as hiring a domestic worker) when they were no longer able to cope with all of those tasks. Traditional solutions, such as hiring private domestic personnel, were thus adopted in an innovative manner (recruiting workers on a global scale) to solve new problems especially due to changing female roles. Further problems were and are due to the booming numbers of elderly people in need of care: the lacking public assistance and the choice by Italians to look for private solutions rather than campaign and struggle to get more public assistance may even have strengthened the role of the family as a provider of care and assistance, though not only through 'private' means but also through public funding ('cash for care'). Moreover, the providers of the assistance are no longer only (mainly female) unpaid family members but also foreign unrelated paid carers. Actually, middle- and upper-class families had traditionally resorted to some help, but the new carers often take on tasks that are those of a nurse. This contributes to changing the role of the family whilst apparently maintaining its traditional role.

It is worth recalling that migration policies contributed to 'constructing' the employment relationship with a migrant domestic worker as a more asymmetric one than that with a national worker. At the same time, the very complicated system for recruiting foreign workers, who, in theory, could only be hired when they were still abroad, encouraged irregular immigration and a large presence of undocumented workers who had only very limited bargaining power until they had an opportunity to be regularized. In short, migration policies provided Italian families with a forcibly 'subservient' and low-cost workforce, thus (paradoxically?) encouraging the recourse to it and (indirectly) the arrival of more migrants, both regular and irregular. Moreover, while migration policies officially tried to limit and regulate immigration, families proved to be 'open' and ready to accept unknown foreigners, even undocumented ones who, working in the private sphere, were particularly well-protected from being discovered by the police. Thus, families contributed to 'protecting' irregular migrants.

Except for short periods, over the last 50 years it has been easier to legally enter Italy as a domestic worker than as a worker in other sectors. Moreover, domestic workers in many cases have had more opportunities to be regularized.[28] This has implied that people who pretended to be domestic workers applied for regularization, both women and men (Sarti, 2004; 2010). However, the high demand for work in the care and domestic sectors has, over time, convinced not only women but also men to actually work as domestics, creating unexpected constellations of gender and national/migrant status (Sarti, 2006; Sarti and Scrinzi, 2010).[29] Despite a considerable percentage of men – up to 30 per cent among registered, foreign domestic workers after the 1996 regularization (Sarti, 2006) – migrant domestic and care workers are largely women.

I have already mentioned the (paradoxical?) outcome of the struggles to get more gender equality by Italian women, which often led to the hiring of a foreign domestic worker. I have also mentioned that migrant domestic workers have been 'constructed' by Italian migration policies as especially 'weak' workers with only limited bargaining power. Yet we can find paradox in the lives of domestic workers too. Actually, despite working in the traditionally female domestic sphere, migrant domestic workers often played and play a role similar to that habitually attributed, until recently, to male migrants who went abroad alone, sent home remittances, were the distant breadwinners for their families, and, when well established abroad, were likely to be joined by their spouses and children. Thus, particularly because of the higher wages that migrant domestic workers earn in Italy when compared to those earned in their country, their work in the domestic sphere may (paradoxically) turn out to be empowering for them and also to lead them to experience a 'contradictory class mobility', especially when they, at home, belong to middle-class families (Parreñas, 2001).

Therefore the domestic sphere turns out to be a crucial place. Because of the relationships and conflicts among its members, as well as its needs, it often seems a prime mover of far-reaching changes that, interacting with others originating in the public arena, have complex and often rather paradoxical consequences. Another rather paradoxical feature of the Italian case is the very fact that, for many Italians, the place where they have met an immigrant for the first time has been precisely their own home. Houses have been places of ethnographic encounters (Signorelli, 2006) and (asymmetric) cultural confrontations (Miranda, 2004).

28 On regularisation strategies see Bonizzoni (2013).

29 The new edition of *Servants of Globalization by* Parreñas (2015) includes two additional chapters on male domestic workers. On gendered aspects of migration and the labour market in Europe see Andall (2013).

While, on the one hand, this openness of the private sphere contrasts with the efforts to control and even close the national borders, on the other hand it does not necessarily contradict the overtly or covertly anti-immigrant discourse which is now rather widespread in Italy. Firstly, one's migrant is often considered as being different from the anonymous mass of 'the migrants' as a whole; secondly, and more importantly, everyday interaction with immigrants within the private sphere does not necessarily prevent prejudice or racialization and ethnicization processes. Often it is rather the contrary (Scrinzi, 2004; 2013). As such, the private sphere represents a crucial place where both gender and national identity are negotiated (with different bargaining powers) by male and female family members as well as foreign domestic workers who are often presented as 'one of the family' to reduce their disquieting 'otherness' and to try to (instrumentally) involve them in the traditional system of family (unpaid) obligations.

To Conclude

Italy, with all its contradictions and paradoxes, thus represents an interesting case to focus on for the unexpected consequences of modernization processes, struggles to improve working conditions, and claims for greater gender equality, which, on the one hand, were strong enough to lead to important legal innovation and social change but, on the other, were too weak and possibly too contradictory to lead to radical change in both gender roles and the role of the family within Italian society. The reactions to these claims and struggles, and the solutions found to cope with the problems that they provoked in the traditional organization of Italian society, have brought about highly contradictory constellations. The question to be addressed by future (actually, already-ongoing) research is to understand how these constellations are changing because of the economic crisis and the new international scenarios.

As a historian interested in long term analysis, before concluding, I would also like to have a look at the remote past. Certainly, foreign domestic and care workers who have arrived in Italy since the 1960s were and are different from domestic workers and servants working in Italian households in previous times, as they generally were Italian nationals. Yet, while today a large number of domestic workers employed by Italian families arrive from Eastern Europe, especially from Romania and Ukraine, some six or seven centuries ago (1300–1400), people arriving from those areas were also to be found among the domestic staff of Italian families. They were only a small percentage, but they were rather visible. Just as they are today, they were mainly women. Unlike today they were generally brought to Italy as slaves (today while there certainly are trafficked women among domestic workers, most of them have chosen to come to Italy, though often 'forced' by problems at home). In the fourteenth and fifteenth centuries, the Italian states were at the forefront of economic development, commercial networking and the creation of colonies in the eastern Mediterranean and the Black Sea region; the slave trade developed alongside this economic growth. In the recent Italian past, migrant domestic workers have been constructed as especially weak workers at a time when national domestic workers were getting new rights; in the Middle Ages, when the trade in foreign slaves developed alongside new commercial networks, in Italy the slavery of nationals had all but completely disappeared; after the Black Death (mid-fourteenth century), which drastically reduced the Italian population and gave surviving workers an unexpected bargaining power, allowing slaves to arrive from abroad and showing that there were affordable alternatives to resorting to Italian workers was probably one of the strategies used to reduce their claims (Sarti, 2015, forthcoming). Is this a sad lesson of history? What would have happened if the Italian authorities had strongly supported the transformation of private domestic workers into public employees, providing care at home to people who needed it, as had been hoped for by some domestic workers in the 1970s, and had developed strong public services to support the claims for more gender equality brought about by Italian feminists?

References

Alemani, C. (2010). Le colf nelle prime indagini sul lavoro domestico nell'Italia repubblicana. In Sarti, R. (ed.) *Lavoro domestico e di cura: quali diritti?*, 137–62. Roma: Ediesse.

Alemani, C. and Castelletti, G. (1994). Introduzione. In Alemani, C. and Fasoli, M.G. (eds) *Donne in frontiera. Le colf nella transizione*, 11–33. Milano: Cens.

Alemani, C. and Fasoli, M.G. (eds) (1994). *Donne in frontiera. Le colf nella transizione.* Milano: Cens.

Ambrosini, M. (1998). Convenienze nascoste. L'inserimento degli immigrati nell'economia informale. *Studi di sociologia*, 36, 233–57.

Ambrosini, M. (2013). *Irregular Migration and Invisible Welfare.* Basingstoke/ New York: Palgrave Macmillan.

Andall, J. (2000). *Gender, Migration and Domestic Service: The Politics of Black Women in Italy.* Aldershot: Ashgate.

Andall, J. (ed.) (2013). *Gendered Mobilities and Work in Europe.* Special Issue of *Journal of Ethnic and Migration Studies*, 39, no. 4.

Anderson, B. (2000). *Doing the Dirty Work? The Global Politics of Domestic Labour.* London: Zed Books.

Badino, A. (2008). *Tutte a casa? Donne tra migrazione e lavoro nella Torino degli anni Sessanta.* Roma: Viella.

Banfi, L. (2008). Lavoro domestico, politiche migratorie e immigrazione filippina. Un confronto tra Canada e Italia. *Polis*, 22, 5–34.

Basa, C. and De la Rosa, R.J. (2007). Me, Us and Them: Realities and Illusions of Filipina Domestic Workers in Italy. In Mongaya Hoegshol, F. (ed.) *In de Olde Worlde: Views of Filipino Migrants in Europe*, 136–59. Philippine Migration Research Network and Philippine Social Science Council.

Billari, F.C. (2008). Lowest-Low Fertility in Europe: Exploring the Causes and Finding Some Surprises. *The Japanese Journal of Population*, 6, 2–18.
Bimbi, F. (1999). The Family Paradigm in the Italian Welfare State (1947–1996). *South European Society and Politics*, 4, 72–88.
Bonizzoni, P. (2013). Undocumented Domestic Workers in Italy: Surviving and Regularizing Strategies. In Triandafyllidou, A. (ed.) *Irregular Domestic Workers in Europe: Who Cares?*, 135–60. Farnham: Ashgate.
Campani, G. (1989). Du Tiers-Monde à l'Italie: Une nouvelle immigration féminine. *Revue européenne de migrations internationales*, 5, 29–49.
Campani, G. (1993). Labour Markets and Family Networks: Filipino Women in Italy. In Rudolph, H. and Morokvasic, M. (eds) *Bridging States and Markets*, 191–208. Berlin: Sigma.
Colombo, A. (2005). Il mito del lavoro domestico: struttura e cambiamenti in Italia (1970–2003). *Polis. Ricerche e studi su società e politica in Italia*, 19, 435–66.
Crippa, E. (1979). *Lavoro amaro. Le estere in Italia.* Roma: Api-Colf.
Dalla Zuanna, G. and Micheli, G.A. (eds) (2004) *Strong Family and Low Fertility: a Paradox?* Dordrecht: Kluwer Academic Publishers.
De Marchi, E. and Sarti, R. (2010). Assistenza pubblica e privata. Un'analisi del ruolo degli enti locali. In Sarti, R. (ed.) *Lavoro domestico e di cura: quali diritti?*, 247–335. Roma: Ediesse.
Degli Esposti, G. (1953). Le domestiche. *Il Mulino*, 15, 54–9.
Del Rio, A. (1979). Filipina Domestic Workers in Italy. *Migration Today*, 24, 20–22.
Einaudi, L. (2007). *Le politiche dell'immigrazione in Italia dall'Unità ad oggi.* Roma-Bari: Laterza.
Esping Andersen, G. (1990). *The Three Worlds of Welfare Capitalism*. Cambridge: Polity Press.
Eurispes (2002). *Il lavoro domestico in Italia: regolare e sommerso*. Roma: Eurispes.
Favaro, G. and Tognetti Bordogna, M. (1991). *Donne dal mondo: strategie migratorie al femminile*. Milano: Guerini e associati.
Ginzburg, N. (1969). I lavori di casa (24 agosto 1969). In *Opere*, vol. II, 68. Milano: Arnoldo Mondadori, 1998 (1987).
Gissi, A. (forthcoming). *The Home as a Factory: The Housewives' Wages Debate in Italy (1968–1980).*
Gjergji, I. (2013). L'infradroit des étrangers: le gouvernement par circulaires et la gestion administrative des mouvements migratoires en Italie. *Migrations société*, 147, 53–68.
Istat (2001). *L'Italia in cifre 2001*. Roma: Istat.
Istat (2002). *Annuario statistico italiano 2002*. Roma: Istat.
Istat (2011). *1861–2011. 150° Unità d'Italia. Italia in cifre 2011*. Roma: Istat.
Istat (2014a). *Noi Italia. 100 statistiche per capire il Paese in cui viviamo.* Roma: Istat.
Istat (2014b). *Migrazioni internazionali e interne della popolazione residente.* Roma: Istat.

Korsieporn, A.P. (1990). L'immigrazione femminile: uno studio sulle lavoratrici domestiche filippine a Roma. In Nassisi, A.M. (ed.) *Il lavoro femminile in Italia tra produzione e riproduzione*, 153–69. Roma: Fondazione Istituto Gramsci.

Luciano, A. (1994). Una presenza che ci interroga. In Vicarelli, G. (ed.) *Le mani invisibili*, 221–6. Roma: Ediesse.

Lutz, H. (2008). Introduction: Migrant Domestic Workers in Europe. In Lutz, H. (ed.) *Migration and Domestic Work: A European Perspective on a Global Theme*, 1–10. Aldershot: Ashgate.

Magat, M. (2004). Women Breadwinners in the Margins: Filipina Domestic Workers in Rome, Italy. In Fauve-Chamoux, A. (ed.) *Domestic Service and the Formation of European Identity*, 351–68. Bern-Berlin: Peter Lang; also published in Pasleau, S. and Schopp, I. (eds) with Sarti, R. *Proceedings of the Servant Project*, vol. 1, 142–57. Liège: Éditions de l'Université de Liège.

Magat, M. (2007). Teachers and 'New Evangelizers' for their Faith: Filipina Domestic Workers at Work in Italy. *Paedagogica Historica*, 43, 603–24.

Marchetti, S. (2011). *Le ragazze di Asmara. Lavoro domestico e migrazione postcoloniale*. Roma: Ediesse.

Marchetti, S. (2014). *Black Girls: Migrant Domestic Workers and Colonial Legacies*. Leiden: Brill.

Miranda, A. (2004). Une frontière dans l'intimité. La confrontation culturelle entre femmes étrangères et femmes autochtones dans l'espace domestique. *Les cahiers du CEDREF*, 12. Available at http://cedref.revues.org/551 (Accessed 1 February 2015).

Näre, L. (2013). Migrancy, Gender and Social Class in Domestic Labour and Social Care in Italy: An Intersectional Analysis of Demand. *Journal of Ethnic and Migration Studies*, 39, 601–23.

Parreñas R.S. (2001). *Servants of Globalization: Women, Migration and Domestic Work*. Stanford: Stanford University Press (new edn 2015).

Parreñas R.S. (2005). *Children of Global Migration: Transnational Families and Gendered Woes*. Stanford: Stanford University Press.

Pasquinelli, S. (2013). Le badanti in Italia: quante sono, chi sono, cosa fanno. In: Paquinelli, S. and Rusmini, G. (eds) *Badare non basta. Il lavoro di cura: attori, progetti, politiche*, 41–55. Roma: Ediesse.

Piperno, F. (2010). Quattro domande sulla sostenibilità del lavoro di cura. In Sarti, R. (ed.) *Lavoro domestico e di cura: quali diritti?*, 337–62. Roma: Ediesse.

Sacconi, R. (1984). Le colf, queste sconosciute. *Politica ed Economia*, 15, 39–46.

Saraceno, C. (1994). The Ambivalent Familism of the Italian Welfare State. *Social Politics: International Studies in Gender, State & Society*, 1, 60–82.

Sarti, R. (2004). 'Noi abbiamo visto tante città, abbiamo un'altra cultura'. Servizio domestico, migrazioni e identità di genere in Italia: uno sguardo di lungo periodo. *Polis. Ricerche e studi su società e politica in Italia*, 18, 17–46.

Sarti, R. (2005). Conclusion. Domestic Service and European Identity. In Pasleau, S. and Schopp, I. (eds) with Sarti, R. *Proceedings of the Servant Project*, vol. 5, 195–245. Liège: Éditions de l'Université de Liège.

Sarti, R. (2006). Domestic Service: Past and Present in Southern and Northern Europe. *Gender and History*, 18, 222–45.

Sarti, R. (2008a). 'Ho bisogno di te'. La protesta degli anziani per la regolarizzazione di carers e lavoratori domestici 'clandestini' (Italia, 2001–2002). In Borderías, C. and Renom, M. (eds) *Dones en moviment(s). Segles XVIII-XXI*, 165–94. Barcelona: Icaria.

Sarti, R. (2008b). The Globalisation of Domestic Service – An Historical Perspective. In Lutz, H. (ed.) *Migration and Domestic Work: A European Perspective on a Global Theme*, 77–98. Aldershot: Ashgate.

Sarti, R. (2010). Lavoro domestico e di cura: quali diritti?. In Sarti, R. (ed.) *Lavoro domestico e di cura: quali diritti?*, 17–131. Roma: Ediesse.

Sarti, R. (2014). Historians, Social Scientists, Servants, and Domestic Workers: Fifty Years of Research on Domestic and Care Work. *International Review of Social History*, 59, 279–314, also published in Hoerder, D., van Nederveen Meerkerk, E. and Neunsinger, S. (2015) (eds) *Towards a Global History of Domestic and Caregiving Workers*, 25–60. Leiden: Brill.

Sarti, R. (2015). Servizio domestico e migrazioni a corto, medio e lungo raggio (secc. XIV-XX) (forthcoming).

Sarti, R. and Scrinzi, F. (eds) (2010). *Men in a Woman's Job: Male Domestic Workers, International Migration and the Globalization of Care*. Special issue of *Men and Masculinities*, 13, no 1.

Sassen, S. (1991). *The Global City: New York, London, Tokyo*. Princeton: Princeton University Press.

Sassen, S. (2002). Women's Burden: Counter-Geographies of Globalization and the Feminization of Survival. *Nordic Journal of International Law*, 71, 255–74.

Scrinzi, F. (2004). Professioniste della tradizione. Le donne migranti nel mercato del lavoro domestico. *Polis. Ricerche e studi su società e politica in Italia*, 18, 107–36.

Scrinzi, F. (2013). *Genre, migrations et emplois domestiques en France et en Italie. Construction de la non-qualification et de la altérité ethnique*. Paris: Petra.

Signorelli, A. (2006). *Migrazioni e incontri etnografici*. Palermo: Sellerio.

Stuppini, A. (2013). Lavoro domestico e politiche migratorie. In Pasquinelli, S. and Rusmini, G. (eds) *Badare non basta. Il lavoro di cura: attori, progetti, politiche*, 183–8. Roma: Ediesse.

Triandafyllidou, A. and Marchetti, S. (2015) (eds) *Employers, Agencies and Immigration: Paying for Care*. Aldershot: Ashgate.

Turri, C. (2010). Le Acli-Colf e l'evoluzione dei diritti delle lavoratrici domestiche. In Sarti, R. (ed.) *Lavoro domestico e di cura: quali diritti?*, 165–90. Roma: Ediesse.

Turrini, O. (1977). *Le casalinghe di riserva. Lavoratrici domestiche e famiglia borghese*. Rome: Coines.

van Hooren, F. (2010). When Families Need Immigrants: The Exceptional Position of Migrant Domestic Workers and Care Assistants in Italian Immigration Policy. *Bulletin of Italian Politics*, 2, 21–38.

Vianello F.A. (2013). Engendering migration. Un percorso attraverso trent'anni di dibattito. *Mondi Migranti*, 7, 49–66.

Vicarelli, G. (1994). *Le mani invisibili. La vita e il lavoro delle donne immigrate*. Roma: Ediesse.

Vitali, O. (1970). *Aspetti dello sviluppo economico italiano alla luce della ricostruzione della popolazione attiva*. Roma: Istituto di Demografia.

Williams F. (2012). Converging Variations in Migrant Care Work in Europe. *Journal of European Social Policy*, 22, 363–76.

World Bank, The (2014). Population ages 65 and above (% of total). Available at http://data.worldbank.org/indicator/SP.POP.65UP.TO.ZS?order=wbapi_data_value_2013+wbapi_data_value+wbapi_data_value-last&sort=asc (Accessed 8 February 2015).

PART II:
Self-Determination, Family and Welfare

Chapter 3
The Third Movement: Family Life for a Fee

Silvia Niccolai

"Have you got children?" "No, thank God. I mean, I had one, but he's dead". She refers to a husband, a sick man she was burdened with for eight years. "He's dead, thank God. Feelings are nice, but life is too hard ..."

(S. Weil, *La condition ouvrière*, 1990a: 192)

What has Feminism Actually Failed?

In recent years, families all over the world have massively turned to paid domestic work, mostly provided by migrant women. What are the causes of such a phenomenon? Academic feminism likes to say that it is due to the failure of the 'Feminist Revolution' (Anderson, 2000; Ehrenreich and Hochschild, 2004; Thomas, 2010). Western women have long fought for their emancipation and they have actually obtained it, more or less, but they haven't been able to teach their men to do their share of the housework. As a consequence, other women have had to take the unwelcome burden on. The result is a vastly growing number of women who, due to a variety of factors of social vulnerability such as race, origin, religion or scarce educational opportunities, are being left behind on the social ladder. 'Global Care Chains' have spread out over the entire world the consequences of a Western trajectory (feminism). At least, this reassures us that the West is still in the leading role.

The picture emerging from such readings is one where, on the one side, there are emancipated, privileged, free women who have successfully entered the marketplace and the public sphere; on the other, there are the less lucky ones, who are bound to a home which isn't even their own, whose situation is ideal in bringing forth sorrowful reflections about multiple discrimination and intersectionality. They are indeed the new slaves of today.[1]

In this chapter, I shall place a very simple and plain criticism on these opinions. The Failed Feminist Revolution theory, applied to the issues of paid domestic work, does not understand that the woman, and man as well, who has no time for family life and therefore hires a housekeeper, a carer, a provider of companionship services or so on, is just as much the victim of the global economy's productive imperatives as their domestic workers. Arguably, that theory properly wants to

1 Literature on new slavery has been impressively growing over the last years: see Mantouvalou (2006 and 2012). The narrative can be traced back to the end of the 1900s: see Macklin (1992).

conceal a sad truth from our view and consciousness. Since society has become entirely and merely an economic resource, contemporary developments of capitalism no longer need to raise boundaries between market and society that keep the two in balance. Family used to be the most important amongst those boundaries, but, today, that family and the connected activities are protected from market mechanisms is becoming pointless and detrimental.

Beyond Polanyi's 'double movement' (Polanyi, 1974) a third one is today coming into view and without the rhetoric of the Failed Feminist Revolution thesis we would recognize it more easily, completely and clearly: family life, superfluous and counterproductive to the interests of contemporary capitalism, is becoming a commercial good, only available at a fee, for those who can pay it and want to.

Capitalistic Feminism or the Damnation of Domestic Work

Despite its choice of words ('failure', 'feminism', 'revolution'), the Failed Feminist Revolution thesis reveals explicitly enough the opposite factual truth: if one looks at its intellectual, academic, political and institutional outcomes, 'feminism' wasn't a 'revolution' at all, it wasn't a 'failure' in any respect and it was 'female' only to a very little extent, if any. What many call 'feminism' (and perhaps for the same reason many others hate) has been the concept of women battling to conquer the roles that once were male, as they represented the best slice of the cake: work, income, career and success.[2] In view of such goals, domestic work is a handicap by definition. For that reason it would have been a victory for women if men had learned to share the housework: this would have established an equal footing in the contest for success within the marketplace (or, better to say, in the contest for entering the marketplace). The Double Burden thesis, deeply rooted in the European context, belongs to the same order of ideas. If women are still disadvantaged in the workplace – the theses reiterate – the unequal distribution of family responsibilities is to blame. These theses embrace the same conceptual couples, bipartite or dichotomic, by which patriarchal rationality reasons: the public sphere is up, superior, male; the private sphere is down, inferior, female

2 Within the feminist debate, many and different itineraries could be traced to find opinions that support the order of ideas I am adopting in the text. With reference to the so called 'second-wave' feminism, Fraser (2009: 2) famously stressed the 'movement's extraordinary successes but also the disturbing convergence of some of its ideals with the demands of an emerging new form of capitalism – post-Fordist, disorganized, transnational'. Feminism can be envisioned as a great incitement to women worldwide to embrace the values of the Western world: see, on this topic, the contrasting views of Kumer (2014) and Tax (2014). For the use of the expression 'institutionalized' feminism see, with peculiar accents, McElroy (2012). Criticism against 'state' feminism (emancipatory and liberal) are distinctive characters of Italian feminist thought known as *Pensiero della Differenza*: see Libreria delle Donne di Milano (1987). Labour issues have always been nevertheless central to it: see Cigarini et al. (2006); Benvenuti et al. (2008).

(Cavarero, 1990). No surprise if feminist academics who think in this way say they are seeking the interest of women. Patriarchal rationality does perpetuate itself by becoming the way of thinking of influential women who take on themselves the function of speaking in the name of other women, while they underestimate and devalue what most women do, have done for decades and – arguably – can't do today, if they want to survive.[3]

Indeed, the Failed Feminist Revolution thesis is a classic account of the ways in which institutional feminism thinks. That is what I call it (institutional feminism), though one could call it 'state feminism' (Buttarelli, 2001) or 'embedded feminism'. It is that 'feminism' that has been feeding, over the last decades, a set of public policies such as European anti-discrimination policies, openly based on a utilitarian rationale and in the interest of the economic performance (Somek, 2011). One could call it 'capitalistic' or 'global' feminism as well. In fact, it spreads the values of capitalistic Western economies all over the world. Actually, together with some anti-discriminatory battles as those linked to sexual orientation, its main issues have become the identity code and the preferred promotional campaign of global corporations. The latter fosters their employees' and customers' loyalties by offering leave on the occasion of employees' same-sex weddings; in order to advertise their cars or cell phones they can indifferently show two lesbian mums or an 'I-Do-Not-Know-How-She-Does-It' juggling mother.[4] Productive work promotes liberty; this is the advertised message: 'don't you see that those who have a job enjoy a set of liberties, and those who are out of the marketplace don't?' Belonging to the marketplace, as workers or as consumers: this is the new citizenship; female emancipation, then anti-discrimination for all, is the key to this message.

---

3 Italian sociologist Luciano Gallino recently observed that the massive entry of women in the marketplace has meant the halving of salaries from the 1970s onwards: what once was earned by the male breadwinner only is today earned by both adult workers as a couple. If one in the family, woman or man, wished to stay at home, that simply wouldn't be possible because 'a salary which has remained unvaried since 1975 can no longer meet a family's needs' (Gallino, 2012: 192). In the American debate, economist Folbre (2006: 41 and 89) denounced in the same terms what she calls the 'fake' Double Burden thesis. According to Folbre, to keep on accusing men for not taking on the housework means hiding the fact that men's ways of behaving have changed, are changing, can change more and more but 'whatever change individuals can make in their behaviour, they have to keep on living and competing in an economy where care work is not rewarded as it should be … What has traumatized families', Folbre adds, 'are capitalism and the growth of waged work'. Italian feminism theorizes that women actually want to say a 'double yes' (both to work and family: Benvenuti et al., 2008). This puts a big and transforming challenge to contemporary organization of work, as well as to the established pro-market 'symbolic order' that assigns to paid work the pivotal role; by repeating the contrary (that women only want to work and aren't interested in domestic work), the Double Burden thesis fights against that revolutionary potential and impedes symbolical change.

4 Reference is made here to A. Pearson's famous novel (Pearson, 2002).

What Does 'Work' Mean?

No one could call contemporary domestic workers 'slaves' if it had not been for the convention that domestic and care work are dreadful things, from which reasonable women must carefully recoil, and from which whoever must escape. If they want to be independent, women need to enter the job market; they need real, dignified work; domestic work, even when paid, does not fit the rule. It is not by chance that the rhetoric weapon used by the pro-market narratives of institutional feminism is the accusation of essentialism, unfailingly addressed against every opinion that claims for the recognition of importance, and value, of domestic work.[5] Essentialism, this veritable anathema of our days, prevents any analyses or discourse in favour of domestic work from gaining ground, as its clear implication is that of criticizing the domination that productive work has on people's lives in the age of global capitalism. Once it has been decided that domestic work is terrible, it is only logical to come to the conclusion that those unfortunate women who do it are being left out: housekeepers and domestic workers are people who must be different from what they are, must do another job – a real job – if they want to be free and have a dignified life.[6] There is, I am arguing, a precise and strong connection between how we consider domestic work and domestic workers, and the way we treat these workers (low wages and humiliation included).

It would be really difficult however, to accuse of essentialism the opinions of German theologian Ina Praetorius. Praetorius's research deeply reconsiders the political meaning that domestic work has when seen *as work.*[7] Domestic work, Praetorius explains, is work in a sense that the equivalence between work and its economic value has made us forget. It is the kind of work that all of us would

5 The accusation of essentialism is today often coupled with the denunciation of a 'new momism', aiming to bring women back to the home and children in the name of a conservative family-values rhetoric which would hide the war of capitalism against welfare: see Roesch (2004).

6 By the way, this is the same mechanism on which the subordination of the workforce – subordination, before being material, is first of all moral and symbolic – was attained at the time of industrial capitalism. French philosopher Simone Weil wrote that the only possibility left to the imagination of labourers who wanted to be free was to become rich; but becoming rich – Weil noted – meant not being labourers any longer, it meant that the individuals they were had to die and disappear (Weil 1990a: 296). Factory workers were the first category to be explicitly told that they could not exist as they were and be free at the same time; they had to die – symbolically – if they wanted to be fully human and dignified. The end of this value-building narrative was clear: only money counts. The narrative goes on to target domestic workers and it says, as I am reasoning in the text, that only to be part of the marketplace makes a life worthy.

7 The English reader can explore Ina Praetorius's thought by reading Praetorius (2006), which contains the self-translation of the speech she gave at the XII Symposium of the International Association of Women Philosophers (IAPh) 'Thinking Experience' that took place in Rome, 31 August–1 September 2006.

like to do; it possesses those qualities that we look for in our jobs, qualities that motivate us to get on with our jobs if feel their presence. In a word, domestic work is work in the sense that it is an activity useful to society and meaningful to those who do it.

> Despite the predominance of measurement techniques oriented only towards the growth of monetary economy, most people still think and feel that work must have a meaning, which goes beyond the economic return. Why, then, don't we start re-defining work from this? (Praetorius, 2013: 36)

Praetorius resumes the main and greatest components of Simone Weil's meditation. Seeking an answer to alienation, desperation, and annihilation of humanity that factory workers' condition provoked, Weil[8] saw only one solution:

> Labourers have to be put in the condition of understanding that they are producing goods demanded by social needs and that they have a limited right to be proud of them. (Weil, 1990a: 287)

Domestic work is the paradigm of 'meaningful work' because it nourishes life. A life, subsequently reduced to a mere resource by the leading economic thought, 'from which the protagonists of economy draw as much as they want whenever they want' (Praetorius, 2011: 55). Cleaning the house, preparing a good meal, taking care of the children: today, many professionals, employees and workers, women or men, hanker after things like these and sigh, 'I wish I had the time for it!' We may or may not be genuinely convinced of this: the fast-flowing images on the iPad do not even give us the chance to contemplate it.

Domestic work, Praetorius says, is a treat for contemporary people, who have only a few odd moments to devote to it, provided that, of course, their working schedule leaves them enough time and energy. Enough time to cultivate friendships, set the table and chat with the children. That time which creates social spaces and gives autonomy, that 'fertile time' (Forenza, 2013: 164) when the texture of social life is interweaved.

---

8 *La condition ouvrière*, the book which reported the experience made by Simone Weil as factory worker in 1934, has never been translated into English. The prominent Italian philosopher of law Giuseppe Capograssi once wrote, 'this book has entered the working force condition so deeply and seriously that it should be quoted entirely [when one talks about that condition]. The originality of its testimony lies in its absolute freedom from prejudices, biases, hidden motives (doctrinal, practical, political, religious), as well as in the absolute innocence with which the experience was dealt with and lived. It is difficult to find a human experience at the purest state. In a subject so treacherous, the case is unique. It is perhaps due to its pure humanity that such a testimony has been left nearly unnoticed, if not ignored by today's literature on the topic, which is, however, mostly political' (Capograssi, 2008: 620).

> I have stopped censoring the pleasure I feel in doing the housework. In fact, I thoroughly enjoy it. It is true, I can afford to, because at this time of my life I have some other income, but I deliberately see my economic independence as the means that allows me to reflect, in theory and in practice, on the domestic place as a work place, a type of work that has been scorned for centuries. It is crazy that today it is mostly the wealthy who are free to carry out these necessary and meaningful activities, reflecting with ease on the sense of everything. This paradox means that the social organization of work is still functioning in the wrong way. (Praetorius, 2011: 105)

The Third Movement: Family as a Cultural Option

Many people in Europe nowadays, certainly in Italy, do not have enough time or tranquillity for domestic work. But they still have some money to pay for a carer, a housekeeper or a babysitter. The home gets cleaned, the meals cooked, the laundry done, clothes ironed and children picked up from school. If working people are no longer the brutalized workforce that Engels described, if we do not live amongst filth and rubbish, it is because we pay a *badante*. We are not paying the bill for a failed feminist revolution; we are paying the bill for a successful turn of capitalism. For most families – and I am speaking from my own personal experience – it would be impossible to exist as such – as families, I mean, bringing children up – without paying someone to do 'the dirty work'. When both parents work, sometimes in different cities, grandparents are too old or live elsewhere, and friends run their hectically busy lives in remote districts of a chaotic metropolis, the hiring of a *badante* has become an imperative.[9] It is not all about scanty services: when you work all hours and places, putting your children in a nursery school won't be enough, because you might not make it for the school bell, or for collecting the children from school, suppertime or bedtime. You need a person, a human being, because the work needed is that of caring for humanity. There is another alternative, of course: not to have children, not to have a family. After all, isn't work far more interesting, far more valuable? By now, we have been told such a story for decades.

---

9 Hochschild (2013) acknowledges that 'careworkers' low-paid jobs form the basis of another and compulsory overtime in which both parents work two, sometimes three or more jobs ... The growing fragility of family ... may increase the desire to enjoy services that promise to deliver the 'spirit' of home'. Widely recognized is the fact that domestic work is nowadays employed mostly by working parents (Williams and Brennan, 2012: 257). A specific aspect of the responsibilities that the capitalistic model of economic and social relationships holds towards the growing resort to paid care and domestic work emerges when one thinks that 'the transnational political economy of care is used by European Countries to reduce their own social expenditure' (Williams, 2012: 363).

Having a family and a family life today depends, first, on the availability of money to pay someone who will look after the family. If this is true, this means that a new inequality is looming up in our times: the inequality between those who can afford a family and those who can't. Secondly, family is a variable which depends on people's imaginaries and desires, and these are fed by notions of normal and dignified life we are given when we grow up and during our lifetime. Everybody has heard about Google offering to pay its female employees the cost of freezing their eggs, so they can concentrate on their career while they are young.[10] The woman who will choose to postpone her pregnancy and maternity probably knows that if she becomes a mother she will lose her job or undermine her career. She hasn't got the material resources to have children and this is the economic component of the issue; neither has she the symbolic resources to do so, that is to say, a form of thought that tells her that having children is better and more important than being Google's servant. And this is another side of the issue. Having a family, I am saying, is a question of symbolic rather than material resources. If this is true, that means that the function that our society assigns to family is shifting: from a natural corollary of human life and capabilities and a basic component of society, family is becoming a cultural option.

Google's announcement confirms that the revolution, called 'failed' by academic feminism, is instead successful: that fake 'revolution' which abominated domestic and care work as the strongest obstacle to women's participation to productive life is the hit of today. Besides, Google's announcement signals one of the most important novelties of our times. These are actually times of great transformations for the family, but the real novelty is a backward movement. Once again, it is becoming less important that the workforce has a family, that is to say, a domestic sphere. Teleworking and perpetual connectivity are at odds with the idea of the domestic sphere as one different and separated from the work (i.e. productive) one. Contemporary capitalism does agree with institutional feminism when it says that domestic and care work hinder productivity. This is so well-agreed that contemporary capitalism has started uprooting the domestic boundaries since their very physical existence (that started long ago, when television entered the home (Marcuse, 1967: 39). If it is 'the entire person' (Marcuse, 1967: 30) that the economic forces of global capitalism demand, what is the point of preserving people's domestic sphere? It has become useless.

10 It has been observed that '[b]y telling their female staff to hold off having babies, companies are demanding their employees to put them before anything else, before their families, before their health … Wouldn't it be nicer if it was totally acceptable to leave work early to pick your kids up from school, or go to a sports day which comes before a board meeting?' (Minter, 2014).

The Contemporary Workplace: Segregation for All

Therefore, a new chapter has to be added to the 'Double Movement' narrative. This story, well-known and extraordinarily told, reminds us that self-regulating capitalism – which started as 'industrial capitalism' – has always been ready to include men, women and even children when it needs them and at any time of their life: it is naturally anti-discriminatory, flexible and dynamic. In the nineteenth century, the socially destructive consequences of such attitudes soon became palpable. With their 'first movement', nation states had made the establishment of self-regulating capitalism possible. Their legislation, burying the institutions of the modern world, had made marketable land and labour. With the 'second movement', they tried to find a remedy. In order to defend society from the socially destructive consequences of self-regulating capitalism, the legislation that we call 'social' was launched. Family in the modern sense was created and constructed upon a gendered division of roles, where the man became the 'standard worker and breadwinner' (Polanyi, 1974). Women were considered the less perfect workers, therefore the less attractive, because of the costly maternity protection schemes they brought with them. Family was born and fostered as a compensation for the uprooting (Weil, 1990b) of people from the solidarity of traditional country life. 'Family life' took the place of the larger relational texture that had connected life and work before the Industrial Revolution (Thompson, 1967, Moffat, 2007). In the new economic-social order men had to go out to work and win bread, but one has to have a home to come back to. Otherwise, one would wander around, get drunk, get into fights or steal. To have a home, you need domestic work. For a family to exist, particular activities are needed: care and time, and a space in which to develop them. In the very distant twentieth century, state housing was introduced, replacing the squalid hovels and straw mattresses on which – for all the capitalists cared – the indiscriminate male-female-adult-infant workforce collapsed to rest and have sex when they could. Some national constitutions of the post-Second World War, like the Italian one, stated that a salary must grant the worker enough to allow 'him and his family' to live with dignity. Such words were still in a 'second movement' mood (Niccolai, 2010: 39). It was not a matter of misogyny or patriarchy: it was a matter of making the family a fundamental right of the person. And it was a matter of seeking a boundary between the market and society. In Michael Sandel's words, family meant that there are things that money can't buy (Sandel, 2012), there are times that production can't dictate, because there are values other than economic growth.

Nowadays, the opposite trajectory is being drawn: family is no longer the key in the definition of the balance between market and society. Or, better, that balance has lost importance, and we no longer see in family anything important which is connected to it. Salaries drop, work is precarious, people spend their lives working or looking for a job. In the global economy, labour is 'feminized': it is becoming more female-like than male-like; it praises female characteristics: being good listeners, empathy, capability of working in a team, unconditioned readiness to devote oneself to no-matter-what cause. Trade unions and political parties are, in their turn, made pointless. They were, with family, the great institutions of solidarity and mutual relationships which supported the balance between market and society. In global capitalism, do they still have any relevance? It can safely swing between its 'cheering, smooth, reasonable un-liberty, evidence of technical progress' (Marcuse, 1967: 21) and its abilities to repress social conflicts, abilities that have become increasingly better. Family, home, political parties, trade unions and each and every dimension of the 'time free from work' are dimensions of autonomy. It is within those places and that time that relationships are built, solidarity flows, and thoughts are developed and shared with others. What relevance do they have in an age where one's entire life is based on work?

One has to turn to a feminism far different from the 'institutional' one to find interpretations that explicitly and consciously recognize how pivotal among contemporary power's devices is the dispossession of women from those times and places that they had protected after men were exiled to factories:

> We do many jobs. They are the most diverse, and are always the same: precarious jobs, if there are any, which make our lives precarious in their turn. Income, housing, health, maternity leave, social security, services: we see all these things as privileges rather than rights.
>
> We work fragmentarily, displaced here and there, for unlimited hours. Work time and life time are mixed together; in this confusion, we are all forever available. Information and communication technologies make it possible to work at home, or on the bus, no matter where, when, or how long.
>
> This ensues the segregation of workers from each other. Governing institutions don't see us, don't trace us, don't catalogue us, they can't. Neither are traditional forms of negotiation such as trade unions capable to do differently. Negotiations on working conditions no longer exist: the whole game is about single workers and their counterparts, who blackmail workers with un-paid or underpaid jobs. (Femministe Nove, 2013: 4)

Historical research tells us that people who had known and still remembered the ways of living and working when society was largely autonomous from the market did not want to bend to the productive imperatives of industrial capitalism. The latter, therefore, had to come into an agreement with societies whose habits were still soaked with the values of the modern and ancient world. Craftsmen and peasants felt humiliated by working in factories and prisoners couldn't provide all the needed workforce. By necessity, the workforce condition was constructed as capable of co-existing with those forms of sociability which people were previously accustomed to. In the city, around the factories, families, homes and forms of social aggregation were re-established. Women's domestic work was crucial in the construction of this balance. It was not about 'gender roles' then, as I have anticipated; it was about the entire order of relationships between society and the market, which lasted for a century-and-a-half (Hoskins, 2010). Such a balance was necessary to the establishment and strengthening of industrial capitalism. But nowadays it has become useless to the deeply transformed production methods, whose premise is the segregation of workers, that it to say, the isolation of every single person.[11] It is not by chance that the European Court of Human Rights, the biggest laboratory where narratives of contemporary public order are being shaped, has never had to reason whether current norms and practices about working conditions – insecurity and precariousness – can actually co-exist with the right to a family. The shifting of the right to have a family to sexual orientation rights signals that the notion of 'family' is being unbundled from the notion of work, which has ever-less to do with the right to have a family life.[12]

What the Failed Feminist Revolution Thesis Does Not Say

The contemporary market economy does not see any utility in the workforce having a home and family or enjoying a domestic life: there are other means to keep the workforce quiet – and the same goes for the jobless. Family is sliding from public concern and having a family is merely an individual choice which, like every choice worthy of respect, one must afford. Commodification of care and domestic work, which makes of a family a commercial good to be paid so much per day, a resource available to those who want it and can pay for it, is a process of subordinating people to a productive order which reproduces itself and flourishes by cutting down the spaces of social autonomy. That's why the Failed Feminist Revolution thesis is misleading. First, it does not understand that devaluing domestic and care work is, on the one hand, co-essential to the establishment of the boundless capitalism of today; on the other hand, it is at the root of the condition of the exploitation of domestic migrant workers, of their low wages and social stigma. Secondly, that thesis does not help us to understand that contemporary domestic and care work, with its conditions of unlimited hours, poor salaries, solitude and segregation that so many times have been described, is the paradigm of the new conception of work in the global era.[13] Moving from domestic

11 The key concept to anti-discrimination analyses, 'segregation' is now becoming the common feature of the entire workforce condition. Acknowledging this warns us of the inherent conceptual limits of the anti-discrimination discourse, functional to capitalism and to the preservation of the latter's symbolic order; see Somek (2011), Niccolai (2014).

12 Curiously enough, recent research noted that one-sex families, especially gay men families, do repeat the 'traditional' division of gender roles; see Mundy (2013).

13 To the 'Failed Feminist Revolution' narrative the equivalence between domestic work and animal labour is central. Thomas (2010: 30) traces it back to H. Arendt's thought. The resurgence of an explicit equivalence between workforce and animality in contemporary capitalism's narratives has been noted by Somers and Block (2014 and 2004).

work to a precarious job? It makes very little difference indeed, but the stigma of care and domestic work prevents us from realizing, all of a sudden, that what is detestable is not domestic work, but 'normal' productive work.[14] That thesis's fatal mistake fuels the illusion – so necessary, however, in order to construct ours as the world of liberty and to protect it from criticism of all sorts – that those who can pay a *badante* and the *badante* stand on different, opposite fronts, the drowned and the saved, the winners and the losers, while instead they both are servants of a productive order which dictates the sacrifice of any social autonomy and the abdication from the freedom to compose one's life.

Domestic work, performed by migrant women who are exploited and deprived of their own family life, does bear today the capitalistic modes of production, as women's domestic work did yesterday. The difference with the times of industrial capitalism that settled the 'breadwinner model' is that today productive logics of efficiency and economic performance have invested the entire society and every moment and aspect of a lifetime. Without a substantial revision of this, without a deep reconsideration of the ways in which our economic order 'assigns value and rewards success' (Folbre, 2006: 64), there won't be any proactive, effective and sincere way to address the many injustices and inequalities suffered by migrant domestic workers.

References

Anderson, B. (2000). *Doing the Dirty Work. The Global Politics of Domestic Labour*. London New York: Zed Books.

Benvenuti, M. et al. (2008). *Lavoro e maternità. Il Doppio sì. Esperienze e innovazioni*. Milano: Libreria delle donne di Milano.

Buttarelli, A. (2001). Quando il linguaggio fa male. *Via Dogana*, 55, 7–8.

14 To the opinion I am expressing in the text the objection could be made that the household is not completely equivalent to the workplace and housework is not fully comparable with a 'true' job relationship (Lutz, 2008: 49). The irreducibility of care and domestic work to 'true' work is, however, a pillar of many studies on the topic. Nevertheless, this assumption lacks of historicization: it takes a historical model of work (paid, to be developed in specialized spaces and according to specialized and well-defined rules), considers that model the 'true' work and, by this way, makes of that historical model a universal and abstract paradigm. Of course, domestic and care work, when compared with that kind of 'true' work, would never fit the size. But one should consider how contemporary work is changing from that 'true model'. Taking this into consideration, domestic and care work, with their characteristics of flexibility, low wages, high emotional involvement and so forth, could be seen as the announcement of transforming dimensions and practices that are taking place within the entire experience that we name 'work'. Typical features of domestic work (as being 'boundless') do parallel, however, those of the so called 'The New Psychological Contract'; see Stone (2001) (I am grateful to PhD student M.F. Carta for signalling Stone's work to me).

Capograssi, G. (2008). Incertezze sull'individuo. In Mercadante, F. (ed.) *Giuseppe Capograssi, La vita etica*, 481–827. Milano: Bompiani (first published 1950–1955).
Cavarero, A. (1990). *Nonostante Platone*. Roma: Editori Riuniti (English trans., 1995. *In spite of Plato*. New York: Polity Cambridge and Routledge).
Cigarini, L. et al. (2006). *Tre donne e due uomini parlano del lavoro che cambia*. Milano: Libreria delle donne di Milano.
Ehrenreich, B. and Hochschild, A.R. (2004). *Donne Globali. Tate Colf e Badanti*. Italian translation by Bellazzi, V. Milano: Feltrinelli (First US edn 2002. *Global Woman: Nannies, Maids and Sex Workers in the New Economy*. New York: Henry Holt and Company LLC).
Femministe nove (2013). *Manifest@F9*. Available at https://femministenove.wordpress.com/manifestofemministenove/.
Folbre, N. (2006). *Il cuore invisibile. La donna la società l'impresa*. Italian. translation by Pretolani, F. Milano: Egea (First US edn 2001. *The Invisible Heart. Economics and Family Values*. New York: The New Press).
Forenza, E. (2013). Libertà precarie e reddito di autodeterminazione. In Burchi, S. and Di Martino, T. (eds) *Come un paesaggio. Pensieri e pratiche tra lavoro e non lavoro*, 158–70. Roma: Iacobelli editore.
Fraser, N. (2009). Feminism, Capitalism and the Cunning of History. *New Left Review*, 56, 1–16.
Gallino, L. (2012). *La lotta di classe dopo la lotta di classe*, interview by Borgna, P. Bari: Laterza.
Hochschild, A.R. (2013). *So How's the Family? And Other Essays*. Berkeley, Los Angeles: University of California Press Berkeley.
Hoskins, C. (2010). The Economic and the Social in EU Gender Policies. In Niccolai, S. and Ruggiu, I. (eds) *Dignity in Change. Exploring the Constitutional Potential of EU Gender and Anti-Discrimination Law*, 23–34. Fiesole: Epab.
Kumer, D. (2014). Imperialist Feminism and Liberalism. *OpenDemocracy*, 6. Available at www.opendemocracy.net.
Libreria delle donne di Milano (1987). *Non credere di avere dei diritti*. Milano: Rosemberg & Sellier.
Lutz, H. (2008). When Home becomes a Workplace: Domestic Work as an Ordinary Job in Germany? In Lutz, H. (ed.) *Migration and Domestic Work. A European Perspective on a Global Theme*, 43–60. Farnham: Ashgate.
Macklin, A. (1992). Foreign Domestic Worker: Surrogate Housewife or Mail Order Servant? *McGill Law Journal*, 37, 681–760.
Mantouvalou, V. (2006). Servitude and Forced Labor in the 21st Century: The Human Rights of Domestic Workers. *Industrial Law Journal*, 35(4), 395–414.
Mantouvalou, V. (2012). The Many Faces of Slavery: The Example of Domestic Work. *Global Dialogue, Special Issue on Modern Slavery*.
Marcuse, H. (1967). *L'uomo a una dimensione. L'ideologia della società industriale avanzata*. Italian translation by Gallino, L. Torino: Einaudi (First

US edn 1964. *The One Dimensional Man. Studies on the Ideology of Advanced Industrial Society*. Boston: Beacon Press).

McElroy, W. (2012). Interview with Wendy McElroy on feminism in America. *Laissez Faire*, 21 February. Available at www.lfb.org/interview-with-wendy-mcelroy-on-feminism-in-americ.

Minter, H. (2014). By offering to freeze their employees' eggs, Apple and Facebook make it clear they do to know what women want. *The Guardian* online, 15 October. Available at www.theguardian.com.

Moffat, G. (2007). Work Life Balance and Employment Law: Cultural Change or Mission Impossible? In Probert, R. (ed.) *Family Life and the Law. Under One Roof.* Aldershot: Ashgate.

Mundy, L. (2013). The gay guide to wedding bliss. *Atlantic Monthly*, 311(5), 56–70.

Niccolai, S. (2010). Changing Images of Normal and Worthy Life. In Niccolai, S. and Ruggiu, I. (eds) *Dignity in Change. Exploring the Constitutional Potential of EU Gender and Anti-Discrimination Law*, 35–68. Fiesole: Epab.

Niccolai, S. (2014). Il dibattito intorno alla svolta universalistica e dignitaria del diritto antidiscriminatorio. *Diritto e Società*, 2, 313–353.

Pearson, A. (2002). *I Don't Know How She Does It*. New York: First Anchor Books.

Polanyi, C. (1974). *La grande trasformazione*. Italian translation by Vigevani, R. Torino: Giulio Einaudi Editore (First US edn 1944. New York: Hotl, Rinehart & Winston Inc.).

Praetorius, I. (2006). Re-Thinking the world. Beginning with everyday life, translated by the Author into 'personal praetorian English', speech presented at the XII IAPh Symposium International Association of Women Philosophers, Rome, 31 August – 3 September. Available at http://host.uniroma3.it/dipartimenti/filosofia/Iaph/english/schedule.htm.

Praetorius, I. (2011). *Penelope a Davos. Idee femministe per un'economia globale*. Milano: Libreria delle donne di Milano.

Praetorius, I. (2013). Il reddito di base incondizionato nell'economia post-patriarcale. In Burchi, S. and Di Martino, T. (eds) *Come un paesaggio. Pensieri e pratiche tra lavoro e non lavoro*, 33–42. Roma: Iacobelli editore.

Roesch, J. (2004). Turning Back the Clock? Women Work and Family Today. *Socialist Revue*, 38. Available at www.isreview.org.

Sandel, M. (2012). *What Money Can't Buy. The Moral Limits of Markets*. New York: Farrar, Straus and Giroux.

Somek, A. (2011). *Engineering Equality*. Oxford: Oxford University Press.

Somers, M. and Block, F. (2004). *The Power of Market's Fundamentalism: Karl Polanyi's Critique*. Cambridge/New York: Harvard University Press.

Somers, M. and Block, F. (2014). Is Cruelty Key to Prosperity? *OpenDemocracy*, 27 October. Available at www.opendemocracy.net.

Stone, K.V.W. (2001). The New Psychological Contract. *UCLA Law Review*, 48, 519–661.

Tax, M. (2014). The Antis: anti-imperialist or anti-feminist. *OpenDemocracy,* 19 November. Available at www.opendemocracy.net.

Thomas, C. (2010). The Economic Family in Global Context: A Case Study of Migrant Domestic Workers in Egypt. *American Journal of Comparative Law*, 58, 978–1022.

Thompson, E.P. (1967). Time, Work, Discipline and Industrial Capitalism. *Past and Present*, 38, 56–97.

Weil, S. (1990a). *La condizione operaia*. Italian translation by Fortini, F. Milano: Arnoldo Mondadori Editore (First French edn 1951. *La condition ouvrière*. Paris: Gallimard).

Weil, S. (1990b). *La prima radice. Preludio ad una dichiarazione dei doveri verso l'essere umano*. Italian translation by Fortini, F. Roma: ES Editore Roma (First French edn 1949. *L'enracinement. Prélude à une declaration des devoirs envers l'etre humain*. Paris: Gallimard).

Williams, F. (2012). Converging Variations in Migrant Care Work in Europe. *Journal of European Social Policy*, 22(4), 363–76.

Williams, F. and Brennan, D. (2012). Care, Markets and migration in a globalizing world. Introduction to the Special Issue of *Journal of European Social Policy*, 22(4), 355–62.

Chapter 4
Autonomy and Self-Realization of Migrant Women: Constitutional Aspects

Laura Ronchetti

Introduction

Examining the relationship between Italian constitutional provisions and the legal status of migrant women offers an opportunity to provide a re-signification to the entire constitutional project and to put its inclusiveness to the test.

From this standpoint, interpretation of the constitution is essential for dealing, with renewed vigour, with the complex power dynamics involving the relationships between gender and migration. A reading of the constitution capable of taking to heart the contributions of feminist legal theory and critical race theory allows us to correlate the person – in his or her dimension of gender, relationships and interdependence – with the constitutional project of self-determination and self-realization.

The proposed approach to constitutional interpretation takes its inspiration from the so-called 'intersectionality' between the multiple grounds that may contribute towards impeding individual and collective self-realization: an interpretive method not founded upon individual qualifications of the person or the social group, but which is aware that each subject – individual and collective –embodies his, her or its own cultural synthesis with internal contradictions and conflicts. The central role of the person and of social groups, in which individual personality is played out, should inspire an approach that looks to subjective positioning in power relationships as a whole, while not splitting the person into his or her various legal qualifications.

An interpretation of the constitutional text in the sense proposed here must, however, come to terms with the tendency of reducing the possible hermeneutic margins afforded by the text itself. The condition of migrant women in Italy, in particular, clearly demonstrates how the devices of exclusion and segregation present in the legal system have repercussions that multiply rather than add to one another certain differences envisaged in the constitution. This concerns in particular the areas of sex (and the correlated differences in terms of sexuality, gender, and gender identity) and personal status (which must include that of being migrants, both regular and irregular).

The exponential effect determined by the synergy among these factors shows the contradiction between the legal *dispositifs* excluding migrant women and their leading role in the Italian migration context.

Constitution as 'Counter-Conduct' against Subordination

In Italy there is no institutionalization of critical legal studies (Carrino, 1992), feminist legal theory or critical race theory,[1] but there has certainly been no dearth of reasoning on law as a tool of oppression to maintain the hierarchical structures of domination. At the very same time, the legal discourse emphasizes how law is an instrument to overturn hierarchies and to give value to differences, especially from the standpoint of gender issues (Gianformaggio, 1993), gendered migration (Pitch, 2004) and the Italian–colonialist experience (Costa, 2004–05 and Bascherini, 2012). The reality of migrations, in fact, has forced us to re-introduce into the legal discourse elements that were long obscured or neglected in the public debate on sexual differences (sexuality, class, race, religion, language and gender identity).

Thus, migrations are the testing grounds for the inclusiveness of the forms of co-existence as prescribed in the constitution.

However, the critical approaches referred to, while on the one hand helping to lay bare the logic and structure of law (Olsen, 1990) and to deconstruct legal categories (Minow, 1990), on the other have contributed to the rise of scepticism towards legislative intervention. In the Italian constitutional system, ordinary law is at a critical juncture, having lost its central importance as, in connection with the crisis of political representation and the strengthening of the executives, sovereignty has been transferred to global institutions. To cope with this, great expectations have been placed on the judiciary, in particular on the case-law of constitutional, international and supranational courts, given case-law's intrinsic aptitude for responding to the needs of the people.

However, it is unsatisfactory to place all expectations for the protection of rights on the conflicting dialogue between courts. Law should try to maintain the promise of overturning social norms, giving those experiencing an unbalanced relationship the tools to not succumb and to afford every person the full development of his or her own personality. Law must then discover its own constitutional dimension: it is therefore appropriate to insist upon the constitution's aptitude to act as an instrument of transformation (Azzariti, 2013), so that constitutional law could fulfil a liberating mission from power relationships based on the differences that, historically and materially, are the source of vulnerability and exclusion and the ground of discrimination.

1 Griffin and Braidotti (2002) problematize using the terms from the English-speaking world, connected with concepts developed in the United States and the United Kingdom, in European women's studies.

In a broader normative conception of the constitution, the idea of 'constitution' should be linked with a dimension of 'counter-conduct' (Foucault, 2004) against the actually existing power relationships and against the statutes that don't comply with this goal (Ronchetti, 2007). Indeed, a re-signification of the constitution can be afforded only investing in the general theory of law and in the conceptualization of the legal subject as a contextualized, gendered person embodied in social and power relationships (Gigante, 2007).

In order to enable a transformation of the individual or collective self, the constitution should be interpreted so as to contain a 'principle of anti-subordination' to the existing power arrangements (Pezzini, 2009a: 16 and 2012: 19) or a principle of anti-subalternity including spaces of autonomy and self-realization for the subalterns (Spivak, 1988). This rereading of the constitutional text would uphold the current transformative capacity of the constitution with regard to the forms of co-existence.

Development of the Personality, Self-Determination and Self-Realization

The Italian constitution not only provides a guaranteeing-fundamental-rights model, but also envisages the free construction of personality in the lived experience of relationships (Rodotà, 2006: 22–3).

The construction of personality is first cited in article 2 of the constitution, which states that 'the Republic recognises and guarantees the inviolable rights of the person, as an individual and in the social groups within which human personality is developed. The Republic requires that the fundamental duties of political, economic and social solidarity be fulfilled'. The universality of inviolable rights enshrined in article 2 is immediately followed by the principle of equality (article 3, paragraph 2, of the constitution) which gives the entire Republic 'the duty … to remove the economic and social obstacles which, by limiting the freedom and equality of citizens, prevent the full development of the human person and the effective participation of all workers in the political, economic and social organization of the country'.

The Italian constitution thus outlines a paradigmatic project of complex social transformation, which is based on two inextricable dimensions: that of the full development of each person's personality and that of the actual participation by all people in the social, economic and political life. These two dimensions – the individual and the social – are hard to separate and, in fact, because they intertwine with and complete one another, enshrine a positive dynamicity.

The Italian constitution, then, goes beyond the idea that 'constitutionalism is a specific method adopted by modern democracies of safeguarding the autonomy on individual self' (Menon, 2004: 1), but aims to restore balance to economic and political social relationships, so as to enable individual and collective self-fulfilment. The linkage between the equal social dignity of the first paragraph of article 3 and the ultimate goal of the principle of substantial equality contained in the second paragraph of the same article (Ferrara, 1974) does not represent merely the foundation of the constitutional welfare state, which finds its various articulations in the recognition of social rights, but is also the basis for a model that may be defined as the pursuit of self-realization. Self-determination is connected to self-realization (Dahl, 1987: 104–8) precisely when the full development of the personality is accompanied, if not also permitted, by actual participation in community life.

It is first of all the actuality of relationships that provides the horizon of meaning for the principle of self-realization: according to the Constitutional Court, article 3 of the constitution, 'in addition to establishing an autonomous principle of 'substantial' equality and of equal opportunity among citizens in social, economic and political life ... expresses a criterion of interpretation ... regarding the actual results produced or which can be produced in real life relationships' (judgment no. 163/1993).[2] But, above all, when referring to what it calls the constitution's 'primary imperative', the Constitutional Court points to 'the ultimate objective of full self-determination of the person' (ibid.) alongside actual participation in community life.

Self-Determination and Self-Realization of Women

And yet, the constitutionalist approach to legal issues involving women's bodies has always been entirely calibrated to protect psycho-physical health (article 32 of the constitution), turning a blind eye to personal freedom (article 13 of the constitution) (Ronchetti, 2006) and therefore to autonomy (Mancini, 2012). The rediscovery of the concept of self-determination was in fact expressed in actions that involved everyone's body, and particularly in the area of informed consent to medical care: in this regard, the Constitutional Court speaks of a fundamental right to self-determination, derived from a combined reading of article 2 and article 13 of the constitution (judgment no. 438/2008).

Only quite recently was the concept of self-determination introduced in reproductive issues: in addition to a health-centred reading of reproductive health pursuant to article 32 of the constitution,[3] in judgment no. 162/2014 the Constitutional Court declared the illegitimacy of the ban of heterologous fertilization – provided for under Law no. 40/2004 on medically assisted procreation – finally speaking of reproductive self-determination as well. It must, however, be noted that, in this regard, reference was made not to article 13 on *habeas corpus*, but to protecting motherhood pursuant to article 31 of the constitution. The judgment in fact states that 'the choice ... of becoming parents and of forming a family that also has children is an expression of the *fundamental*

2 All Constitutional Court judgments are available at www.cortecostituzionale.it/actionPronuncia.do.

3 See Constitutional Court, judgment no. 151/2009.

and general freedom of self-determination … since it concerns the private and family sphere … the most intimate and intangible sphere of the human person [that] can only be incoercible' and is characterized by 'the free and voluntary nature of the act' (my italics).

And it is precisely women's sexuality and reproductive self-determination, as the Estrela Report to the European Parliament underscored (2013: para 66), that can have a 'long-term impact on women's and girls' sexual and reproductive health, as well as on their self-esteem and empowerment', especially for young, poor and migrant women (with a particular degree of seriousness for the Roma people) who 'are disproportionately affected by a lack of SRHRs[4] due to the nature of human reproduction, and the gender-based social, legal and economic context in which it occurs'.

Not only, however, was the Estrela Report not approved by the European Parliament but, for Italy, some cases of cultural resistance reverberating at the constitution's interpretive margins bear mentioning. One example of the conflict involving the constitution's text, its interpretation and its aptitude to interact with the materiality of life concerns the institution of marriage. This allows us to grasp how much the conflict between the various ways of understanding coexistence has shifted to interpretation of the constitution itself: according to the Constitutional Court, the 'heterosexual paradigm of marriage' – as declared by judgment no. 138/2010 – 'cannot be overcome hermeneutically, because it would not be a matter of a mere rereading of the system, or of abandoning a mere practice of interpretation, but of proceeding with *a creative interpretation*' (my italics) (judgment no. 170/2014). And yet, upon closer examination, article 29 of the constitution contains no reference to the sex of the 'spouses',[5] so that this indeterminacy has left open the possibility of a different interpretation, one which, in the perspective of a 'dignity in change' (Niccolai and Ruggiu, 2010), would not rule out the equal social dignity of homosexual unions.

The aforementioned judgment in particular considered legitimate the automatic dissolution of marriage in the event of the 'sex reassignment' of one of the spouses. Indeed, in the court's opinion, a joint reading of articles 29 and 30 of the constitution would underscore the 'constitutional importance given to the legitimate family and to the (potential) procreative purpose of marriage, which sets it apart from homosexual union'. However, again with regard to article 30, it must be pointed out that the constitution goes no further than to establish the 'duty and right of *parents*' (my italics) to 'support, raise and educate their children', with no reference to the parents' being of different sexes.

To be sure, in both of these decisions, lawmakers were called upon to regulate forms of 'homosexual union, understood as a stable cohabitation between two

4 Sexual and reproductive health and rights.

5 'The Republic recognizes the rights of the family as a natural society founded on marriage. Marriage is based on the moral and legal equality of the spouses within the limits laid down by law to guarantee the unity of the family'.

persons of the same sex, entitled to the fundamental right of freely living a condition as couple, while obtaining – in the time and manner and within the limits established by law – legal recognition thereof with the related rights and duties … in the context of giving value to the pluralistic model' (judgment no. 170/2014). However, in the Constitutional Court's view, this legislation would not be a new and better implementation of article 29 of the constitution so much as an evolution of how to understand those social formations in which the personality of the individual is developed, as protected by article 2 of the constitution.

Intersectionality as New Interpretation of the Italian Constitution

Article 3 of the constitution opens by affirming that 'all citizens have equal social dignity and are equal before the law, without distinction of sex, race, language, religion, political opinion, personal and social conditions'. This non-comprehensive list, which includes every difference understood as specificity, must by all means be broadened to include at least all the diversities mentioned in the EU Charter of Fundamental Rights: colour, ethnic or social origin, genetic features, belief, opinions, membership of a national minority, property, birth, disability, age or sexual orientation and nationality.

Besides the differences just mentioned, from the constitutional point of view, gender differences and gender identity issues are likewise important. These personal and social differences, that may all coexist in a given person and in a given group, may determine very peculiar social circumstances for migrant women. It must be carefully considered differences strictly intersecting the condition of migrant women.

A very important differentiation is between regularly and irregularly residing migrants (Sassen, 1996).

While gender, sexuality and gender identity would appear more appropriately to be based upon sex differences, contrary to what was established by the European Court of Justice from the *Grant* case onwards[6] (Pezzini, 2012: 139–140), on the other hand, being a regular or irregular migrant, as much as being an unaccompanied minor, are new forms of classic personal status, just the same as being married, unmarried, widowed or orphan.

However, all of these diversity factors show that each individual incorporates within himself or herself a plurality of special characteristics which, beyond

6 ECJ, *Grant v South West Trains Ltd*, Case C-249/96, 17 February 1998. The applicant, Ms Grant, claimed that, because unmarried opposite-sex partners were given social benefits, the refusal of those benefits to her partner (a woman) constituted sex discrimination. The ECJ did not find discrimination on the basis of sex, because male workers and female workers would be affected identically by the denial of benefits. According to the Court, it is an issue related to the personal status based on the position of same-sex couples. It is for the legislature alone to change it.

nationality, makes him or her a unique cultural synthesis. This is why a theoretical transition is starting to take place from a single-ground approach, which construes each ground of discrimination separately from all of the others, to an intersectional approach (McCall, 2005; Carbin and Edenheim, 2013). Taking intersectionality as 'theory' (Minow, 1990), 'politics' (Crenshaw, 1991) or 'normative paradigm' (Hancock, 2007), the aim is to go beyond a simplistic sum of possible discriminations in order to grasp the true dynamics of power relationships, which may also cut across sex and gender (class, race, nationality, age, sexuality and sexual identity differences).

In this regard, especially since the introduction of article 13 of the Treaty of Amsterdam, we have begun to speak of multiple forms of discrimination. Similarly, the Beijing Declaration and Platform for Action, adopted at the 1995 UN Fourth World Conference on Women, makes the recommendation to 'intensify efforts to ensure equal enjoyment of all human rights and fundamental freedoms for all women and girls who face *multiple barriers* to their empowerment and advancement because of such factors as their race, age, language, ethnicity, culture, religion, or disability, or because they are indigenous people' (my italics).[7]

Actually, the European directives adopted pursuant to the aforementioned article 13 – the Racial Equality Directive and the Employment Equality Directive[8] – contain no explicit definition of multiple discrimination, although they mention it precisely with regard to the intersection between sex and racial and ethnic origins in 'whereas' clause number 14: 'in implementing the principle of equal treatment irrespective of racial or ethnic origin, the Community should … aim to eliminate inequalities, and to promote equality between men and women, especially since women are often the victims of multiple discrimination'.[9]

It is to be kept in mind that discrimination on the basis of sex or nationality is excluded from the field of action of the two anti-discrimination directives; indeed, the latter prohibits discrimination based on religion, convictions, disability, age and sexual orientation, but exclusively with reference to the area of employment,

---

7 The Fourth World Conference on Women was a conference convened by the United Nations in Beijing, China, on the Convention on the Elimination of All Forms of Discrimination Against Women (CEDAW). Available at http://www.un.org/womenwatch/daw/beijing.

8 Council Directive 2000/43/EC of 29 June 2000, implementing the principle of equal treatment between persons irrespective of racial or ethnic origin, and Council Directive 2000/78/EC of 27 November 2000, establishing a general framework for equal treatment in employment and occupation.

9 In Italy, the transposition of the directives with Legislative Decrees no. 215/2003 and no. 216/2003, although not establishing the concept of multiple discrimination, introduced the simplified version of double-discrimination (Gottardi, 2007), in which any one of the factors of discrimination is associated with that of gender. Legislative Decree no. 150/2011 (article 28) subsequently unified in a single proceedings the legal actions against different grounds of discrimination, with the significant exception of cases of gender discrimination that maintain a special proceeding.

while the former provides protection from discrimination due to racial or ethnic origins in fields other than employment and work. On the one hand, this discrepancy establishes a sort of 'hierarchy' or 'asymmetry' between the grounds of discrimination; on the other, 'this differentiation in scope also makes it difficult to deal with multiple discrimination' (European Union Agency for Fundamental Rights, 2013: 3).

There is, disappointingly, no legal or jurisdictional instrument to combat those enhanced multiple barriers upon the full development of personality, thus resulting in uncertainties as to the very definition of multiple discrimination (Committee on Economic, Social and Cultural Rights 2009: 17–27). Despite this, the ambiguity of positive law does not prevent the theory of legal interpretation from adopting a method that takes into account the contribution of the literature on intersectionality. In fact, a renewed proposal of meaning of and on the constitution remains to be tried: by respecting the constitution's text, it might be possible to trigger its interaction with the actual forms of co-existence and to foster an approach that recognizes (and turns against) the upsetting effects of certain forms of vulnerability, exclusion and subordination.

The translation of the intersectional approach into the constitutional theory of interpretation might be a keystone for a rereading of the constitution fitting for the questions to be dealt with. In fact, it could help to identify the mechanisms which contribute towards defining social groups and to overcome the monolithic vision of the disadvantaged group in favour of a dynamic and conflictual vision. The 'claim of cultural identities' (Benhabib, 2002) often implies the crystallization of the group's characteristics, creating an intertwinement of provisions that threatens to weaken the subjective position of men and women belonging to that group, and of young women in particular (Okin, 1997). By contrast, intersectionality accommodates the perspective – also adopted by such other critical approaches as postcolonial theory (Mohanty, 1988), diaspora studies (Brah, 1996) and queer theory (Butler, 1990) – of seeking 'alternatives to static conceptualization of identity', towards 'multiple and shifting identities' (Davis, 2008).

In fact, the intersectional approach allows us to focus attention on the most vulnerable persons, even within the disadvantaged social groups themselves (Olivito, 2007), thus raising the question of subjection to several systems of subordination (Crenshaw, 1991).

In 2005, the European Court of Human Rights judged an emblematic case (*Siliadin v. France*[10]) which involved a young migrant woman reduced to slavery and required to perform forced household work by persons – men and women – of

10 European Court of Human Rights, Second Section, *Case of Siliadin v. France*, Application No. 73316/01, 26 July 2005. The Court notes that, although the applicant was not threatened by a 'penalty', 'she was in an equivalent situation … [s]he was an adolescent girl in a foreign land, unlawfully present on French territory and in fear of arrest by the police. … she was not given any choice … As a minor, she had no resources and was vulnerable and isolated … and was completely dependent on Mr and Mrs B'. So the

the same ethnic or geographical origin. Taking advantage of her dearth of resources, her vulnerability and her isolation, a French couple of Togolese origin had been charged with having obtained household and care services without payment or in exchange for payment that was manifestly disproportionate to the work carried out by the young woman. She was subjected to working and living conditions that were incompatible with human dignity, as the couple took advantage of her state of dependence, aggravated by the circumstance that she was unlawfully present in French territory.

It is to be kept in mind that, in the negotiations between the couple and the young woman, the household and care work that she was to perform were to compensate the family's support for her school attendance, which was never permitted. The young woman's migration plan hinged entirely upon the expectation of being able to develop her personality and to effectively take part in the country's social life – an expectation betrayed to a great degree not only due to her being a young woman of Togolese origin, but also because of her condition as an illegal immigrant, which decisively contributed to worsening her vulnerability.

Constitutional Citizenship of Migrant Men and Women

The constitutional interpretation of the issues involving differences of gender, sexuality and gender identity still stands at a certain distance from a reading that takes the free development of personality and actual participation in community life as a primary interpretative criterion. In this context, the viewpoint of migrant women must be introduced in order to grasp the close connection that exists between guaranteeing inviolable individual or collective rights, the development of personality and full participation in the country's economic, social and political organization.

The Constitutional Court, before Italy went from being a country of emigration to one of immigration, in fact stated that 'those who remember the grave wounds inflicted upon the right to emigrate for militaristic, nationalistic or racist reasons, will want to recognize the need for a man's [*rectius*: a person's] right to the full expansion of his or her own personality, and thus the right to take part in the community life of peoples, to be preserved from other dangers tomorrow' (judgment no. 269/1986). Emigration, as a characteristic of free transnational circulation, is thus ascribed by Italian constitutional case-law to the legal system's ultimate aim: the full development of personality and the full participation in all fields of social co-existence in the territory, which at times only a migration plan can make possible.

The significant stabilization of the migrant population in Italy (Istat, 2014), which contains within it a strong degree of feminization (Ponomareva, 2014),

applicant was 'subjected to forced labour and was held in servitude within the meaning of Article 4 of the Convention'. See Naddi, 2012.

requires a profound rethinking, above all, of the migrant's position in the Italian constitutional system.

Of central importance to this was the Constitutional Court's interpretation of the principle of equality established in article 3 of the constitution: in judgment no. 120/1967, contrary to what took place in the cases referred to earlier, the court overcame the constitution's text in favour of a systematic and evolutionary interpretation. In fact, notwithstanding that the principle of equality refers expressly to 'citizens', the court affirmed that this provision cannot be considered 'in isolation', but must be placed in 'connection' with other constitutional provisions. Above all, these provisions are article 2 of the constitution, which guarantees inviolable rights to each person, and article 10 of the constitution, which links the foreigner's legal status to international law. Pursuant to this synergy, 'when it is a matter of respecting … fundamental rights', the word 'citizens' contained in the principle of equality includes every person, even if foreign.

Since then, however, there has persisted a margin of interpretative uncertainty as to whether foreigners possess certain constitutional rights considered to belong to citizens exclusively, such as the right of entry into the Italian territory and the right to vote.

From this standpoint, in giving value to the text of the constitution itself, which refers to 'citizens', this judgment might be considered the leading case of a sort of constitutional citizenship (Ronchetti, 2014), because, even before distinguishing state and foreign citizenship, the constitution is held to indicate the forms of co-existence among constitutional citizens. In this perspective, the adjective 'constitutional' is to be understood as upholding an idea of citizenship's connotation as participation in co-existence, thereby restoring solemnity – in an inclusive vision of territoriality – to the forms of sharing. The assumption of a constitutional citizenship also aims to underscore the expansive force of the constitution's provisions, which can provide a new basis for people's basic rights, including those typically deemed to belong to citizens alone. Pursuant to the citizenship recognized by the constitution, and regardless of national citizenship, anyone present in national territory is immediately a holder of every legal status guaranteed by the constitution.

The most recent decisions of the court seem to be going in this direction. Indeed, it has affirmed that the fundamental rights must be recognized and guaranteed 'also for foreigners, whatever their position is with respect to the provisions governing entering and staying in the country, although lawmakers may decide upon different procedures for the exercise thereof' (judgment no. 252/2001). It has also held that the fundamental rights 'also belong to foreigners without valid residence permits, until an expulsion measure is issued and enforced against them, without this being asserted to legitimate their presence in national territory' (judgment no. 299/2010).

This case-law appears to reinforce the constitutional citizenship of migrants that was referred to, precisely because it is 'consistent with the natural expansive propensity of the need to guarantee respect for (which can mean nothing other than actual implementation of) the fundamental rights to which the person is entitled' (judgment no. 61/2011).

And yet, among all the possible sources of subordination, the condition of irregularity is often a determining factor in exacerbating this disadvantaged position when it is intertwined with other grounds of discrimination. In the *Siliadin* case, as has been shown, the irregularity of the stay was a decisive factor in exposing a young, migrant woman to mandatory labour in a condition of slavery.

Irregularity, Nationality and Gender

Since illegal stay is a personal condition determined by law itself (Rigo, 2007), it represents a very fertile ground for assessing what are – in a constitutional perspective – the effective conditions for providing migrant women with a path of self-fulfilment.

The possible paths of self-realization, understood as full participation in community life, include the acquisition of the national citizenship, that every constitutional citizen should be able to access, on the basis of a reasonable assessment of the bond he or she has established with the legal system: national citizenship – understood as a particular status – is in fact an outcome that constitutional citizenship should reasonably make attainable by reassessing the (forgotten) right to change citizenship and the related freedom of movement.

Although, in Italy, citizenship acquisitions based on permanent residence now outnumber those gained through marriage, for women of non-EU citizenship, getting married has remained the largely prevalent condition of access to Italian citizenship (Istat, 2014).[11]

In 2009, the Parliament interpreted those data as a result of the so-called marriages of 'convenience', which is to say, unions contracted solely as a basis for acquiring Italian citizenship by those lacking the requirements to do so through residence: the 'irregular' migrant. The acquisition of citizenship through residence is, in fact, significantly marked by the strong legal correlation between the labour contract, regular residence permit and a 10-year legal residence, understood as not merely dwelling in the Italian territory but as being entered in the civil registration lists (Morozzo della Rocca, 2014). Therefore, Law no. 94/2009 had subordinated the right to marry to possession of a regular stay, but this requirement was declared unconstitutional (Constitutional Court, judgment no. 245/2011).

From the standpoint of gender, what could represent direct discrimination against irregular migrants could result in indirect, and thus more insidious,

11 In the perspective of migrant lesbians it means that the Italian heterosexual paradigm of marriage has a negative impact on access to national citizenship, and that same-sex marriages and civil unions recognized in other countries are irrelevant for the purposes of being granted visas or residence permits.

discrimination against migrant women, disproportionately disadvantaged by that illegitimate provision.

Indirect Discrimination against Migrants

Although the aforementioned anti-discrimination directives do not involve nationality,[12] it was already undisputed that the principle of equal treatment based on nationality prohibits

> not only overt discrimination by reason of nationality but also all covert forms of discrimination which, by the application of other distinguishing criteria, lead in fact to the same result. Accordingly, conditions imposed by national law must be regarded as indirectly discriminatory where, although applicable irrespective of nationality, they affect essentially migrant workers or the great majority of those affected are migrant workers, where they are indistinctly applicable but can more easily be satisfied by national workers than by migrant workers or where there is a risk that they may operate to the particular detriment of migrant workers. (*O'Flynn* case, paragraphs 17–18)[13]

Moving in this direction were the aforementioned European anti-discrimination directives, according to which indirect discrimination is any apparently neutral provision, criterion, or practice that places anyone in a condition of particular disadvantage compared with other persons and which can drain the abstract ownership of rights of all effectiveness.

The evolution of the concept of indirect discrimination is in fact the chief success of second-generation anti-discrimination law,[14] because the definition of indirect discrimination 'fits in a substantive concept of equality' (Howard, 2010: 148). It has a close connection with the *de facto* conditions that, by limiting freedom and equality, prevent the full development of the human person and effective participation in the political, economic and social organization of the country (article 3, paragraph 2, of the constitution).

---

12 In particular, article 3(2) of Directive 2000/43 provides that it 'does not cover difference of treatment based on nationality and is without prejudice to provisions and conditions relating to the entry into and residence of third-country nationals and stateless persons on the territory of Member States, and to any treatment which arises from the legal status of the third-country nationals and stateless persons concerned'.

13 ECJ, Fifth Chamber, *John O'Flynn v Adjudication Officer*, C-237/94, 23 May 1996.

14 Council Directive 97/80 established, however, that there was indirect discrimination when 'an apparently neutral provision, criterion or practice disadvantages a substantially higher proportion of the members of one sex'.

In the Italian case, the limitation upon access to fundamental rights – and to social rights in particular – was pursued by relying on an exclusionary way of conceiving settlement in the territory.

As for migrants' access to welfare benefits, the Constitutional Court has repeatedly repealed conditions relating to the duration of residence in national territory;[15] in particular, it deemed arbitrary that access to social benefits would require the long-term residence permit,[16] the possession of which is dependent on 'requirements that range from income parameters to others that pertain to general living conditions, thereby ending up with a merely temporal requirement linked to the period of stay in Italy with a regular residence permit' (judgment no. 40/2013).

Moreover, since the Constitutional Court declared that the fundamental rights are granted to the person as such, regardless not only of citizenship but also of the regularity or irregularity of the residence permit, many regional lawmakers have begun to introduce indirect discrimination against foreign nationals by subordinating access to social benefits to a temporally qualified stay in regional territory. Length of residence or of working activity in the regional territory as a criterion for accessing benefits is a particularly insidious device for excluding migrants.

In some cases, the strengthening of the residence criterion was expressly established for migrants alone. The *Kamberaj* case,[17] for example, in a preliminary ruling before the European Court of Justice, involved an Italian provincial law that, in order to be eligible for housing benefits – in addition to the obligation to have resided for more than five years in the territory of the province – required only third-country nationals to satisfy the further condition that they should have completed three years of work in that territory.

In many other cases, however, only in an ostensibly neutral fashion did regional legislation link social benefits to the requirement of a qualified residence in the region's territory (Ronchetti, 2012).

In this regard, the Constitutional Court declared unconstitutional the 'absolute exclusion of entire categories of persons' from the integrated system of social services, 'on the basis either of lacking possession of European citizenship or upon the lack of long-term residence', because 'it fails to respect the principle of equality, as it introduces into the legislative system arbitrary elements of distinction' (judgment no. 40/2011). Since then, it has been stressed that 'there is no correlation whatsoever between satisfying the primary needs of the human being who has settled in regional territory and the duration of settlement over time' (judgments no. 40/2011 and no. 187/2010).

---

15 See the Constitutional Court's case-law in judgments no. 11/2009 and no. 324/2006, no. 306/2008, no. 40/2013, no. 187/2010 and no. 329/2011.

16 The card has been now replaced by the EC residence permit for long-term residents.

17 ECJ, Grand Chamber, Servet Kamberaj v Istituto per l'Edilizia sociale della Provincia autonoma di Bolzano and Others, C-571/10, 24 April 2012.

Reliance on the criterion of length of residence, therefore, by impeding the effective enjoyment of fundamental rights, amounts to indirect discrimination against migrants (Pezzini, 2009b) – and, as will be underscored, against migrant women in particular.

Multiple Discrimination against Migrant Women

Length of residence impacts migrants more for the structural difficulty migrants have in fulfilling the requirements of long-term residence in the regional territory: it is sufficient to consider that, in 2014, in at least half of cases their province of residence changed from the one where they regularized their status (Istat, 2014).

But not only does the criterion of long-term residence in the region translate into indirect discrimination against all migrants; upon closer examination, this discrimination puts migrant women at a greater disadvantage.

Even if migrant women have a more stable presence in Italy than men do, there is in fact a strong difference in mobility behaviours within national territory between the two genders, as well as between the migration patterns typical of different groups. In particular, there is a greater propensity for movement among non-national women (Bonifazi, Franz and Tucci, 2014), for whom breadwinner migrations are more common (Italian women are breadwinners in 8.4 per cent of couples with children: Istat, 2014).

Therefore, a migrant breadwinner woman shows greater-than-average mobility in the territory. This means that, although she will frequently change where she lives, she can change her legal residence only if she has a regular labour contract. The numerous legislative provisions adopted in recent years that, through the criterion of long-term residence in regional territory, have the effect of limiting migrants' access to social rights and therefore to the economic benefits established to relieve situations of disadvantage and need, thus have particular impact upon migrant women, rising to the level of multiple discrimination.

It must also be considered that many migrant women are also mothers, often of children born in Italy, making a 12 per cent contribution to Italy's total fertility rate (Bonifazi, 2013: 249–50). And, yet, the Constitutional Court, with judgment no. 222/2013, considered the birth allowances and other economic benefits for families to be 'measures that go beyond the intangible nucleus of the fundamental rights of the human person, and that reward, not arbitrarily, the contribution the family makes to the moral and material progress of the community established on a regional basis', thereby justifying in this case subordinating these benefits to long-term residence in the territory.

Moreover, judgment no. 432/2005 confirmed the special regime of the housing policy and the corresponding constitutional validity of the long-term residence criterion. It suggests that migrant women, characterized by their strong mobility within Italy, are thus disproportionately more affected by social benefits restrictions such as those for housing and family support services.[18]

From this standpoint, we need to carefully assess the professional gender segmentation that characterizes the Italian labour market; indeed, in 2012, more than half of foreign employed women were engaged in just two professions (caregivers and domestic workers)[19] and, in more than eight cases out of ten, the increase in foreign employment has been in household services (Sabbadini, 2013).

As concerns the protection of labour and motherhood, migrant domestic workers also suffer a form of discrimination unique to our system: unlike for all other female workers, the ban on dismissal during maternity does not apply to domestic workers. It also means that after five months of compulsory maternity leave they can be fired; they are not entitled to the so-called six-month optional maternity leave, breastfeeding leave and leave for illnesses of children up to three years of age (article 62 of Law no. 151/2001).[20]

For these reasons, in Italy the case of domestic workers was expressly pointed to (Andall, 2000), alongside the grave situation for Roma women (European Union Agency for Fundamental Rights, 2014), as a typical one of multiple discrimination:

> Migrant women working in domestic/care services bridge the gap in the social welfare system and are exposed to the risk of exploitation and discrimination by their employers – primarily because of fear of deportation in case of revocation of their contracts. In many households they are exposed to multiple forms of discrimination and prejudices because of their nationality; their generic work contracts and diverse labour conditions and responsibilities, which often go beyond the provision of caregiving to include other housework; their working hours are irregular; their salaries are not paid regularly; and there are no opportunities for career development. (Manjoo, 2012, para 83)

Also of importance from this standpoint is the intersectionality of race and gender for asylum-seekers, given the multiple forms of discrimination suffered by refugee women who often head single-parent families. The gender dimension that often characterizes the experiences of refugee women doubtlessly finds an

18 However, the eight-year residence limit recently established by a regional law was considered an 'unreasonable discrimination' in comparison with Italian citizens because it was 'clearly disproportionate to the purpose and inconsistent with the very aims of public housing' (judgment no. 168/2014).

19 In 2008 they were instead engaged in five professions, because they also entered the workplace as waitresses, salespeople or cleaning workers.

For an analysis of the juridical profiles, in particular of regularization of irregular migrants, of the massive outsourcing of housework and care giving to migrant women in Italy, see Bascherini and Niccolai, 2010.

20 Precisely for this reason, in the latest national collective bargaining agreement (2013–2016, article 24) trade unions made a statement indicating that this regulation infringes ILO Convention no. 189/2011.

obstacle in the 1951 Refugee Convention, which does not include an explicit reference to women, sex, gender, homosexuality or gender identity. All the same, the UN Refugee Agency has stressed that

> persecution for reasons of race may be expressed in different ways against men and women. For example, the persecutor may choose to destroy the ethnic identity and/or prosperity of a racial group by killing, maiming or incarcerating the men, while the women may be viewed as propagating the ethnic or racial identity and persecuted in a different way, such as through sexual violence or control of reproduction. (2002)

Furthermore, in 2012 it adopted a similar text on 'sexual orientation and/or gender identity' (UNHCR, 2012).[21]

From this standpoint, it bears mentioning that gender identity has recently been added to sexual orientation among the characteristics for identifying the 'particular social group' in which membership may be considered grounds for persecution (Legislative Decree no. 18/2014). It clearly shows that it is essential to identify the intersection between different forms of discrimination, with particular reference to those connected with gender identity (lesbian, gay, bisexual, transgender, queer and intersex: LGBTQI),[22] also given their ability to escalate into full-blown persecution (LaViolette, 2011).

In conclusion, the many issues involving (migrant) women help towards a more general re-signification, in intersectional terms, of the constitutional project. A project which, starting from the relationship between the public and private spheres and between social production and reproduction, can allow each person to pursue his or her own self-realization.

References

Andall, J. (2000). *Gender, Migration and Domestic Service: The Politics of Black Women in Italy*. Aldershot: Ashgate.

Azzariti, G. (2013). *Il costituzionalismo moderno può sopravvivere?* Roma-Bari: Laterza.

---

21 '3. Intersecting factors that may contribute to and compound the effects of violence and discrimination include sex, age, nationality, ethnicity/race, social or economic status and HIV status. Due to these multiple layers of discrimination, LGBTI individuals are often highly marginalized in society and isolated from their communities and families ... Because of these and other factors, they may be inhibited from informing asylum adjudicators that their real fear of persecution relates to their sexual orientation and/or gender identity'.

22 See Lorenzetti, 2013.

Bascherini, G. (2012). *La colonizzazione e il diritto costituzionale. Il contributo dell'esperienza coloniale alla costruzione del diritto pubblico italiano*. Napoli: Jovene.

Bascherini, G. and Niccolai, S. (2010). Regolarizzare Mary Poppins. Lavoro nello spazio domestico e qualità della cittadinanza. *Rivista del Diritto della Sicurezza Sociale*, 3, 499–534.

Benhabib, S. (2002). *The Claims of Culture: Equality and Diversity in the Global Era*. Princeton: Princeton University Press.

Bonifazi, C. (2013). *L'Italia delle migrazioni*. Bologna: il Mulino.

Bonifazi, C., Franz, H. and Tucci, E. (2014). Le migrazioni interne in Italia nel 2011–2012. In Colucci, M. and Gallo, S. (eds) (2014). *L'arte di spostarsi. Rapporto 2014 sulle migrazioni interne in Italia*, 3–20. Roma: Donzelli.

Butler, J. (1990). *Gender Trouble: Feminism and the Subversion of Identity*. NY: Routledge.

Carbin, M. and Edenheim, S. (2013). The intersectional turn in feminist theory: A dream of a common language? *European Journal of Women's Studies*, 20, 3, 233–48.

Carrino, A. (1992). *Ideologia e coscienza. Critical legal studies*. Napoli: ESI.

Committee on Economic, Social and Cultural Rights (2009). *General Comment No. 20, Non-Discrimination in Economic, Social and Cultural Rights*, UN Doc. E/C.12/GC/20.

Costa, P. (2004–05). Pagina introduttiva. *Quaderni fiorentini*. L'Europa e gli 'Altri'. Il diritto coloniale fra Otto e Novecento, 33/34, 1–9.

Crenshaw, K. (1991). Mapping the margins: intersectionality, identity politics, and violence against women of color. *Stanford Law Review*, 43(6), 1241–99.

Dahl, D.T. (1987). *Women's Law. An introduction to Feminist Jurisprudence*. Oslo: Norwegian University Press.

Davis, K. (2008). Intersectionality as buzzword. A sociology of science perspective on what makes a feminist theory successful. *Feminist Theory*, 9, 1, 67–85.

EP Committee on Women's Rights and Gender Equality (2013). *Report on Sexual and Reproductive Health and Rights* (2013/2040(INI)). Available at www.europarl.europa.eu/.

European Union Agency for Fundamental Rights (2013). *Inequalities and multiple discrimination in access to and quality of healthcare*. Available at http://fra.europa.eu/en/publication/2013.

European Union Agency for Fundamental Rights (2014). *Discrimination against and living conditions of Roma women in 11 EU Member States*. Available at http://fra.europa.eu/en/publication/2014/.

Ferrara, G. (1974). La pari dignità sociale (Appunti per una ricostruzione). *Studi in onore di Giuseppe Chiarelli*, 1089–1105. II. Milano: Giuffrè.

Foucault, M. (2004). *Sécurité, territoire, population. Collège de France (1977–1978)*. Paris: Gallimard.

Gianformaggio, L. (1993). Identity, Equality, Similarity and the Law. In Karlsson, M.M., Jónsson, O.P. and Brynjarsdóttir, E.M. (eds) *Recht, Gerechtigkeit und der Staat*, 121–34. Berlin: Duncker&Humblot.

Gigante, M. (ed.) (2007). *I diritti delle donne nella Costituzione*. Napoli: Editoriale Scientifica.

Gottardi, D. (2007). La discriminazione razziale. In Barbera, M. (ed.) *Il nuovo diritto antidiscriminatorio*, 1–42. Milano: Giuffrè.

Griffin, G. and Braidotti, R. (2002). *Thinking Differently: A Reader in European Women's Studies*. London: Zed Books Ltd.

Hancock, A.-M. (2007). Intersectionality as a normative and empirical paradigm. *Politics and Gender*, 3(2), 248–54.

Howard, E. (2010). *The EU Race Directive: Developing the Protection against Racial Discrimination within the EU*. London: Routledge.

Istat (2014). *Cittadini non comunitari regolarmente presenti*. Available at http://www.istat.it/it/archivio.

LaViolette, N. (2011). Les identités multiples et le droit des réfugiés. *Canadian Ethnic Studies/Études Ethniques au*, 35(3), 39–55.

Lorenzetti, A. (2013). *Diritti in transito. La condizione giuridica delle persone transessuali*. Franco Angeli: Milano.

Mancini, S. (2012). *Un affare di donne. L'aborto tra eguale libertà e controllo sociale*. Padova: Cedam.

Manjoo, R. (2012). *Report of the Special Rapporteur on violence against women, its causes and consequences*, Addendum Mission to Italy, A/HRC/20/16/Add.2. 15 June 2012.

McCall, L. (2005). The Complexity of intersectionality. *Chicago Journals*, 30(3), 1771–800.

Menon, N. (2004). *Recovering Subversion. Feminist Politics Beyond the Law*, Ranikhet: Permanent Black.

Minow, M. (1990). *Making All the Difference: Inclusion, Exclusion, and American Law*. Ithaca: Cornell University Press.

Mohanty, C.T. (1988). Under Western Eyes: Feminist Scholarship and Colonial Discourses. *Feminist Review*, 30, 61–88.

Morozzo della Rocca, P. (2014). La residenza degli stranieri: un diritto speciale? In Ronchetti, L. (ed.) *La Repubblica e le migrazioni*, 63–77. Milano: Giuffrè.

Naddi, E. (2012). All'incrocio di genere e altri fattori di discriminazione. In Pezzini, B. (ed.) *Genere e diritto. Come il genere costruisce il diritto e il diritto costruisce il genere*, 207–35. Bergamo: Sestante edizioni.

Niccolai, S. and Ruggiu, I. (eds) (2010). *Dignity In Change. Exploring the Constitutional Potential of EU Gender and Anti-Discrimination Law*. Fiesole: EPAP.

Okin, S.M. (1997). Is Multiculturalism Bad for Women? *Boston Review*, 22, 25–8.

Olivito, E. (2007). Primi spunti di riflessione su multiculturalismo e identità culturali nella prospettiva della vulnerabilità. *Politica del diritto*, 1, 71–109.

Olsen, F. (1990). Feminism and Critical Legal Theory: An American Perspective. *International Journal of the Sociology of Law*, 18, 199–215.

Pezzini, B. (2009a). L'uguaglianza uomo-donna come principio anti-discriminatorio e come principio anti-subordinazione. In Brunelli, G., Pugiotto, A. and Veronesi, P. (eds) *Scritti in onore di Lorenza Carlassare, Il diritto costituzionale come regola e limite al potere*, 1141–58. Napoli: Jovene.

Pezzini, B. (2009b). Lo statuto costituzionale del non cittadino: i diritti sociali. *Rivistaaic*, 1–35. Available at http://archivio.rivistaaic.it/materiali/convegni/aic200910.

Pezzini, B. (ed.) (2012). *La costruzione del genere. Norme e regole*. Bergamo: Sestante edizioni.

Pitch, T. (2004). *I diritti fondamentali: differenze culturali, disuguaglianze sociali, differenza sessuale*. Torino: Giappichelli.

Ponomareva, O. (2014). La dimensione femminile dell'immigrazione in Italia. In Idos (ed.) *Dalle discriminazioni ai diritti*, 165–8. Pomezia: Consorzio Age.

Rigo, E. (2007). *Europa di confine. Trasformazioni della cittadinanza nell'Unione allargata*. Roma: Meltemi.

Rodotà, S. (2006). *La vita e le regole: tra diritto e non diritto*. Milano: Feltrinelli.

Ronchetti, L. (2006). Donne e corpi tra sessualità e riproduzione. *Costituzionalismo.it*, 2, 1–20. Available at www.costituzionalismo.it.

Ronchetti, L. (2007). *Il* nomos *infranto: globalizzazione e costituzioni. Del limite come principio essenziale degli ordinamenti giuridici*. Jovene: Napoli.

Ronchetti, L. (ed.) (2012). *I diritti di cittadinanza dei migranti. Il ruolo delle Regioni*. Milano: Giuffrè.

Ronchetti, L. (2014). La 'cittadinanza costituzionale' degli stranieri: una questione d'interpretazione costituzionale. In Ronchetti, L. (ed.) *La Repubblica e le migrazioni*, 25–63. Milano: Giuffrè.

Sabbadini, L.L. (2013). Aumentano le donne breadwinner, ma il mercato del lavoro è ancora maschile. *Reset*, 146. Available at www.reset.it.

Sassen, S. (1996). *Losing Control? Sovereignty in the Age of Globalization*. New York: University Press.

Spivak, G.C. (1988). Can the subaltern speak? In Nelson, C. and Grossberg, L. (eds) *Marxism and the Interpretation of Culture*, 271–313. Urbana/Chicago: University of Illinois Press.

UN High Commissioner for Refugees (UNHCR) (2002). *Guidelines on International Protection No. 1: Gender-Related Persecution*. 7 May 2002. HCR/GIP/02/01. Available at http://www.unhcr.org.

UNHCR (2012). *Guidelines on International Protection No. 9: Claims to Refugee Status based on Sexual Orientation and/or Gender Identity*, 23 October 2012, HCR/GIP/12/01. Available at http://www.unhcr.org.

Chapter 5

The Case of Healthcare and Social Services for Migrant Women: Between Anti-Discrimination and Anti-Subordination

Anna Lorenzetti

Preliminary Remarks

In the twofold prospect of gender and migration, migrant women's capability to access healthcare and social services represents a focal issue because of the particular vulnerability they may experience.

The disadvantage of migrant women emerges not only in comparison with migrant men, on the ground of gender, but also in comparison with non-migrant women, thus on the grounds of status and citizenship.

In the first perspective, women represent the most vulnerable migrant 'group':[1] being often employed in a temporary job (domestic and care works), their status generally depends on a male counterpart (typically a husband or father).

On the other hand, compared to Italian women, migrant women face a vulnerability which hinges on their legal status and the precariousness of residence permits, as well as on socio-cultural reasons. Migrant women are often exposed to hard working and living conditions which may result in poor health and point to the tight link between socio-economic and health status.[2] In addition, they also have reduced access to healthcare for a number of political, administrative and cultural reasons which do not generally apply to 'native' women.

---

1 Considering women as a 'collective' is questionable indeed, given that this viewpoint ignores that women are themselves a heterogeneous 'group'. Nevertheless, this expression will be used for descriptive purposes, bearing in mind its underlying contradictions.

2 See Ministero della Salute (Health Ministry), 2005 and 2006; Istat (National Statistical Institute), 2013.

Migrants' Access to Health Services

In order to fully grasp the width of this issue, it is important to first describe the conditions under which migrants gain access to health and social services.

In Italy, access to healthcare and social services rests on citizenship and on the legal arrangements related to immigrants' entrance and stay (Pezzini, 2010: 163 ff; Biondi Dal Monte, 2013: 197 ff). Applying to the national health service is compulsory for most foreign citizens[3] and the benefits of state-provided healthcare also apply to relatives. Emergency and essential healthcare is available to all migrants, although people who are not official residents may be liable to pay a fee.[4] In fact, in the so-called 'Immigration Act' (Legislative Decree no. 286/1998), access to non-emergency healthcare is not guaranteed for migrants who are not official residents.

Even within a theoretical framework which recognizes health as a fundamental right[5] and a general public interest striving to prevent disease and contagion, the notion and borders of 'essential and emergency care' are not clear at all, and even critical prescriptions are not (or may not be) considered necessary.[6]

The Italian Constitutional Court also tried to provide a legal definition to this notion, acknowledging that there is a 'hard core' in social services and in healthcare provision that must be guaranteed to all foreigners, irrespective of their being illegally residents, notwithstanding eventual discrepancies in the legislative implementation.[7] The court did not specify, though, under which terms a healthcare service should be considered essential and necessary, deferring the choice to medical practitioners and their 'discretion' in any specific case (Cocco, 2009: 87).

It is important to stress that 'necessary and emergency care' does not imply a minimum level or a predetermined standard, given that any concrete case should be considered by doctors according to the actual medical circumstance of each individual.

3 'Foreign citizens' are those who hold residency permits for work or family reasons, asylum-seekers or refugees and so on.

4 Literally, the norms refer to 'inpatient or outpatient care, urgent or essential, as well as ongoing care following an illness or injury'. Urgent treatments are those that cannot be postponed pending one's life or worsening one's health; essential care is that treatment that, if too long delayed, could affect one's health up to endangering one's life. See article 35, co. 3–6, Legislative Decree no. 286/1998; article 43, co. 2–5, 8, Presidential Decree (D.p.r.) no. 394/1999.

5 Access to health and social services is considered a fundamental right and a key element of the so-called European social model and of the national welfare state model, as is explicitly stated in several Member State constitutions (in the Italian constitution, see article 32) and incorporated into the European Union Charter of Fundamental Rights (article 35).

6 This is the case of insulin for diabetes.

7 Corte costituzionale, judgments no. 252/2001, no. 306/2008, no. 11/2009.

Besides the legal framework, we should consider that non-EU migrants may face economic, socio-cultural and geographical barriers in accessing healthcare services, such as the inability to meet the financial costs of care and the lack of several resources such as mobility, language skill, correct nourishment, appropriate housing, work stability and access to information (Cocco, 2009: 87). In addition, inadequate broader immigration and integration policies can add to migrants' difficulty in accessing sanitary services.[8]

Not only is access to health and social services for migrants sometimes significantly restricted or conditional, but the range of services provided might be inappropriate for some social groups and, further, be affected by the context in which people live.

Another aspect that should be highlighted is that health issues are not always a matter of individual choice. Access to health services and the quality of the service that can be attained are determinants of health in their own right and have a rooted social dimension.

In conclusion, it is well recognized that differences in health status are closely linked to socio-economic status and, in general, to legal status and citizenship in an ongoing relationship and feedback loop.

However, and paradoxically, in the European system (that is in the European Union context), the most socially disadvantaged groups stand in an unequal position concerning health and access to healthcare.

The Access to Health Services in Anti-Discrimination Law

The access to healthcare and the supply of health goods and services as experienced by migrant women need to be considered in the context of the 'second-generation' anti-discrimination EU legislation.

With this expression we refer to the new package of anti-discrimination directives adopted, since 2000, throughout the EU on the basis of article 19 of the TFEU (former article 13 of the TEC) (Bell, 2002; Ellis, 2005; Barbera, 2007; Favilli, 2008). These directives formed part of an unprecedented wave of anti-discrimination law reforms carried out across the Member States which expanded the field of EU protection significantly in two principal areas. First, it expanded beyond gender to cover race, ethnic origin,[9] disability, age, sexual orientation, religion and personal beliefs.[10] Secondly, it began to address spheres beyond the traditional gender-equality realm of the labour market.[11]

8 See footnote no. 2.

9 Directive 2000/43.

10 Directive 2000/78.

11 Directive 2000/43 for race and ethnic origins, Directive 2004/113 for gender and COM (2008)426 for other grounds.

These so-called 'second-generation directives' led to the creation of new European anti-discrimination laws and, consequently, to new national laws.

Taking into consideration studies which revealed a framework of existing gender-discriminatory practices and rules in the access and supply of goods and services, in 2004, in the midst of a new 'golden age' of anti-discrimination legislation (Barbera, 2003: 399), the EU approved a directive to contrast discrimination and introduced the principle of equal treatment based on sex in the access and supply of goods and services, including social and health services.

EU Directive 2004/113, the 'Goods and Services Directive', and its Italian implementation[12] were contested because of their many exceptions and exemptions. For instance, differences in treatment are not prohibited if the exclusive or primary provision of goods and services to a particular gender is justified by a legitimate aim, and if the means of achieving that aim are appropriate and necessary (article 4, paragraph 5). This exception has been objected to as it risks becoming discriminatory for women, reinforcing gender stereotypes and, in some way, providing a sort of 'unofficial legitimization' for discriminatory practices (Lorenzetti, 2011; McColgan, 2009).

An interesting example of a practical application of Directive 113/2004 in health services concerns the refusal of medical staff to perform legal abortions (or to prescribe the abortion pill, also referred to as RU486) and of pharmacists to sell contraceptives because of their religious beliefs: both cases disclose a general disadvantage of women's positions.[13]

Bearing in mind that discrimination occurs when a person is treated less favourably than other people in a comparable situation because of a personal characteristic and when such treatment cannot be objectively and reasonably justified (Bell, 2002; Ellis, 2005), this case has been considered a form of discrimination based on sex because it weakens the position of women in the use of health services.

The Situation of Migrant Women: Exploring Gender Differences

In the above context, the condition of migrant women shows a particular vulnerability, specifically concerning health and social services,[14] although these are considered fundamental rights in the European social model.

In general, the health condition of women coming from developing countries tends to be precarious, due to their household responsibilities and lifestyles, together with the social discrimination they may endure. Migrant women habitually suffer

12 Legislative Decree no. 198/2006, the so-called Equal Opportunity Code.

13 On this topic, see the position of the European Court of Human Rights: ECHR, *Tysiac v Poland* (Case No. 5410/03, 20 March 2007).

14 Compared to Italian citizens, foreign citizens show an opposite trend, since their wellbeing is perceived to be higher among men than women. See Istat (2014).

worse health conditions than either migrant men or 'native' women (Dotti and Luci, 2008; Genova, 2014: 145).

We should consider that healthcare staff often lack adequate experience and training to address the cultural and religious issues posed by migrant women, pitfalls which altogether reduce the accessibility of these services for migrant women. In most countries, there is also a shortage of information material available in minorities' languages and there is a need to develop interpreting and mediating services to assist foreign women in hospitals and care facilities.

Migrant women face strong difficulties also in accessing long-term social and healthcare services, due to persistent language difficulties, cultural differences and poor knowledge of the national service system.[15]

The already-frail condition of female partners of migrants in accessing health services is emphasized in the context of reproductive care and contraception, also as a consequence of the different impact of gender differences on each cultural group.[16]

In fact, certain traditions and cultural practices can yield further problems for some groups of migrant women and for women of different ethnic origins when they try to access health facilities and information on sexual and reproductive health (Cocco, 2009: 91 ff).

According to the specific situation, the law considers the condition of pregnant migrant women within the social protection of pregnancy and maternity[17] (including abortion), which needs to be guaranteed as for Italian women nationals, even in the cases of non-regular residence in Italy.

As for the non-migrant women, abortions for undesired pregnancy reveal the general weakness of the women's position. Not only is this incidence more frequent among migrant women, but it also proves their lack of knowledge of legal instruments to counteract the denial from medical staff to perform legal abortions (or prescribe the abortion pill) and from pharmacists to sell contraceptives because of their religious beliefs.[18]

In addition, we should consider that this difficult access to health services may entail the risk of performing a clandestine abortion and using illegal contraceptive

---

15 See the National Health Program (Ministero della Salute, 2011). This complies with the framework set by the FRA (2011 and 2013).

16 For example, migrant women, or their partners, may be reluctant or may even refuse to be treated by male medical doctors in hospitals. They also often request the assistance of female social workers when in need of healthcare.

17 See, article 35, co. 3, Legislative Decree no. 286/1998.

18 See National Report on the abortion law application (Ministero della salute, 2014).

Actually, the studies on migrant women's abortions in Italy have not separated data according to geographical origins, but they overall indicate a steady pace for 'foreign' women who decide to interrupt their pregnancies compared to a decrease in 'natives' rates (Bonfanti, 2012).

pharmaceuticals, eventually creating a perilous divide between the official health system and the social position of migrant women.

Migrant Women as a Case for Multiple Discrimination?

Given the particular and weaker position of migrant women, it is interesting to analyse whether it is possible to consider them as an emblematic example of multiple discrimination,[19] that is, discrimination on the basis of multiple grounds: gender and status or citizenship.

According to relevant studies, this form of discrimination is considered especially treacherous, not simply because it generates negative outcomes proportionally higher than a mere 'addition' of singular discriminations for personal social conditions. Since 'multiple discrimination' refers to a condition often uneasy to detect and demonstrate, the synergic action of the diverse identity-markers of the victim of such a discrimination is hardly recognized and thus legally addressed and protected. In fact, the discrimination test demands the comparison with a *tertium comparationis*, that is, with an individual who does not have the personal attribute of the victim and who can be real or either potential or hypothetical. But the way in which the anti-discrimination test works is not applicable in the case of multiple discrimination.

Given that discrimination is contrasted on the basis of different events and different grounds, actual legal instruments appear inadequate as they require the so-called 'single ground approach'. When a person has endured multiple discrimination, he or she needs to choose one of his or her personal aspects and base the claim only on one ground of discrimination with different legal instruments.

The specific situation of those who have been victims of multiple discrimination, where more than one ground interact with each other in such a way that they are completely indivisible, remains invisible because each ground of discrimination is considered on its own and the comparative test does not work out.

Considering migrant women on the whole, the outcome of the comparative test could perhaps result as being non-discriminatory. Compared to migrant men, migrant women are not treated in a different and discriminatory manner because they have the same treatment, depending on their (same) status. Compared to

19 It is important to note that, generally, scholars shape three different types of multiple discrimination: multiple discrimination, when two or more grounds operate separately; compound or additive discrimination, when a person is discriminated on the basis of two or more grounds at the same time; and intersectional discrimination, when several grounds of discrimination operate simultaneously and interact in an indivisible way. However, in this work, I use the umbrella expression of 'multiple discrimination', as including all three types of multiple discrimination (Schiek, 2009: 12–13; Makkonen, 2002: 10–11; Burri and Schiek, 2009: 3).

non-migrant women, the treatment is not discriminatory either, because it could be considered on the basis of gender.

Thus, in a theoretical approach, gender and migration status continue to be conceptualized independently, leaving migrant women in a sort of limbo.

In a practical legal perspective, the failure in protecting migrant women from multiple forms of discrimination reflects (but at the same time produces) their particular vulnerability.

Indeed, the anti-discrimination rule limits itself to enforce the application of the same treatment to ideally neutral individuals, without taking into account those personal conditions which may situate them in unequal starting points. Therefore, the anti-discrimination judgment is not based on the actual fairness of the treatment, that is, on establishing whether a discriminatory treatment has been inflicted or not, but it limits itself to verifying that the specific personal attribute has not been influential on the withstood treatment. In fact, the anti-discrimination judgment is based on, and limited to, the evidence of a correspondence between the treatment undergone by the alleged victim of discrimination and a pre-set standard, a 'normality' standard. It is thus verified that such treatment would be equivalent to that withstood by an individual who does not display the same personal attribute protected by European law. The anti-discrimination judgment instead remains unable to detect those inequalities and differentiated treatments whenever they are based not on a specific personal attribute but, rather, on the pre-existing conditions which such attribute entails, on the different social positioning or status that may be associated to that specific personal attribute.

When gender is concerned, the issue turns ever more relevant if one considers that often it is not sexual belonging, that is, the biological match to either the male or the female sex, to be at stake, but, rather, those cultural attributes which are socially and historically tallied with it (sex/gender).

In dealing with multiple discrimination, the gender approach is imperative, because gender (along with age) is the one and only cross-cutting ground for discrimination.

A typical case that shows the relevance (and the invisibility) of multiple discrimination is the workplace.

The legal agenda needs to address the issue of its blindness to gender dynamics: the apparent gender neutrality that refers to 'the (male) worker' is clearly unsuitable for fields, such as domestic jobs, in which the vast majority of employees are migrant women.

This stresses the hidden mechanism that acts to reinforce intra-ethnic hierarchies, based on the unequal position of women compared to migrant men, and because of the stigma attached to domestic care work. In addition, the 'direct call' and 'quotas' systems[20] do not satisfy the stability needs for domestic and care workers. Thus, domestic (women and migrant) workers continue to remain

20 That is the legislation regarding immigration entry and the acquisition of legal status.

marginalized when compared to other types of employees, with regard to the guarantee of access and supply of social and health services.

The weaker juridical condition of migrant women could be interpreted as the consequence of the narrow recognition of multiple discrimination. When they are considered like any other (male) worker, without the awareness of gender dynamics which create and reinforce gender stereotypes, women are unequally situated in the labour market and consequently in the access and supply of services.

In addition, we should note that the different treatment could be considered as not discriminatory under the European anti-discrimination framework because 'migrant' usually identifies a non-EU citizen and a third country's citizenship is not covered by anti-discrimination law.

This shows not only the drawback of the multiple discrimination *ex se* but also the ambiguous shadow of the comparative analysis, that is, the strategic axis of anti-discrimination judicial procedures, which requires a *tertium comparationis* to compare with the potential victim.

In addition, it also shows that the EU anti-discrimination framework neglects legal protection for third countries' citizens.

At the national level, one notices a detachment from the protection of individual rights, considering that the constitution, and namely article 3 of the Constitution stating equality principle, does not need to demonstrate the different treatment compared to someone or something else, because the protection is based on the individual and on the reasonable judgment of the different treatment.

The Role of Regions

In the effort to overcome the vulnerability of migrant women, a central issue that needs to be considered is the potential role of regional legislation and good practices.

In Italy, in fact, regions have legislative power over the healthcare system,[21] and in many cases this leads to strong and deep differences between territories, also depending on the political orientation of each regional government.

---

21 Since 2001, a significant reform of Title V of the Constitution introduced a new division of legislative powers among the state and the regions. The state holds exclusive legislative powers in specified matters, while other matters are covered in the so-called 'concurrent legislation'; thus, regions hold legislative power except in the case of certain fundamental principles which are reserved for state law in many significant matters (for instance, health protection). In addition, regions have residual legislative power in all non-specified matters and they are also expressly empowered to contrast gender discrimination by article 117 of the constitution. The state is competent in the 'determination of the basic standards of welfare related to those civil and social rights that must be guaranteed in the entire national territory': thus, the power balance between the state and the regions in such matters remains somewhat unclear.

In particular, the condition of migrants and specifically of migrant women (but the same could be said for other minority groups) seems to be an arena for regional political debates.

In brief, there is a double-edged national context: some Italian regions are playing an innovative and supporting role in combating discrimination according to their legislative powers;[22] some other regions are taking advantage of their margins of manoeuvre to cut down and limit access to health services for migrants.[23]

Actually, in order to guarantee the same treatment at the national level, there exists a 'state-regions agreement',[24] which is supposed to be compulsory, but whose implementation rests in the hands of each region. This means that where the region does not implement the agreement, there could be an actual lack of protection.

This is the case, for instance, of the Lombardy region, where the non-transposition of the state-region agreement means that pregnancy assistance for new EU citizens (namely intra-EU migrants from Romania and Bulgaria) may be subject to payment. This seems a paradox because it would assume that pregnancy assistance is not a 'necessary and emergency' healthcare. In addition, family counselling is often arranged through pro-life family planning centres[25] that preclude or hamper the possibility of getting in contact for non-Catholic migrant women.

On the contrary, some regions introduced positive measures and carried out trials of good practices. This is the case of Emilia Romagna, which first provided leaflets and brochures in foreign languages (like Arabic and Romanian) concerning freedom in reproductive and health choices, offering a complete information package.[26]

Undeniably, the rising autonomy of Italian regions in the management of sanitary services has not generally played out in a civil-libertarian perspective; it has instead increased inequalities in access to health services (Cocco, 2009: 87) and it has empowered discretion in the recognition of rights and freedoms for migrant women.

---

22 Genova (2014) describes the regional contexts of Marche and Emilia Romagna, which are considered the most advanced regions on this topic, in particular concerning intercultural mediation in health services.

23 For instance, Lombardy region had passed a rule which excluded foreign citizens from some economic benefits regarding public transportation. The Constitutional Court, though, recognized grounds for discrimination and it declared the rule contrary to principles of the Italian constitution (Corte costituzionale, judgment no. 432/2005).

24 The so-called *Conferenza Stato-Regioni* is an institution, created for dialogue between the state and the regions, which represents the privileged arena for the negotiation on regional issues. The 'conference' realizes agreements and mutual understanding.

25 CAVs (in Italian, *Centri di aiuto per la vita*) are Catholic-orientated birth-care facilities.

26 See Genova (2014). Also, the Piedmont region implemented a number of measures and legislations aimed at eliminating discrimination.

Roma Women: the Least-Advantaged European Citizens

In a work focused on the access to social and health services by migrant women, the situation of Roma women calls to be considered because they stand at the hub of the 'intersection',[27] constantly travelling and moving in an uncertain social and legal condition.

Consistently, the situation of Roma women has been recently defined as 'a case for gender equality' in the European context.[28]

Roma are perhaps the most universally disadvantaged group and generally stand at the very bottom of the socio-economic ladder, hidden from society due to several interacting factors. First, they are under-represented in local and national governments; secondly, their communities are socially isolated and fragmented; and thirdly, they come from a history of discrimination and repression that has impacted on their political alienation (Bonetti et al., 2011). The Roma have no defined homeland as a result of their historic wide dispersion throughout Europe, thus they represent a minority everywhere.[29] Consequently, they suffer worse health conditions than other national or ethnic minorities, because of their higher exposure to a range of health-damaging factors[30] such as poverty, inadequate education, unemployment and low levels of social integration. Also, their unregulated civil status (including lack of personal documents, birth certificates and insurance[31]) gives way to a number of additional barriers that make it difficult

27 Following Crenshaw (1989), multiple discrimination, like traffic through an intersection, may flow in one direction and it may flow in another. If an accident happens at a crossroad, it can be caused by cars travelling from any number of directions and, sometimes, from all of them.

28 See European Commission Directorate-General for Employment, Social Affairs and Equal Opportunities (2008). Together with the Council of Europe, other EU institutions such as the European Union Agency on Fundamental Rights and other bodies have recognized that visible minorities such as Roma are more likely to suffer multiple discrimination than other minorities.

29 Roma people constitute the largest ethnic minority group in Europe with an estimated population of 10–12 million and very heterogeneous communities. In many countries, the Roma are neither recognized as a national minority nor as an ethnic minority.

30 WHO (World Health Organization, 2006). The European Commission recognizes 'for the first time that the Roma face a very specific situation across the EU' and that 'the main priorities are pretty clear: education, employment, health and housing' (European Roma Summit Memorandum 08/559, 2008).

31 Many Roma are not registered with a general medical practitioner, which may be due to a lack of documents, as well as reluctance on the part of health service providers to accept Roma patients. Their access to health services may also be influenced to a certain extent by their beliefs and cultural norms: for instance, Roma people tend to access services for severe problems only, as hospitalization is sometimes perceived as preceding death.

for Roma to access health services,[32] in particular when regular use of healthcare is required (for instance due to chronic disease or old age).

In such a general framework, compared to men, Roma women are more vulnerable than other members of their community and their situation has been recognized, in the international context, as a priority, particularly in relation to discrimination and violence, including those forms of domination experienced in their own community, ranging from forced and child marriages[33] to coercive sterilisation.[34]

More than Roma men, Roma women display a lower level of health[35] and they are likely not to have an ID card, the lack of which in turn excludes them, for instance, from pre-natal care and birth assistance.[36]

Although the situation of Roma women is particularly disadvantaged, the comparative test has shown significant limits. Indeed, in the event that we assumed the condition of a Roma man as a *tertium comparationis*, according to the anti-discrimination law on the ground of sex/gender we would disregard the vulnerability intrinsic to ethnic belonging. The evaluation or judgment would not record the peculiar disadvantage experienced by a woman who has withstood a differentiated treatment on the grounds not only of her gender, but also of her Roma ethnic identity.

Likewise, according to the anti-discrimination law on the ground of ethnic identity, if the *tertium comparationis* were a non-Roma woman, the anti-discrimination judgment would be hindered, since the treatment could be deemed non-discriminatory because of ethnic identity. It is critical that the multiplying effect of being simultaneously Roma and a woman, a condition which determines a tangled social frailty, would not then come to the surface.

What are the Possible Solutions?

The particular vulnerability of migrant women seems to be linked to a number of interacting factors which act both in a legal and in a non-legal dimension. In order to guarantee equality of treatment for migrant women, the reflection

32 For instance, Roma people cannot benefit from health-screening programmes and Roma children cannot take advantage of health checks or immunizations.

33 See Recommendations of the European Forum of Foundations for Roma Inclusion, 2010.

34 ECHR, *V.C. v. Slovakia*, Application no. 18968/07, 8.2.2012; *N.B. v. Slovakia*, Application no. 29518/10, 12.09.2012; and *I.G. and others v. Slovakia*, Application no. 15966/04, 29.04.2013.

35 This seems a paradox, given that women are usually in a better health condition than men.

36 Differences in language, culture and religious beliefs, practices and interpretations may lead to less effective care for Roma women: European Commission, 2008: 58–9.

should be orientated towards possible solutions. Heading for this aim, many options seem to be feasible.

Positive Actions and Good Practices: The Proactive Impact of Non-Juridical Solutions

Such a legislative vacuum and a challenging framework suggest the need for positive actions and promotional measures that can meet the cultural differences borne by migrant women in accessing healthcare and social services. These could overcome barriers such as inadequate information and confidence, limited language knowledge, lack of access to transport and inadequate mobility,[37] misunderstanding as to entitlement to some services, and social isolation and marginalization.

A positive action could lead to implement more suitable organizations, so as to ensure the presence of female sanitary staff and the opportunity to create health and sanitary services responding to specific cultural beliefs and behaviours or even to create separated services for migrant women, although such a strategy would likely result in a form of discrimination because of such separation.[38] However, we must emphasize the possible downside of cultural bias, stereotypes and lack of awareness among healthcare providers themselves, in particular concerning the needs of migrant women and the specific care they require (Bonfanti, 2012).

Some regions experimented with day-care centres for foreign women and children[39] in order to guarantee appropriate and reserved treatments and specialized personnel. The creation of *ad hoc* services assumes the knowledge and awareness of the specific needs of migrant women, in order to contrast those prejudices and stereotypes that often affect this domain.

In addition, we should recognize the fundamental role of a correct and comprehensive communication of the protective measures provided by the national health service.

Lastly, Italian legislation ignores the possible role of cultural mediators and cultural mediation in health and social services, which are crucial for enabling participation in health prevention by those who would otherwise be barred from

37 In general, a number of studies recognize that lack of accessible and affordable transport is more likely to affect socio-economically disadvantaged groups. See the report on immigration and access to health national services (CNEL, National Council for Economics and Labour, 2000) and Istat (2008).

38 We should also be aware that the provision of services or facilities reserved for foreign women who belong to ethnic or religious minorities does not only impinge on pre-existing group separations from the host society (further affecting integration processes), but it also risks to essentialize the social condition of migrant women.

39 *Direzione Sanitaria dell'Azienda Unità Sanitaria Locale Città di Bologna. Centro per la salute delle donne straniere e dei loro bambini*, General directorate of local health care in Bologna municipality. Health centre for migrant women and their children.

doing so by cultural and religious attitudes towards decency, or by embarrassment or fear. Thus, cultural mediators could facilitate migrant women in accessing and making use of social services; they could provide culturally competent training for service providers and assist in the design of customized informative materials.[40]

At large, this could help to overcome cultural barriers which are particularly strong and resistant in the case of migrant women.

A further positive action could be the organization of training, both for minority communities and for their service providers in the health, social services, mediation and translation sectors, in order to bridge the communicative flow between service providers and recipients who are members of minority groups. Some regions created *ad hoc* professional training for sanitary personnel where a section is committed to 'immigration and health' in a multi-ethnic society: a learning project which focuses on foreign women and their relationship with body, fertility, maternity, sanitary features, and social and psychological issues.[41]

A concrete aid could come forward from 'migration medicine', a socio-culturally aware medical practice which unravels the complexity of health for migrant people in relation to both their cultures of origin and their experiences of mobility (Geraci and Marceca, 2002).

Finally, it should be considered that good practices aimed at filling such health gaps need to be accompanied by a more general effort to reduce inequalities and to promote the full participation of migrant women in mainstream society.

Multiple Discrimination and its Conceptualization: Looking in the Wrong Direction?

Moving towards an enhanced protection for migrant women in accessing social and healthcare services, a more viable solution may be found within the theoretical legal framework.

Tackling migrant women's vulnerability in accessing social and healthcare services, we could call upon the conceptualization of multiple discrimination as a separate form of discrimination, with specific judicial procedures and remedies. This approach could overcome the actual weakness of multiple discrimination, which seemed so far unable to protect people from discrimination based on more than one personal condition.

However, the topic question is whether it is necessary and useful to introduce a new form of discrimination in order to guarantee stronger protection for victims of multiple discrimination like migrant women.

Indeed, the act of codifying *ad hoc* norms and specific bans and legal forms does not guarantee a complete and comprehensive protection. Instead,

---

40 Similar initiatives were realized in Ireland (Lowe and Dimola, 2010: 206 ff). See Genova (2014) for the Italian context.

41 This is the case of the Veneto region.

paradoxically, inserting a new set of rules to determine and protect from multiple discrimination might even generate a step backward from the legal protection so far upheld. Moreover, this being a European anti-discrimination norm which applies to European citizens only, it would leave foreign migrant women aside and unattended.

Very likely, this option would risk to reify those differences pertaining to migrant women, creating stiff definitions which may not match with their lived experiences and thus with judicial tools hard to put into practice.

Thus, the issue turns now to validating possible solutions under the national constitutional protection, emphasizing the constitutional equality framework, which does not question individual personal conditions whilst offering protection against a non-reasonable treatment.

Equality Principle, Anti-Discrimination and the Right to Differ

In the light of the above critical issues and given the shortage of good practices, an analysis of the multifaceted character of constitutional equality appears to be necessary in order to verify the condition of migrant women in accessing and being supplied with health provisions and services under the anti-discrimination perspective.

As noted, from the EU perspective, the anti-discrimination legislation aims to include a discriminated person or group in a space that would otherwise be barred. Although this operation removes the ongoing discrimination, it does not reshape the public space so as to include the person or the group discriminated against, as the principle of equality potentially being applied to this person or group may be at the expense of other or similar persons or groups in different circumstances (Pezzini, 2009).

The deficiency of the EU anti-discrimination legislation emerges in the way equality works with regard to the access to and supply of goods and services for migrant women: contrasting discrimination seems an immediate solution but it does not guarantee any change in the conditions or pre-conditions which determined such bias, or any future development towards a more equal structural position. We should also mention the standpoint of those who have intended anti-discrimination protection as a means to determine, perhaps swiftly, improved access to power by those people who were previously excluded from it. Despite a clear positive impact as far as legal protection is concerned, such a measure left unquestioned those power relations and social values which remain unaltered and keep being exercised by those who were (and still are) in charge of some material (and symbolic) authority (Ruggiu, 2012: 103).

In the light of these critical issues, research should focus on the formulation of a legislation which will help to redefine not only the subjects but also the social spaces involved, so that change can be implemented in the lives of all individuals with the ultimate goal of undermining a power structure which identifies the male as superior and the female as subordinate.

Such legislation will be rooted in the anti-subordination principle, which in particular refers to the gendered 'dilemma of difference' (Minow, 1984: 1990; Morondo Taramundi, 2004) and to social rights.

It may therefore be interesting to interpret the existing legislation (for instance, Directive 2004/113) in different ways, in connection with the analysis of the equality principle, not only from an anti-discrimination perspective but also on the grounds of diversity (Niccolai, 2007; Ruggiu, 2009 and 2010).

Thus, the law could contribute to challenge not only the legal framework, but even the symbolic horizons this is embedded within, which continuously tend to reinforce and legitimate patterns of social exclusions (Repetto, 2010: 149).

An interpretation of equality as a consideration of diversity should allow for protective measures which will reduce or remove any negative impact (through the protection of migrant women as 'particularly vulnerable individuals'). It should also allow for promotional measures that recognize cultural differences (as is the case with measures which emphasize the recognition of identity) and be founded on a multicultural view of society (measures which emphasize specificity) (Gianformaggio, 1997: 2005).

This approach could legitimate gender separation by enabling access to services by those who would otherwise be prevented from partaking because of cultural or religious attitudes towards decency, embarrassment or fear of sexual harassment. In this way, gender-separated services or *ad hoc* services might encourage migrant women's full access to the public sphere.

Although an analysis of equality as anti-discrimination could cast doubt on the legitimacy of different treatment (which could potentially be interpreted as discrimination against men), the need for protecting diversity forces us to accommodate occasional instances of different treatment.

These distinctions are particularly helpful in the protection and development of individuals and their personal differences (as in the case of decency); on the other hand, however, the non-consideration of these differences could limit their freedom and lead to the exclusion of certain individuals from social and community life.

The Emergence of the Anti-Subordination Principle

Given the unsatisfactory dimension of the anti-discrimination perspective, Pezzini (2009) outlines an anti-subordination principle, which recognizes the importance of eradicating the subordination of women to men, reading the gender relations as a power structure.

Pezzini finds the legal basis of that principle in the constitutional norms related to gender, or, rather, in gender-sensitive interpretations of the Italian constitution; indeed, a general reading of the Italian constitution and, in particular, of the norms on women's work (article 37), family (article 29 ff) and political rights (article 48) stresses the importance of transforming gender relations. It also foresees the end of women's subordination to men, reversing the 'direction' in the construction of gender relations. In fact, until the approval of the Italian constitution in 1948, gender relations had been characterized by discrimination against women and the subordination of women to men. This social order was considered 'natural' and so it became legalized: gender differences produced by gender disparities were used as a justification for further inequalities introduced by the law itself (Pezzini, 2012).

Following Pezzini, I would propose a similar route concerning the access to and supply of health provisions and services for migrant women.

In the EU context, the main difficulty is that the European Community law was (and in part still is) characterized by the economic goal of avoiding social dumping (Bell, 2002; Ellis, 2005). Only in recent times, with the Charter of Nice (2000) and the Lisbon Treaty (which came into force in 2009), did the European legal framework start to consider the social dimension of equality as a general principle, also coming to incorporate the concept of individual dignity.[42]

As seen above, the anti-discrimination legislation (see Directive 2004/113) admits exceptions to the general principle of equal treatment when a legitimate aim is present (and the means of achieving it are appropriate and necessary). Thus, we should reflect on the possibility of allowing specific services targeting women migrants and of permitting certain single-sex provisions according to specific situations.

In the anti-discrimination perspective, it does not seem admissible to apply this exception because a different access for women could be considered to be discrimination against men.

By contrast, following the anti-subordination principle, this exception seems appropriate when the ground of gender is used to break down traditional gender roles, contest the unequal position of (migrant) women in society, fight against stereotypes or promote women's full access in the public sphere. In fact, this may indeed contribute to redefine power relations between genders and to cast a new light on roles and social spaces that are experienced differently by the two genders.

This change in perspective goes beyond the issue of anti-discrimination policy, which is itself a sphere where gender hierarchy is expressed and performed. In fact, the anti-discrimination perspective confirms and legitimates a comparative process which identifies the masculine as the universal benchmark and stigmatizes the feminine as different, 'other' and implicitly inferior (Pezzini, 2009; Barrère Unzueta, 2004).

42 In fact, the jurisprudential attitude of the European Court of Justice had already severely affected the legislator's work, forging new notions of discrimination (such as the notion of indirect discrimination) and moreover steering towards social meaning the interpretation of the original rule in article 119 of the Treaty.

Conclusions

Wrapping up our arguments, we may draw some general conclusions.

Given the interrelation between status and economic stability on the one side, and health conditions and social divide between migrant and non-migrant on the other, the condition of migrant women is a conundrum which questions equality overall and the way this may work out in an inclusive perspective.

The situation of migrant women can be represented as a form of double seclusion or marginalization. In fact, women are not generally involved in the networks to which male migrants belong in their country of origin; at the same time, because of intra-ethnic hierarchies, women do not succeed in building new social networks in the country of resettlement. As a result, they may experience a double exclusion: in their community, from the males who may consider them as second-class members, and in the society of residence, where they will hardly create a real network with other women.[43]

This social exclusion is mirrored in their legal vulnerability, which is even reinforced by the anti-discrimination perspective.

We have seen, indeed, that the legislative reference standard, introduced by Directive 2004/113, disclosed a pitfall in assuming a gender 'neutral' individual, a feature that prevents us from grasping those power relations and interactions that situate women in a subaltern and vulnerable position never experienced by men.

Meanwhile, it is significant to underline how the European legislative framework hardly tenders its protective umbrella over non-European citizens, leaving almost all regulation at the discretion of singular Member States.

Even immigration law generally addresses migrant men and it has so far struggled in protecting migrant women, who bear gender specificities hard to recognize and attend to.

Some of the suggested solutions – implementation of good practices, actions taken by the regions – lay bare the substantial limit of relying on the legislators' discretion, who in turn might remain silent and thus leave migrant women in a state of frailty (social as well as juridical).

On the contrary, the theoretical frame for protecting equality through the promotion of diversity and against gender hierarchy could have a greater impact, also steering public policies and upholding legal judgments.

Once this issue has been reviewed, we may conclude that, in dealing with the access to healthcare by women migrants, one has first to take into account their actual social condition. In fact, what we argued so far on migrant women's frailty and vulnerability applies to those who experience poverty and social weakness, not to those who migrate within a structural frame of social and economic stability.

The above statement gains greater significance when we consider that, together with the issue of healthcare access for migrants under a gender perspective, the

---

43 *Mutatis mutandis*, this reflects the concept of 'marginal man' (Park, 1928) and 'double absence' (Sayad, 2002).

possibility for migrant women to benefit from social and health services crosses a further contingent matter, which is the effect of austerity measures on healthcare.

In the light of the current economic downturn, the so called 'spending review' period, the Italian government has already decided to trim down spending on social and public matters, and the health service is one of the fields that has been targeted for cuts. This will probably have a stronger impact on migrant women and, in general, on people (or groups) with low and uncertain resources, increasing once again their vulnerability.

Less affordable and accessible health services will inevitably mean increased inequalities with a negative impact on the substantive dimension of the equality principle. In this respect, we ought to highlight that the perspective emerging from the accessibility of health and social services by migrant women shows some disquietude, as it interrogates the role played by the anti-discrimination rule and its relation to the constitutional principle of equality.

We have seen that, largely, the idea of gender equality in the European law framework is narrower than the Italian fundamental principle of equality.

For this reason, it seems to me paradoxical that the development of a common European anti-discrimination law has led to the levelling of internal (national) rules against discrimination.

In practice, this levelling has caused a sizable lack of protection for migrant women and has put back into question rights and prerogatives which once seemed secure, and which could have been better shielded in a constitutional framework.

Under a theoretical view, this levelling has instead triggered the ultimate desertion of a possible fertile contamination between EU anti-discrimination law and constitutional principles, which could have yielded a wider network of legal protections.

Drawing to a conclusion, we ought to plead for a review of the European principles and system of anti-discrimination. This renewal seems to be possible if one adopts the constitutional equality in its substantive dimension, which only full access to social rights can guarantee. This could be an antidote to existing forms of domination that place migrant women in unfair starting points when they demand access to social and health services. And it would certainly contribute to offer migrant women a more reliable legal framework, which would not only apply to that realm, but would also improve their overall participation in the public sphere.

References

Barbera, M. (2003). Eguaglianza e differenza nella nuova stagione del diritto antidiscriminatorio comunitario. *Diritto del Lavoro e delle Relazioni Industriali*, 99–100, 399–422.

Barbera, M. (ed.) (2007). *Il nuovo diritto antidiscriminatorio*. Milano: Giuffrè.

Barrère Unzueta, M.A. (2004). Diritto antidiscriminatorio, femminismo e multiculturalismo. Il principio di uguaglianza di donne e uomini come strategia per una rilettura giuridica. *Ragion pratica*, 23, 363–80.

Bell, M. (2002). *Anti-discrimination Law and the European Union*. Oxford: Oxford University Press.

Biondi Dal Monte, F. (2013). I diritti sociali degli stranieri. Politiche di appartenenza e condizioni di esclusione nello stato sociale. In Cavasino, E., Scala, G. and Verde, G. (eds) *I diritti sociali dal riconoscimento alla garanzia. Il ruolo della giurisprudenza,* 189–233. Napoli: Editoriale Scientifica.

Bonetti, P., Simoni, A. and Vitale, A. (eds) (2011). *La condizioni giuridica di Rom e Sinti in Italia*. Milan: Giuffré.

Bonfanti, S. (2012). Farsi madri. L'accompagnamento alla nascita in una prospettiva interculturale, *Quaderni di Donne&Ricerca*, 27, 1–75. Available at http://www.cirsde.unito.it.

Burri, S. and Schiek, D. (2009). Multiple Discrimination in EU Law. Opportunities for legal responses to intersectional gender discrimination? European Commission Directorate-General for Employment, Social Affairs and Equal Opportunities Unit EMPL/G/2. Available at http://ec.europa.eu/justice/gender-equality/files/multiplediscriminationfinal7september2009_en.pdf.

CNEL (2000). Immigrazione e accesso ai servizi sanitari nazionali. Available at www.portalecnel.it.

Cocco, G. (2009). In direzione ostinata e contraria: spunti in materia di diritto alla salute e immigrazione. In Balduzzi, R. (ed.) *Sistemi costituzionali, diritto alla salute e organizzazione sanitaria*, 85–108. Bologna: Il Mulino.

Crenshaw, K. (1989). Demarginalising the Intersection of Race and Sex: A Black Feminist Critique of Antidiscrimination Doctrine, Feminist Theory and Antiracist Policies. *The University of Chicago Legal Forum*, 140, 139–67.

Dotti, M. and Luci, S. (2008). *Donne in cammino. Salute e percorsi di cura di donne immigrate*, Milano: FrancoAngeli.

Ellis, E. (2005). *EU Antidiscrimination law*. Oxford: Oxford University Press.

European Commission Directorate-General for Employment, Social Affairs and Equal Opportunities (2008). *Ethnic minority and Roma women in Europe. A case for gender equality?* Available at http:// ec.europa.eu/social/BlobServlet?docId=4833&langId=en.

Favilli, C. (2008). *La non discriminazione nell'Unione europea*. Bologna: il Mulino.

FRA, Fundamental Rights Agency (2011). Fundamental Rights of Migrants in an Irregular Situation in the European Union. Available at http://fra.europa.eu/sites/default/files/fra_uploads/1827-FRA_2011_Migrants_in_an_irregular_situation_EN.pdf.

FRA, Fundamental Rights Agency (2013). Inequalities and multiple discrimination in access to and quality of healthcare. Available at http://fra.europa.eu/sites/default/files/inequalities-discrimination-healthcare_en.pdf.

Genova, A. (2014). Policy to tackle health inequalities in accessing health services for migrant women in Italy: A regional comparative analysis in Marche and Emilia Romagna. *Sociologia del diritto*, 1, 145–65.

Geraci, S. and Marceca, M. (2002). La promozione della salute per gli stranieri: normativa nazionale sull'accesso ai servizi e politiche locali. In *Atti della Conferenza nazionale 'Migrazioni e salute' – Bari, 3–4 maggio 2002*, 36–51. Lecce: OER Puglia.

Gianformaggio, L. (1997). L'eguaglianza e le norme. In Gianformaggio, L. and Jori, M. (eds) *Scritti per Uberto Scarpelli*, 373–406. Milano: Giuffré.

Gianformaggio, L. (2005). *Eguaglianza, donne e diritto*. Bologna: il Mulino.

Istat (2008). Rapporto annuale 2008. Available at http://www3.istat.it/dati/catalogo/20090526_00/rapporto_annuale_2008.pdf.

Istat (2013). Cittadini stranieri: condizioni di salute, fattori di rischio, ricorso alle cure e accessibilità dei servizi sanitari. Anno 2011–2012. Roma: Istat (Statistiche Report). Available at http://www.istat.it/it/archivio/110879.

Istat (2014). Rapporto annuale 2014. La situazione del Paese. Available at http://www.istat.it/it/files/2014/05/cap4.pdf.

Lorenzetti, A. (2011). Case law on the access and supply of goods and services. Equal is not enough: Moving towards a formulation of an antisubordination principle. In Motmans, J., Cuypers, D., Meier, P., et al. (eds) *Equal is Not Enough: Challenging Differences and Inequalities in Contemporary Societies*, 44–59. Antwerpen: PRCEO.

Lowe, A.M. and Dimola, S. (2011). Combating 'ghost discrimination' against hidden populations: best practices for EU inclusion policies in the pilot project for Roma inclusion. In Motmans, J., Cuypers, D., Meier, P., et al. (eds) *Equal is Not Enough: Challenging Differences and Inequalities in Contemporary Societies*, 200–215. Antwerpen: PRCEO.

Makkonen, T. (2002). Compound and Intersectional Discrimination: Bringing the Experiences of the Most Marginalized to the Fore. Åbo Akademy University. Available at http://www.ilga-europe.org/content/download/24688/157174/version/1/file/multiple,+compound+and+intersectional+discrimination.pdf.

McColgan, A. (2009). The Goods and Services Directive: A curate's egg or an imperfect blessing? *European Gender Equality Law Review*, 1, 16–24.

Ministero della Salute (2005). Relazione sullo stato sanitario del Paese 2003–2004. Available at http://www.salute.gov.it/imgs/C_17_pubblicazioni_506_allegato.pdf.

Ministero della Salute (2006). Piano Sanitario Nazionale 2006–2008. Available at http://ape.agenas.it/documenti/Normativa/PSN_2006-08.pdf.

Ministero della Salute (2011). Piano Sanitario Nazionale 2011–2013. Available at http://sanita.formez.it/sites/all/files/Schema_PSN_2011_2013.pdf.

Ministero della Salute (2014). Relazione del ministro della salute sulla attuazione della legge contenente norme per la tutela sociale della maternità e per l'interruzione volontaria di gravidanza (Legge 194/78). Available at http://www.salute.gov.it/imgs/C_17_pubblicazioni_2226_allegato.pdf.

Minow, M. (1984). Learning to live with the Dilemma of Difference: Bilingual and Special Education. *Law and Contemporary Problems*, 48 (2), 157–211.

Minow, M. (1990). *Making all the Difference. Inclusion, Exclusion, and American Law*. Ithaca/London: Cornell University Press.

Morondo Taramundi, D. (2004). *Il dilemma della differenza nella teoria femminista del diritto*. Pesaro: Esa.

Niccolai, S. (2007). Differenze come cose o come valutazioni. In Cerrone, F. and Volpi, M. (eds) *Sergio Panunzio. Profilo intellettuale di un giurista*, 475–531. Napoli: Jovene.

Park, R.E. (1928). Human migration and the marginal man. *The American Journal of Sociology*, 33, 6, 881–93.

Pezzini, B. (2009). L'uguaglianza uomo-donna come principio anti-discriminatorio e come principio anti-subordinazione. In Brunelli, G., Pugiotto, A. and Veronesi, P. (eds) *Scritti in onore di Lorenza Carlassare. Il diritto costituzionale come regola e limite al potere*, 1141–76. Napoli: Jovene.

Pezzini, B. (2010). Una questione che interroga l'uguaglianza: i diritti sociali del non cittadino. In *Lo statuto costituzionale del non cittadino. Annuario AIC – Associazione italiana dei costituzionalisti 2009*, 163–228. Napoli: Jovene.

Pezzini, B. (2012). Costruzione del genere e Costituzione. In Pezzini, B. (ed.) *La costruzione del genere. Norme e regole*, 15–73. Bergamo: Sestante.

Repetto, G. (2010). Discrimination against Homosexuals and 'Integration by Reasonableness': Suggestions from the *Maruko* case. In Niccolai, S. and Ruggiu, I. (eds) *Dignity in Change. Exploring the constitutional potential of EU Gender and Anti-discrimination Law*, 137–49. Florence: European Press Academic Publishing.

Ruggiu, I. (2009). Effettività del diritto e protezione delle minoranze. Per un principio costituzionale della diversità. *Polemos*, I, 27–40.

Ruggiu, I. (2010). Diversity as a Public Good? Cultural Identity in Legal Narratives. In Niccolai, S. and Ruggiu, I. (eds) *Dignity in Change. Exploring the constitutional potential of EU Gender and Anti-discrimination Law*, 151–84. Florence: European Press Academic Publishing.

Ruggiu, I. (2012). *Il giudice antropologo*. Milan: FrancoAngeli.

Sayad, A. (2002). *La doppia assenza. Dalle illusioni dell'emigrato alle sofferenze dell'immigrato*. Milano: Raffaello Cortina Editore.

Schiek, D. (2009). From European Union non-discrimination law towards multidimensional equality law for Europe. In Schiek, D. and Chege, V. (eds) *European Union Non-Discrimination Law. Comparative Perspectives on Multidimensional Equality law*, 3–28. London-New York: Routledge-Cavendish.

WHO, World Health Organization, Regional Office for Europe and Council of Europe Development Bank (2006). *Health and Economic Development in South-Eastern Europe*. Available at http://apps.who.int/iris/mobile//bitstream/handle/10665/107777/E89184.pdf?sequence=1.

Chapter 6
Migration and (Legal) Irritants: Italian Family Law and Gender Equality

Elisa Olivito

Introduction: Gender, Migration and Italian Family Law

As migratory flows continue to grow, Italy, too, has had to cope with the formation and reunification on national territory of migrant families. For a country that as late as a few decades ago had a case-law not only inattentive towards gender relationships but even discriminatory in several points, the rise of problems regarding family, women and migration has meant taking a look in the mirror. In Italy, in fact, family law has taken time to gain awareness of gender issues – an awareness that has passed through an evolving interpretation of constitutional provisions, as well as through major legislative reforms in the matter of marriage, divorce and parental authority.

From the constitutional standpoint, it must first be remarked that Italy's 1948 constitution refers numerous times to family and to the role played by women within it. However, these references are by no means unambiguous and they long received conservative and sexist interpretations. Indeed, article 29, paragraph 2, of the constitution provides that marriage is based on the moral and legal equality of the spouses, but also adds that this takes place 'within the limits laid down by law to guarantee the unity of the family'. Moreover, article 31, paragraph 2, states that '[t]he Republic protects mothers, children and the young by adopting the necessary provisions'. Lastly, while the first paragraph of article 37 provides that '[w]orking women have the same rights and are entitled to equal pay for equal work', its second paragraph specifies that '[w]orking conditions must allow women to fulfil their essential role in the family and ensure special appropriate protection for the mother and child'.

It may then be inferred from these articles that the constitutional guarantee of equality between men and women is balanced – at least nominally – by an ambiguous emphasis upon the unity of the family and upon the reproductive and care functions associated unilaterally with the woman/mother/wife. Because of this, in the first years of the constitution's implementation, the sexualized and stereotyped language of these provisions became the source of a reactionary interpretation. They were detached from other constitutional principles, such as those of the equal social dignity of citizens, gender equality and the Republic's duty to remove the obstacles to the full development of the human person (article 3). At the beginning, the result was maintaining numerous openly discriminatory legal provisions and perpetuating the image of women as guardians of the domestic hearth.

That attitude is, for example, revealed by some judgments from the early 1960s, in which the Italian Constitutional Court (*Corte costituzionale*) adopted the idea of 'the unity of the family' based upon the unequal treatment of spouses and upon the husband's leading position. It is sufficient to recall judgment no. 64/1961, in which the constitutional judges first rejected the question of the constitutionality of article 559 of the criminal code, which at that time criminalized adultery only by wives and not by spouses in general.[1] Judgment no. 71/1966 moved in the same direction, declaring groundless the question of the constitutionality of article 260, paragraph 2, of the civil code, which established that if a natural child was recognized by both parents, the rights derived from parental authority, then called *patria potestà*, were normally exercised by the father.[2]

It was to take several more years before the patriarchal interpretation of the constitutional provisions just mentioned was slowly abandoned to make way – in both constitutional case-law and in legal doctrine – for considerations of greater openness in the matter of family, gender relations and reproductive functions. These changes were also followed by numerous legislative reforms, thanks to which, starting from the early 1960s, significant changes were introduced with regard to divorce, filiation and spousal relationships (Rodotà, 1975; Pocar and Ronfani, 1978; Ferrando, 2005: 8 ff).

However, the legislative and judicial framework of Italian family law became far more complex when, also as a consequence of the massive increase in migratory flows to Italy, lawmakers, judges and legal scholars found themselves having to cope with different family models. The rise of legal and political issues concerning the recognition of the 'migrant family of migrants' thus drew back the veil on certain idiosyncrasies of multiculturalism à l'italienne (Ferrari, 2008: 141), bringing its limits and hypocrisies to light (Azzariti, 2013: 92). And while the media's attention has been catalysed by multicultural conflicts deemed more sensational because involving criminal law, on the level of family relations a more silent but no less significant representation of the migrant as the 'other' has entered the scene. A dual order of difficulties thus quickly emerged in how the problems of migration family law are dealt with: (1) difficulties deriving from the increasingly transnational features of migrant families, given the several intertwinements and movements in the creation of family networks (Baldassar et al., 2014; Baldassar

1 Article 559 of the criminal code was then declared unconstitutional, due to violation of articles 3 and 29 of the constitution, by judgment no. 126/1968 and by judgment no. 147/1969. All Constitutional Court judgments are available at www.cortecostituzionale.it/actionPronuncia.do.

2 Article 260 of the civil code was later abrogated by article 109 of Law no. 151/1975 (Reform of family law).

and Merla, 2014) and (2) cultural and legal difficulties in confronting the foreign system which, based on the provisions of private international law, would be called upon to regulate the cases.

Unlike other European legal systems, in which control over migrants' families was soon translated into *ad hoc* legislative measures (Pearl and Menski, 1998: 87–9; Shah, 2003), the Italian system long exercised this control by relying on its judges and civil registrars. As a consequence of a migration flow that only in recent decades has taken on important dimensions, the related issues and problems passed through courtrooms and civil servants before going through Parliament (Olivito, 2012). This certainly contributed to the development of seesawing case-law and gave rise – despite certain recent legislative provisions – to a decidedly patchy picture.

Nonetheless, there is one element of the interaction between Italian family law and migration law that the Italian experience shares with that of other Western legal systems. The resistance against recognizing 'family models' other than the predominant one have often been (and continue to be) motivated by the need to protect the rights of women and children belonging to migrant families. Thus, for example, in dealing with migrants' claims to recognize marriages and divorces performed in ways other than those governed by Italian law, the 'multiculturalism is bad for women' refrain (Okin, 1999) has been taken up, quickly and uncritically, in the area of migrant family law as well. In fact, when legal questions have cropped up and the element of cultural diversity claimed by the migrant has touched upon the sphere of family relations, the dismissal of the cultural argument has been supported by the unavoidable safeguarding of migrant women's rights against supposed patriarchal family models.

Paradoxically however, the rejection of claims for multicultural accommodation not only passed through simplistic biases associated with foreign family laws, but, above all, it helped reinforce an 'orientalist' – and thus distorted – idea of migrant women and their position within the family. Therefore, in Italy as well, by rehashing the old saw of 'feminism versus multiculturalism'[3] instead of offering tools to grasp the complex questions to be dealt with, the real needs and perspectives of migrant women have often been lost sight of: so much for the 'other feminisms' of which these women may consciously be an expression, and for the actual gender dynamics within migrant family groups.

It should first be noted that the formation and reunification processes of migrants' families have raised serious difficulties for the Western systems of private international law, casting doubt upon their actual openness to foreign systems and to legal and cultural diversity (Foblets, 2000). In particular, the formation of transnational family groups has laid bare the fact that the age-old

3 For a critique of this assumption, see Volpp (2001).

forms of European family law are still affected by the legacy of Christianity in the matter of marriage and divorce.[4]

In Italy in particular, the dissonance between migration, family law and gender issues arises on two closely linked levels.[5] In certain cases, conflicts with the Italian legal system (and the consequent attention given to the position of migrant women) occur: (1) when applying the provisions of foreign law referred to by Italian law to govern relationships that have cross-border implications, or (2) when recognizing and enforcing foreign judgments handed down on the basis of these provisions. In other cases, however, problems arise when the foreign law comes into play on a preliminary basis when applying family reunification law (Clerici, 2009: 199).

To dwell on the first case for the moment, it bears keeping in mind that under Law no. 218/1995, which reformed the Italian system of private international law, many issues related to family, such as, for example, the conditions for marriage to be valid, formed and dissolved, are governed by the national law of the spouses or by the law in the state in which their married life prevalently takes place (articles 26 and following). However, article 16 of Law no. 218 also establishes that the foreign law has no application if its effects are contrary to public order, thus giving broad manoeuvring room to the judiciary, which has to establish whether there is incompatibility.[6] And it is precisely international public order that is mentioned whenever the legal institution provided for by the foreign system is deemed contrary to the principle of equality of spouses.

Italian Marriage Law in the Multicultural Diaspora: Gender, Polygyny and the 'Utilitarian' Recognition of its Effects

For migrants residing in Italy, the question is first raised of the validity and legal effects of polygamous marriages celebrated abroad, in the event that these marriages take on the form of polygyny (plural marriage in which only the man is allowed to have more than one wife). Although polygyny is practised in a number of different cultures and religions (Zeitzen, 2008), in Italy it tends to be associated chiefly with Islam, as the questions as to its compatibility with the Italian legal system have arisen above all as a consequence of the increased numbers of Muslim migrants. However, connection with Islamic law alone is not without consequences, not only because it affects the possibility of opening marriage to other cultural models,

4 One need only consider the assumptions concerning consent to marriage, the involvement of a third party in formalizing the marriage, and restrictions on divorce (Shah, 2013: 613).

5 For a critical approach to the complex relationship between transnationalism, gender and migration, see, however, Salih (2001).

6 On the uncertainties and risks connected with the limit of public order, see, more generally, Büchler (2011: 41 ff).

but also – for that which is of interest here – because it brings with it several preconceptions about the role and agency of migrant Muslim women.

The problems related to polygyny involve only marriages celebrated in the country of origin of the migrant man or woman: the monogamous principle upheld in Italian civil law and enforced through criminal law rules out polygamous marriage (polygynous or polyandrous) being validly celebrated in Italy. Article 86 of the civil code establishes in this regard that whoever is bound by a prior marriage may not contract a marriage,[7] while article 556 of the criminal code punishes the crime of bigamy.[8] However, although the ban of polygamous marriage is historically and culturally due to the preference Western systems have for monogamous marriage, given the increasing multiculturalism of Italian society, nowadays the prohibition is justified with the aim of protecting women from the deprivation and abuse to which they would be subjected in polygamous marriages (critically in this regard, see Marella and Marini, 2014: 118).

Nevertheless, while on the domestic level the ban on polygamy remains firm, as the possibility of the institution's legal transplant[9] within the Italian legal system is excluded, the picture becomes patchier when considering the judicial implementation of private international law. In this regard, it has been observed that

> [i]n today's globalized societies, diffusion of family law is sometimes indirectly achieved through the vehicle of private international law … Nevertheless, in moving from the periphery to the core of the world, there are pieces of the peripheral legal package that are left behind … [N]on-westernized law (law from the periphery) can travel to the core as long as it is compatible with the rhetoric and politics of the core's human rights (that is, with the individualist paradigm). On the contrary, the core rejects such peripheral law as long as the non-westernized law enforces the communitarian value of solidarity, evoking a patriarchal (or "non-civilized") image, as in polygamy. (Marella, 2011: 740–41)

Despite this, in this movement of family law from the periphery to the core, the Italian system shows a less rigid attitude, as the approach followed for polygamous

7 For the foreign national who wishes to celebrate a marriage in Italy, article 116 of the civil code provides that it is necessary to 'submit to the civil registrar a declaration by the competent authority in his or her own country, stating that according to the laws to which the foreign national is subjected, nothing precludes the marriage' and that he or she, too, is subject, among other things, to the 'single status' requirement as provided for by article 86 of the civil code.

8 Article 556, paragraph 1, of the criminal code: 'Whoever, when bound by a marriage having effects under civil law, enters into another marriage also having effects under civil law, is punished by one to five years' imprisonment. The same penalty is applied to any unmarried person who enters into a marriage with a person bound by marriage having effects under civil law'.

9 On the possibility of legal transplants, see Watson (1974); for the opposing view, see Legrand (1997).

marriages celebrated abroad may be considered a way – albeit a partial way – to focus attention on the interests actually in play, beyond formalistic understandings of gender equality.

A first opinion given by the Italian Council of State (*Consiglio di Stato*) to the Ministry of Justice and the Ministry of Foreign Affairs first of all excluded, as being contrary to international public order, the transcription by civil registrars not of the potentially polygamous marriage (one celebrated in accordance with a law that, like the Islamic one, admits polygyny), but only of the actual polygamous marriage (in which one of the spouses is already bound by a prior marriage).[10] Later, when cases touched incidentally upon the question of polygamous marriages, solutions able to exploit the flexibility of international public order were set out: thus, application of the foreign law providing for polygamy was excluded, while the effects already produced abroad by the relationship established within the terms of that law were recognized.[11] In this way, an abstract notion of public order was kept from resulting – for women involved in polygamous marriages – in the rejection of their actual interests.

This approach, which owes a lot to the French doctrine of attenuated public order (Lagarde, 2010), was, for example, adopted in the first (and only) judgment in which – albeit incidentally – the legal effects of polygamy came under discussion.[12] The case concerned a woman, a Somali national, who had entered into marriage with an Italian citizen in Mogadishu. Following her husband's death, she brought suit against her husband's daughters to establish her inheritance rights. However, the daughters made the objection that the marriage, although it had been transcribed in Italy, was contrary to the principles of internal public order and thus without effect, as the marriage had been celebrated under Islamic law, which permits repudiation and polygamy. Faced with this objection, the Italian Supreme Court (*Corte di Cassazione*) affirmed, however, that

> as it is uncontested … that the marriage was contracted according to the forms established by Somali law and the requirements of status and capacity of the parties were met, there is no reason for our legal system to exclude its validity, and thus its effectiveness with regard … to the inheritance right …
>
> … the unsustainability of the thesis according to which a marriage entered into by an Italian citizen abroad – although in compliance with the forms established there and in the presence of other persons – might not be accorded any legal effect, in those places where the *lex loci* contains elements that run counter to

10 Consiglio di Stato, Section III, opinion no. 640/1988.

11 These were, moreover, cases in which 'the validity of the base relationship [was] only a preliminary question, to be resolved in accordance with the provisions of the foreign legal system, which, however, are not introduced into the Italian system and therefore exclude the enforceability of the public order limit' (Colaianni, 2000: 135–6).

12 Corte di Cassazione, Civil Section I, judgment no. 1739/1999.

> the bedrock principles of our own system, arises from the principle of what is called *favor matrimonii*, according to which the act does not lose validity if it has not been contested on one of the grounds indicated in articles 117 and following of the civil code (which must include that of marriage contracted in accordance with a ritual that allows polygamy and/or *ad nutum* dissolution of the marriage) and no ruling of nullity or annulment has taken place. It follows that, by virtue of the interim validity of the marriage entered into by an Italian citizen abroad, albeit in accordance with a law that permits polygamy and/or repudiation, but in compliance with the forms established there and with the substantial requirements of status and capacity of persons having been met, its suitability for producing effects in our legal system cannot be disregarded, until such time as its nullity is inferred and a ruling on the point is made.

Here, however, it is a matter of a marriage that was only potentially polygamous (and therefore duly transcribed), for which the argument was actually over whether the Italian citizen's only wife had inheritance rights.[13] The case (and perhaps the ruling, too) would have been different if the recognition of the effects connected with the spouse's status were to have been requested by the second or third wife married abroad (or by her children), if it were a question of their inheritance rights or in the event that they had claimed welfare benefits.[14]

Although there are currently no judgments in this regard (aside from those on the family reunification of second wives, to be discussed below), it bears keeping in mind that, at least with regard to filiation, the barriers to recognizing polygamous marriages should not come at the expense of the children of polygamous couples. This may also be seen from a 1992 note on 'birth reports submitted by polygamous foreign nationals' (Directorate-General of Civil Affairs and Free Professions at the Ministry of Justice). Addressed to the Prosecutor General (*Procuratore generale*) before the Bologna Court of Appeal (*Corte d'Appello di Bologna*), the note states that recognizing the status of legitimate filiation for the daughter of a polygamous Nigerian couple,

> since specific reference is made to a foreign legal system, does not conflict with the provisions of Italian law, (nor does it) clash with the principles of public order, because it goes no further than to acknowledge, by adopting it within the

13 For critical remarks on this judgment, see, among many, Campiglio (2008: 58).

14 In these cases, the barrier to the openness of national family law would be even more problematic, because to prevent the discrimination that would be engendered within the family, it would be necessary to cope with the financial costs of the welfare state (Mattei, 1992: 468–9). Indeed, two documents of the National Institute of Social Security (INPS) - circular no. 190 of 22 July 1992 and message no. 25928 of 29 September 2009 - respectively provide that, in the case of polygamous marriages, the marriage leave allowance (*assegno per congedo matrimoniale*) and the family allowance (*assegno per il nucleo familiare*) are granted only for one spouse (Durisotto, 2015: 373 ff).

system regulated by private international law, the attribution of legitimacy that the Nigerian system grants with regard to its own citizen.[15]

There is lastly an additional element to be taken into consideration as regards the relationship between impediments to marriage, foreign law and gender discrimination. The question, in fact, has come up over celebrating in Italy marriages of Muslim women to citizens of another religion or to atheists. Since Islamic law does not permit marriages of this kind, while the Hanafi school admits those between a Muslim man and a Christian or Jewish woman (Esposito, 2001: 19; Nasir, 2002: 69–70), the problem arose when Italian civil registrars refused to celebrate these marriages, given that the authority in the Muslim woman's country of origin had not issued its *nulla osta* (certificate of non-impediment).[16] At first, Italian judges and the Constitutional Court itself[17] tried to overcome this obstacle by invoking the instrument of international public order: in fact, the civil registrars could have relied on it to celebrate the marriage even without this certificate. However, the Ministry of the Interior took action against the registrars' refusal to use this means,[18] and, in a ministerial circular, asked that no account be taken of the requirement of religious faith that may be contained in the certificates issued by countries like Morocco. This requirement was deemed inapplicable because it was contrary to the freedom of religion enshrined in the constitution (and therefore not so much because it ran counter to spousal equality).

15 The note's text is reported by Campiglio (2008: 59–60). Moreover, the case concerned granting legitimate status to the daughter of two Nigerian nationals, both bound by prior marriages, as polyandry is also permitted in Nigeria. Another case concerning filiation is that of a woman, a Moroccan national, who, having had an extramarital relationship with an Italian citizen, had submitted an application for the natural filiation of her son (born from the relationship) to be recognized. However, the child's father had contested the admissibility of the lawsuit brought against him, since the Moroccan law (the *lex patriae* of mother and child) did not have an institution similar to the Italian judicial declaration of paternity. In this case, the Supreme Court ruled against the applicability of the *lex patriae* precisely because, by denying importance to natural filiation and also establishing criminal consequences for the woman, it ran counter to *favor filiationis*, which is instead a principle of international public order: Corte di Cassazione, Civil Section I, judgment no. 1951/1999.

16 According to article 116 of the Italian civil code, '[t]he foreign national who wishes to celebrate marriage in the Republic must submit to the civil registrar a declaration by the competent authority in his or her own country, stating that according to the laws to which the foreign national is subjected, nothing precludes the marriage'.

17 Corte costituzionale, order no. 14/2003.

18 Ministry of the Interior, circular no. 46 of 11 September 2007. Available at http://servizidemografici.interno.it/it/content/circolare-n462007.

Unilateral Male Repudiation and Women's Agency

While the most problematic issues for establishing or recognizing migrants' family models have concerned polygamy, conflict with public order has been asserted for unilateral repudiation as well. Islamic law, albeit with forms and limitations that vary according to legal school or country of origin,[19] has a form of unilateral marriage dissolution, which can be accessed only by the husband upon the pronouncement of a formula (*talaq*) and the consequent economic compensation of the wife. However, just as polygamous marriages cannot be celebrated in Italy, in the same way, Italian judges are not allowed to pronounce divorces in application of foreign provisions that permit unilateral repudiation.[20] Given this, the problem instead arises when repudiation has been pronounced in the migrant's country of origin and recognition of its effects, or recognition of the foreign judgment validating the unilateral male divorce, is requested. While, on the one hand, article 31, paragraph 1, of Law no. 218/1995 establishes that 'personal separation and divorce are governed by the common national law of the spouses at the time of the divorce or separation application' and that, when lacking, 'the law of the State where the married life prevalently takes place is applied', articles 64 and 65 establish that the foreign judgments and the foreign measures concerning the existence of family relationships produce effects in the Italian legal system only when they are not contrary to public order and the basic rights of defence are respected.

Although there are many more rulings in the matter of repudiation than polygamy, these rulings have nevertheless yielded a seesawing trend in Italian case-law. Alongside judgments in which the judges opted to sharply reject this form of divorce, justifying their decision with the discriminatory nature of the act,[21] there have also been decisions in which the public order limit was not brought into play, so as not to result in counterproductive effects precisely against women. In an early judgment – in fact preceding the law introducing divorce[22] – the Rome Court of Appeal (*Corte d'Appello di Roma*), in denying any effect of a repudiation taking place between two Syrian spouses in Syria, did not refrain from making remarks with an orientalist flavour.[23] The judgment states that repudiation

19 For the other forms of dissolution of marriage that Islamic law grants to the husband (*zihar* and *ilaa*) see Nasir (2002: 106). Wives, on the other hand, can divorce their husbands, either consensually (*khul* or *mubaraat*) or in court (*tafriq*).

20 Corte d'Appello di Milano, judgment of 17 December 1991; Tribunale di Milano, judgment of 24 March 1994; Tribunale di Milano, judgment of 11 March 1995.

21 In one case, however, the application for recognition of repudiation was rejected, because it had been done without examination by a foreign judicial body: Corte d'Appello di Milano, judgment of 14 December 1965.

22 Law no. 898/1970.

23 Corte d'Appello di Roma, judgment of 29 October 1948.

> is repugnant to the moral and legal mentality of the peoples who have achieved a higher degree of civilization, and who have a far more advanced ethical and social concept of marriage than that produced by the Oriental peoples.

Among the rulings in which the refusal to recognize the legal effects of repudiation was engendered by a concern for the wife's disadvantaged position,[24] one judgment by the Rome Court of Appeal in 1973,[25] however, stands out for the paradoxical outcome reached by the judges. In insisting upon the discriminatory nature of the repudiation under discussion, they failed to notice that they were dealing with a form of marriage dissolution other than unilateral repudiation. The act of divorce was in fact denied effect due to its being contrary to public order, even though the *talaq* formula had been pronounced by the Egyptian husband at the initiative of the Italian wife, who in exchange had renounced alimony and dowry.[26] For the judges, the act was to be considered discriminatory all the same and therefore unenforceable due to the fact that, in formal terms, the dissolution of the marriage derived from the declaration of the husband only, thereby reducing the wife to being a 'passive subject of his determinations'. In this way, the woman's alleged legal inferiority under Islamic law came to be invoked against her, resulting in consequences less favourable to her: remaining married to a man who, moreover, had legally remarried in the meantime (Schwarzenberg, 1974: 655).

Nevertheless, there are decisions in which judges appear to have considered that an unconditioned denial of the legal effects of repudiation risks impacting the very party that is supposed to be protected. The categorical refusal may in fact have the effect of keeping 'bound to a marriage a woman who, having consented to the repudiation or having even requested recognition thereof in Italy (perhaps in order to be able to marry), believes the rupture of conjugal life is now irremediable' (Campiglio, 2008: 66). Noteworthy, then, is the solution followed by the Brescia Court of Appeal (*Corte d'Appello di Brescia*) in a case where the husband had pronounced the repudiation of his (Italian) wife before the Qadi's Court in the city of Meknès.[27] On that occasion, the judges, although not recognizing the repudiation in and of itself, still attributed to the (Italian) wife 'single status', as well as the right to maintenance for herself and her daughter, based on article 4,

24 Corte di Cassazione, Civil Section I, judgment no. 3881/1969; Corte d'Appello di Torino, judgment of 9 March 2006.

25 Corte d'Appello di Roma, judgment of 9 July 1973.

26 It was therefore not *talaq* but *mukhala'a*, a form of divorce by mutual consent or by renunciation of outstanding rights, also practised in Egypt. It had been the wife to propose dissolving the marriage, by pronouncing before the tribunal's *Maazun* the formula 'I exempt you from paying the dowry and alimony under the condition that you repudiate me', to which the husband responded 'You are repudiated based on the aforesaid'.

27 Corte d'Appello di Brescia, judgment of 9 November 1973.

no. 4, of the code of civil procedure,[28] 'since, in its effects, the act of repudiation is equal to dissolution of the marriage by divorce'. In another case, in which the repudiation – once again of an Italian woman – had been pronounced instead before the Egyptian consul in London,[29] the Court of Rome (*Tribunale di Roma*) took the act of repudiation into consideration for the purposes of applying article 3, no. 2, letter e), of Law no. 898/1970[30] and of consequently recognizing the wife's 'single status'.[31]

Further reflection is provided by the Cagliari Court of Appeal (*Corte d'Appello di Cagliari*),[32] which declared effective and ordered the transcription of a divorce decree obtained in Egypt through the *talaq* procedure, even if the formula had been pronounced by the husband in the wife's absence. Once they were no longer bound by marriage, both spouses had in the meantime celebrated a second marriage: this proves how the continuous flows of migrants' family relationships is not halted by the legal barriers placed upon their recognition in the host country. Moreover, according to the judges, recognition of the divorce decree based on repudiation was contrary neither to public order nor to the wife's right of defence, because

> the pronunciation of the husband's desire to divorce was brought to the knowledge of Ms. R., who thus had the opportunity, in accordance with the provisions of Egyptian law, to bring to the knowledge of the competent authority, and to defend before the Courts, her economic claims, and to achieve reconciliation with her husband.

28 This article, prior to being repealed by Law no. 218/1995, under no. 4 provided a principle of reciprocity, based on which the foreign national could be sued through Italian courts if the judges in the foreigner's country could rule on lawsuits filed against an Italian citizen. The judges in Brescia, then, affirmed that, since the foreign judgment (or the equivalent act) of divorce could not be asserted in Italy, it was logical to allow the wife to go before her own national court to apply for divorce.

29 Tribunale di Roma, judgment no. 70/1979.

30 It provides that the dissolution or termination of the civil effects of marriage can be applied for by one of the spouses when 'the other spouse, a foreign national, has obtained annulment or divorce abroad or has celebrated another marriage abroad'. At first established to 'remedy the situations of the so-called "limping" marriages created by Italy's lack of a divorce law (and by a judiciary taking refuge behind the indissolubility of marriage beyond all reason), it is now becoming essential for regulating the traumatic cases that may arise from contact with Islamic law' (Galoppini, 2005: 968).

31 It bears mentioning, however, that in both cases the judges were able to find an alternative solution – the dissolution of marriage in accordance with Italian legislation – because the wife was Italian. Had it been a case of a foreign woman repudiated by a husband of the same nationality, their national law would have had to be applied, with the paradoxical outcome of keeping the woman in a limping marriage: Islamic law would have allowed her to remarry, while under Italian law she was still married (Sona, 2014: 131).

32 Corte d'Appello di Cagliari, judgment no. 198/2008.

> …
>
> As has been seen, the divorce decree in question comes at the end of a procedure in which the wife's opportunity to attend is safeguarded; the irreversible dissolution of the bond or the end of the spouses' common life and affection is ascertained; and the wife's economic rights are regulated.
>
> Moreover, it is useful to recall that under Egyptian civil law, the wife has an equal (unilateral) right to free herself from marriage even in the absence of her husband's consent, according to the so-called Khola procedure, so there would be no violation of gender equality even in principle.

What is unconvincing, however, is the equivalence that the Cagliari Court of Appeal draws between the repudiation pronounced by the husband and the *khul* (or '*khola*'), which is to say the instrument that since 2000 has allowed wives to unilaterally dissolve the marriage (Oberto, 2012: 416). The judges, in neglecting that differences still exist in Egypt – even only on the level of 'law in books' (Dupret, 2007) – between repudiation by the husband and the wife's right to divorce, failed to consider that while the husband's repudiation is still unconditioned and does not have to be pronounced before a judge, a woman may unilaterally ask for divorce, but only before a judge and by financially compensating the husband in return for the divorce.[33] Therefore, what they should rather have noted, for the purposes of recognizing the repudiation decree, was whether, in this case (and not in the abstract), family life and affection had ceased for both spouses and whether the wife's economic rights were regulated.

Restrictions on Family Reunification: in Whose Best Interest?

Transnational families of migrants receive special attention from the law when applying for family reunification in the host country. In this case, while legal restrictions on reunification are a matter of controlling and containing immigration, they are also a tool to admit solely those families which respond to the host country's cultural and social patterns (Sirianni, 2006: 67). Legislation on family reunification is thus intertwined with private international law, insofar as legal institutions and rules of the migrant's country of origin represent a preliminary question for exercising the right in question. Consequently, limitations upon the application of foreign laws, put in place to safeguard spousal equality, re-emerge

33 On the social, economic and cultural barriers that Egyptian women come up against in obtaining the *khul* introduced by Law no. 1/2000, see Bernard-Maugiron and Dupret (2008). On the complex reform process of the Islamic family law, with respect to the position of women, see, more generally, Hallaq (2009: 118).

in the form of denying reunification to migrant women who have family relations deemed intrinsically discriminatory.

On this point, Italy has shown considerable uncertainties, due not only to oscillations in case-law, but also and above all to significant restrictions introduced to migration law. Nonetheless, these uncertainties allow us to see first-hand how legal devices adopted in the presumed interest of migrant women often risk backfiring on them badly, both in terms of actually guaranteeing their rights and for the consequent disregard of their agency. Often, behind laws enacted to support the family unity of migrants lies not so much a need to maintain firm bedrock principles of the legal system as a rejection of family models lying outside the (supposed and at times dated) cultural and legal tradition of the majority.

In Italy, if at first the right to family reunification was extended through case-law and legislation, the pendulum began slowly to swing in the other direction. In fact, Law no. 943/1986 had recognized family reunification with the spouse and dependent children only for workers from outside the European Community, residing legally in Italy, who performed paid work (article 4, paragraph 1). However, the Constitutional Court, called upon to rule on the violation of articles 29 and 30 of the constitution, declared that

> work performed within the family, given its social and also economic value, may also be included, albeit with the special features that characterize it, under the protection that art. 35 of the Constitution ensures for work "in all its forms".
>
> This is a kind of working activity that has already been recognized in a variety of ways given its social and also economic importance, due also to the indisputable advantages that society as a whole draws from it and, at the same time, to the burdens and responsibilities that descend from it and, to this day, are borne almost exclusively by women (due also to widespread unemployment).

The contested provision was thus to be interpreted

> in the sense that the non-EC national who, in our country, performs her work in her own family must also be listed among workers entitled to reunification with minor children residing abroad.[34]

Thereafter, the Consolidation Act of provisions on immigration (Legislative Decree no. 286/1998, art. 29) extended the range of individuals admitted to apply for family reunification, adopting the idea of a family unit broader than the nuclear

34 Corte costituzionale, judgment no. 28/1995. The question of constitutionality had been raised in the context of proceedings concerning the claim by a Brazilian woman married to an Italian citizen, who had been denied family reunification with her minor son because in Italy she performed the unpaid work of a housewife.

one and therefore closer to the structure of migrants' families.[35] However, a few years later, in line with the legislative trend aimed at progressively containing migratory flows, the right to family reunification also began to be gradually downsized and, starting with the 'Bossi-Fini Law',[36] the number of people entitled to this right has been considerably reduced and limited to within the nuclear family.[37]

Nonetheless, legal issues immediately arose in Italian case-law, as a consequence of the fact that the status of spouse, child, or parent must be established according to the foreigner's national law, but without prejudice to the limit of public order (article 16 of Law no. 218/1995). The problem was thus raised as to whether, for the purposes of family reunification, the status of spouse could also be granted to a second (or third) wife or to a repudiated wife. In some cases, the judges, in line with two circulars from the Ministry of the Interior,[38] denied family reunification to both wives of a polygamous husband, maintaining that otherwise a polygamous marriage contrary to public order – because it most certainly ran counter to the principle of spousal equality – would have been allowed to be reconstituted in Italy.[39] Different conclusions, however, were reached when the polygamous marriage came into discussion, not as such, but as a legal requirement for producing further effects beyond the recognition of the marriage. Thus, for example, when reunification of the second wife was requested because she was the mother of a three-year-old who had been staying in Italy since birth, reunification was allowed only so as not to deprive the minor of a two-parent family.[40] The

---

35 The original version of the article granted the right to family reunification:

a) to the spouse who was not legally separated;

b) to dependent minor children, including those of the spouse or those born out of wedlock, unmarried or legally separated, under the condition that the other parent, if existing, has given his or her consent;

c) to dependent parents; and

d) to relatives to within the third degree of kinship unable to work in accordance with Italian legislation.

36 Law no. 189/2002.

37 This restriction was also confirmed by the Constitutional Court, which endorsed the lawmakers' decision to once again limit the right to family reunification to the nuclear family alone (spouse and minor children), consequently excluding parents and adult children. In fact, the judges – in particular with judgment no. 224/2005 – in drawing a distinction between the constitutional right to family unity and a mere interest in family affection, contributed towards excluding from reunification the more extended bonds of affection that often characterize the migrants' family networks.

38 Circular no. 599/443/1512756/A16/88, 1 October 1988, as well as circular no. 5599/443/186378/5/11/3/1/2/I Div., 7 October 1988.

39 Regional administrative court (TAR: *tribunale amministrativo regionale*), Emilia-Romagna/Bologna, Section I, judgment no. 926/1994.

40 The woman was in Italy on a residence permit issued to her because she was pregnant.

mother's stay in Italy was therefore conditioned not only upon the persisting grave reasons connected with the minor's psycho-physical development, health and age (article 31, paragraph 3, of Decree no. 286/1998), but also upon the absence of parental activities incompatible with the minor's needs or with staying in Italy.[41] In the reverse case of a mother's reunification applied for by her son, the competent authority had initially denied approval to entry into Italy because the father was already living there with his first wife and the reunification would have meant reconstituting a polygamous union. The Court of Bologna (*Tribunale di Bologna*), however, declared the authority's denial illegitimate because no claim had been submitted by the husband to have the civil effects of the polygamous marriage recognized. Instead, the request had been submitted by the son, who was asserting only the indirect effects of the polygamous marriage as the mere *de facto* and *de jure* requirement for reunification.[42]

The interest of (minor) children was the reason why, in 2005, the Court of Cassation granted to a Moroccan woman family reunification with her second husband and her children born from her first marriage, although this marriage had been dissolved by an act of repudiation and the *Moudawana* (the Moroccan code of personal status) entrusts legal guardianship to the father alone.[43] In rejecting the arguments of the two appealing ministries, which had insisted upon the Moroccan attribution of parental authority (and of legal representation) to the father alone, the judges decided to take a different road:

> When, as in this case, the father who, for the law of the Kingdom of Morocco, is the only holder of parental authority, uncontestedly does not live with the minor children who, based on what was ascertained by the local court, are maintained

41 Corte d'Appello di Torino, decree of 18 April 2001.

42 Tribunale di Bologna, order of 12 March 2003.

43 Corte di Cassazione, Civil Section I, judgment no. 12619/2005. The case concerned a Moroccan woman holding a valid Italian residence permit. Although having obtained approval from the Perugia Police Headquarters (Questura) for the reunification of her second husband and her minor children born from her first marriage, she was denied entry for her children by the Italian Embassy in Rabat. The documents showed that, upon repudiation, her first husband had excluded the woman from guardianship over the minors, reserving it for himself. Nonetheless, the court of first instance upheld the woman's claim, given that she had seen, at a distance, to maintaining her children, who therefore were to be deemed her 'dependents', and that the father had given his assent to their expatriation. The Ministries of the Interior and of Foreign Affairs appealed the ruling before the Perugia Court of Appeal (Corte d'Appello di Perugia): they invoked the lack of legal representation for the woman because, according to Moroccan law – applicable to relations between parents and children on the basis of article 36 of Law no. 218/1995 – the father alone would have been entitled to legal representation. However, the appeal by the two ministries was rejected due to the Moroccan law's being contrary to the public order, as it was discriminatory against the mother. The ministries then appealed to the Court of Cassation, which confirmed the second-instance judgment.

> by the mother alone, and she does not live with them only because she emigrated to Italy for reasons of work, there is no reason to refuse the visa on the passport for the children's entry into Italy, given that the assent to the expatriation by the father who holds parental authority is incompatible with the prior revocation of guardianship for the mother in the act of repudiation, and in fact annuls it.

However, the openness and the most thought-out decisions by the Italian judges in the area of family reunification and spousal equality suffered a setback following some legislative changes. It must first be recalled that, with Directive no. 2003/86/EC on the right to family reunification, the European Union assumed an attitude entirely contrary to polygamy. That attitude, however, does not exclude more careful assessments by the Member States when the interests of minor children come into play. Indeed, article 4, point 4, provides that

> [i]n the event of a polygamous marriage, where the sponsor already has a spouse living with him in the territory of a Member State, the Member State concerned shall not authorise the family reunification of a further spouse.

Nonetheless, it also adds that

> [b]y way of derogation from paragraph 1(c), Member States *may limit* the family reunification of minor children of a further spouse and the sponsor. (My italics)

The restriction upon the reunification of the minor children of polygamous families is therefore not mandatory but is applied at the discretion of the Member States,[44] although the mere addition of this option shows an inclination to penalize children for their parents' supposed 'cultural shortcomings' (Morozzo Della Rocca, 2004: 67).

---

44 In terms of possibility, points 10 and 11 of the preamble provide as follows:

'It is for the Member States *to decide whether* they wish to authorise family reunification for relatives in the direct ascending line, adult unmarried children, unmarried or registered partners as well as, in the event of a polygamous marriage, minor children of a further spouse and the sponsor. Where a Member State authorises family reunification of these persons, this is without prejudice of *the possibility*, for Member States which do not recognise the existence of family ties in the cases covered by this provision, of not granting to the said persons the treatment of family members with regard to the right to reside in another Member State, as defined by the relevant EC legislation.'

'The right to family reunification should be exercised in proper compliance with the values and principles recognised by the Member States, in particular with respect to the rights of women and of children; such compliance justifies *the possible taking of restrictive measures* against applications for family reunification of polygamous households' (my italics).

In implementing the European directive, Italy did not rely on the power to limit the reunification of minor children in the case of polygamy.[45] Lawmakers, however, took action thereafter, banning family reunification when it is applied for by someone who is married to a foreign national legally residing in Italy with another spouse or when it is requested by an adult for a dependent parent, if polygamous (a prohibition not provided for by the directive).[46] Following the entry into force of the new and more restrictive legislation, the claim of a Moroccan national requesting reunification for his mother, as she had neither means of subsistence nor other children in the country of origin, was thus dismissed. The woman, in fact, was married to the claimant's father, who lived in Italy and had already submitted a family reunification request for another wife.[47]

Family, Migration and Gender Equality: The Missing Terms

As the analysis thus far has shown, attention to the connections between gender and migration from the perspective of family law lays bare some paradoxes in how gender equality is framed and guaranteed. Indeed, when the problems concerning family law involve migrants, a tendency of legal actors to excessively simplify the issues emerges, unveiling an equality that, instead of being gender-sensitive, risks becoming gender-blind. In response to claims to recognize other family patterns, the legal system's dismissals, justified by the need to respect women's rights, may in fact be counterproductive, helping to perpetuate not only imbalanced gender relations, but above all a stereotyped image of migrant women (Mohanty, 1986; Narayan, 1997). In this regard, the above examination of Italian case-law shows how the frequent resort to the egalitarian argument to dismiss migrants' claims often goes hand-in-hand with a low awareness of the complex interests in play. Two elements in particular are striking: on the one hand, the lack of attention to the inherently conflicting nature of family relationships and to the complex dynamics they give rise to; on the other, the overlooking of the difficulties that migrant women encounter on levels other than gender (economic barriers, cultural barriers, class barriers, etc.).

Above all, there is no awareness of the fact that '[t]he study of law in general, and personal status law in particular, needs focusing more on practices. It should capture the language of law in action and not only of law in the books. Law as a social phenomenon cannot be reduced to the mere provisions of a legal code (law on the books)' (Bernard-Maugiron and Dupret, 2008: 74). It must then be

45 Legislative Decree no. 5/2007.

46 Article 1, paragraph 22, letter s), of Law no. 94/2009, which modified article 29 of Consolidation Act no. 286/1998. In the intent to prevent fictitious or forced marriages, reunification is now generally excluded not only for the legally separated husband, but for the minor-age one as well.

47 Corte di Cassazione, Civil Section VI, order no. 4984/2013.

seen whether formalistic assumptions regarding the equality to be guaranteed for migrant women are such as to produce only symbolic effects and not effects in terms of family relations as actually lived. Thus, for example, when the enforceability of foreign laws on marriage or divorce is countered by the public order barrier, the conflict with the principle of gender equality must be assessed not in the abstract, but by thinking of the effects that actually stem from the failure to recognize the acts adopted according to these laws. If dismissal results in a denial of the rights connected with the conjugal status, an impediment to regain single status or a denial of the right to family reunification, all in the name of a blind equality for migrant women, the cost becomes quite high.

It is necessary instead to devote attention to the strategic behaviours that migrant women maintain in and out of the courtroom to obtain the pursued outcomes and maximize the benefits that can be had from laws and practices that are discriminatory in the abstract. These women demonstrate they know how to navigate the multiple 'legal archipelagos' that govern the family law of migrants and that otherwise risk trapping them in a sort of legal limbo (Sona, 2014). However, to make sure that Italian family law fosters and does not hinder (or disregard) these strategies,[48] the judges must have complete knowledge of the foreign laws to be applied, by seeking out, especially in the case of Islamic law, the law in practice and the litigants' actual interests (Fournier, 2010: 7–8, 29). In this way, they will avoid taking foreign legal institutions to be compact bodies, unambiguous in meaning and impermeable to change (Giunchi, 2014: 1 ff).

Moreover, the assertive and formalistic appeal to gender equality whenever legislation on migration intersects with Italian family law is an unsatisfactory solution from another standpoint as well. It leads to underestimating the fact that the vulnerable position of migrant women is determined by multiple factors which do not stem necessarily or exclusively from the personal status acquired in the country of origin. The problems they find themselves coping with often depend also on the fact that whether or not their claims are upheld is conditioned by their being mothers and by their actual carrying out of care functions.[49] Emblematic of

48 Albeit with reference to a different context, but based on considerations that could be extended to Italy as well, it was indeed specifically observed that '[i]t is quite obvious that if the State wishes to protect women against discriminatory practices, it is not possible to ignore dynamic legal pluralism. Otherwise, other than being unable to protect the members of society, the State could also possibly lose its official control over the socio-legal domain as a result of the growth of unofficial legal alternatives' (Yilmaz, 2003: 41).

49 It is also to be kept in mind that article 19, paragraph 2, letter d), of the Consolidation Act on immigration prohibits the expulsion of women during pregnancy or in the six months following the birth of the child they are caring for. The Constitutional Court, with its judgment no. 376/2000, declared the unconstitutionality of the provision in the part where it does not extend the expulsion prohibition to the husband living with the woman, holding this legislative omission to be in violation of the minor's right to the unity of family. However, with orders no. 192/2006 and no. 444/2006, the Constitutional Court declared as manifestly groundless two questions of constitutionality raised with regard to

this, for example, is the propensity in Italian case-law to grant family reunification to the second wife who is the mother of minor children, while denying it to a woman who is dependent upon children of full age. The first case, in fact, discriminates against childless wives, while the second case shows that the reunification of a mother, even if she is polygamous, is admitted only insofar as she must still attend to childcare functions. In this way, the mother/wife may enjoy only the indirect and temporally limited effects that the legal system associates with motherhood, while no weight is given to her decision to re-join her husband in order to reconstitute family relations that she was not necessarily subjected to (Petralia, 2013: 17).[50]

Legal tools should thus be developed that do not leave migrant women at the sole mercy of the judges' (or public officials') assessments and oscillations. They might allow us to lend value to the choices migrant women make in family matters and to consider the ways in which they manage and intersect multiple identities and forms of belonging (Crenshaw, 1991), by implementing strategies of adaptation, of resistance and of providing family relationships with new meaning (Landuzzi, 1995).

References

Azzariti, G. (2013). *Il costituzionalismo moderno può sopravvivere?* Roma-Bari: Laterza.

Baldassar, L. and Merla, L. (eds) (2014). *Transnational Families, Migration and the Circulation of Care*. New York/London: Routledge.

---

this provision, in the part where it provides that the expulsion decree must also be carried out against the foreign national who has a *de facto* relationship with a pregnant woman. The court affirmed that 'the question of constitutionality, although set out in terms of protecting the *de facto* family and the consequent rights/duties, actually draws a comparison between treatments applied in very different situations – that is, that of the husband of the pregnant foreign national and that of the foreign national who states he is the natural father of an unborn child – that lawmakers have, not unreasonably, regulated in different ways'.

50 On the other hand, the risk that concern for vulnerability and for the interests of migrant women is only a facade is also demonstrated by a recent legislative amendment which, in the wake of certain current events, provided for the residence permit for victims of domestic violence (article 18 bis of Legislative Decree no. 286/1998, as introduced by Decree Law no. 93/2013). Not only is the issuance of the residence permit (and, where applicable, its revocation) subjected to a discretionary assessment by the police commissioner (*questore*), but it is granted only in cases of real and present life-threatening danger, where there is non-episodic violence and under the condition that the victim has lent active cooperation in the criminal proceedings. The provision, moreover, does not speak of women, but falsely uses a neutral formula ('situations of violence or abuse against a foreign national').

Baldassar, L., Kilkey, M., Merla, L. and Wilding, R. (2014). Transnational families. In Treas, J., Scott, J. and Richards, M. (eds) *The Wiley-Blackwell Companion to the Sociology of Families*, 155–75. Chichester: Wiley.

Bernard-Maugiron, N. and Dupret, B. (2008). Breaking up the family: Divorce in Egyptian law and practice. *Journal of Women of the Middle East and the Islamic World*, 6, 52–74.

Büchler, A. (2011). *Islamic Law in Europe?: Legal Pluralism and its Limits in European Family Laws*. Farnham-Burlington: Ashgate.

Campiglio, C. (2008). Il diritto di famiglia islamico nella prassi italiana. *Rivista di diritto internazionale privato e processuale*, 1, 43–76.

Clerici, R. (2009). La compatibilità del diritto mussulmano con l'ordine pubblico internazionale, *Famiglia e diritto*, 2, 197–211.

Colaianni, N. (2000). *Tutela della personalità e diritti della coscienza*. Bari: Cacucci.

Crenshaw, K. (1991). Mapping the margins: intersectionality, identity politics, and violence against women of color. *Stanford Law Review*, 43(6), 1241–99.

Dupret, B. (2007). What is Islamic law?: A praxiological answer and an Egyptian case study. *Theory, Culture & Society*, 24, 79–100.

Durisotto, D. (2015). Poligamia e ordinamenti europei. In Cardia, C. and Dalla Torre, G. (eds) *Comunità islamiche in Italia. Identità e forme giuridiche*, 357–80. Torino: Giappichelli.

Esposito, J.L. (2001). *Women in Muslim Family Law*, 2nd edn. New York: Syracuse University Press.

Ferrando, G. (2005). *Manuale di diritto di famiglia*. Roma-Bari: Laterza.

Ferrari, A. (2008). Laïcité et multiculturalisme à l'italienne. *Archives de sciences sociales des religions*, 141, 133–54.

Foblets, M.-C. (2000). Migrant women caught between Islamic family law and women's rights. The search for the appropriate 'connecting factor' in international family law. *Maastricht Journal of European & Comparative Law*, 7(11), 11–34.

Fournier, P. (2010). *Muslim Marriage in Western Courts. Lost in Transplantation*. Farnham: Ashgate.

Galoppini, A. (2005). Il ripudio e la sua rilevanza nell'ordinamento italiano. *Diritto di famiglia e delle persone*, 969–89.

Giunchi, E. (2014). Muslim family law and legal practice in the West: An introduction. In Giunchi, E. (ed.) *Muslim Family Law in Western Courts*, 1–13. London-New York: Routledge.

Hallaq, W.B. (2009). *An Introduction to Islamic Law*. Cambridge: Cambridge University Press.

Lagarde, P. (2010). Reference to public order ("ordre public") in French private international law. In Foblets, M.-C., Gaudreault-Desbiens, J.-F. and Dundes Renteln, A. (eds) *Cultural Diversity and the Law: State Responses from Around the World*, 521–46. Bruxelles: Bruylant.

Landuzzi, C. (1995). La donna nella famiglia immigrata. In Landuzzi, C., Tarozzi, A. and Treossi, A. (eds) *Tra luoghi e generazioni: migrazioni africane in Italia e in Francia*, 83–104. Torino: L'Harmattan.

Legrand, P. (1997). The impossibility of legal transplants. *Maastricht Journal of European & Comparative Law*, 4, 111–24.

Marella, M.R. (2011). Critical family law. *American University Journal of Gender Social Policy and Law*, 2, 721–54.

Marella, M.R. and Marini, G. (2014). *Di cosa parliamo quando parliamo di famiglia*. Roma-Bari: Laterza.

Mattei, U. (1992). Ai confini della Terra Promessa: immigrazione, povertà, razzismo ed i limiti del diritto. *Foro italiano*, V, 458–71.

Mohanty, C.T. (1986). Under western eyes. Feminist scholarship and colonial discourse. *Feminist Review*, 30, 61–88.

Morozzo Della Rocca, P. (2004). Il diritto all'unità familiare in Europa: tra 'allargamento' dei confini e 'restringimento' dei diritti. *Diritto, immigrazione e cittadinanza*, 1, 63–85.

Narayan, U. (1997). *Dislocating Cultures. Identities, Traditions and Third World Feminism*. New York: Routledge.

Nasir, J.J. (2002). *The Islamic Law of Personal Status*, 3rd edn. The Hague, London, New York: Kluwer Law International.

Oberto, G. (2012). Matrimonio misto, ordine pubblico e principi sovranazionali. In Queirolo, I., Benedetti, A.M. and Carpaneto, L. (eds) *La tutela dei soggetti deboli tra diritto internazionale, dell'Unione europea e diritto interno*, 401–17. Roma: Aracne.

Okin, S.M. (1999). *Is Multiculturalism Bad for Women?* Princeton: Princeton University Press.

Olivito, E. (2012). Giudici e legislatori di fronte alla multiculturalità. In Cavino, M. and Tripodina, C. (eds) *La tutela dei diritti fondamentali tra diritto politico e diritto giurisprudenziale*, 149–98. Milano: Giuffré.

Pearl, D. and Menski, W. (1998). *Muslim Family Law*, 3rd edn. London: Sweet & Maxwell.

Petralia, V. (2013). Ricongiungimento familiare e matrimonio poligamico. Il riconoscimento di valori giuridici stranieri e la tutela delle posizioni deboli. *Online Working Papers-Università di Catania*, 49. Available at http://www.cde.unict.it/sites/default/files/Quaderno%20europeo_49_febbraio_2013.pdf.

Pocar, V. and Ronfani, F. (1978). Family law in Italy. *Law & Society Review*, 12(4), 607–44.

Rodotà, S. (1975). La riforma del diritto di famiglia alla prova. *Politica del diritto*, 661–83.

Salih, R. (2001). Moroccan migrant women: Transnationalism, nation-states and gender. *Journal of Ethnic and Migration Studies*, 27(4), 655–71.

Schwarzenberg, C. (1974). Ordine pubblico e riconoscimento in Italia dello scioglimento di matrimonio islamico per ripudio. *Diritto di famiglia e delle persone*, 653–60.

Shah, P. (2003). Attitudes to polygamy in English law. *International and Comparative Law Quarterly*, 52(2), 369–400.

Shah, P. (2013). Transnational family relations in migration contexts: British variations on European themes. In Juss, S.S. (ed.) *The Ashgate Research Companion to Migration Law, Theory and Policy*, 599–616. Farnham: Ashgate.

Sirianni, G. (2006). *Il diritto degli stranieri all'unità familiare*. Milano: Giuffrè.

Sona, F. (2014). Defending the family treasure chest: Navigating Muslim families and secured positivistic islands of European legal systems. In Shah, P., Foblets, M.-C. and Rohe, M. (eds) *Family, Religion and Law: Cultural Encounters in Europe*, 115–41. Farnham: Ashgate.

Volpp, L. (2001). Feminism versus multiculturalism. *Columbia Law Review*, 101(5), 1181–218.

Watson, A. (1974). *Legal Transplants*, 2nd edn. Edinburgh: Scottish Academic Press.

Yilmaz, I. (2003). Non-recognition of post-modern Turkish socio-legal reality and the predicament of women. *British Journal of Middle Eastern Studies*, 30(1), 25–41.

Zeitzen, A.M. (2008). *Polygamy: A Cross-Cultural Analysis*. Oxford: Berg.

PART III:
Culture, Patriarchy and Religion

Chapter 7
Gender and Culturally Motivated Crimes: The Italian Perspective

Valentina Masarone

Migratory Phenomena, Multi-Ethnic Societies and Women's Role in Identity Politics

'Multiculturalism' may be briefly defined as 'a complex of phenomena related to the co-existence of different cultural identities … aiming to claim membership in a community' (Bernardi, Pastore and Pugiotto, 2008: 22). With reference to the cultural diversity that finds deep roots in belonging to a certain ethnicity or national community,[1] a society's 'multiculturalism' may stem from its 'multinational' character – which is to say, from the presence of native national minorities, originally autonomous and then absorbed into the state by the effect of colonization, conquest, or confederation – or from its 'multi-ethnic' composition, due mainly to the immigration of individuals and families (Basile, 2007: 1301 ff; Basile, 2010: 43 ff; de Maglie, 2010: 26–7). Due to the intense migratory flows in recent decades, Europe – and Italy in particular – is now increasingly multi-ethnic in character.

Europe, and Italy in particular, has seen a growing presence of 'minority ethnic groups, formed by immigrants. In addition to their work, these immigrants are also importing their "cultural difference" to European soil' (Basile, 2008: 150); this has raised the problem of the relevance the 'cultural factor' is to be given in the multiple spheres of social life. It is an issue that, with particular reference to the criminal law sector, takes on a special complexity. In fact, 'cultural diversity' may in some cases be expressed through behaviours incorporating values – ethical, religious, political and cultural in a broad sense – different from and even contrary to those of the locally majority culture. It may then occur that conducts tolerated, authorized or even imposed in the cultural setting from which the subject comes may violate the norms of the host legal system, thereby offending legal interests protected in that setting under criminal law.

Criminal law is not ideologically or culturally 'neutral' (Basile, 2010: 89 ff) because it is and must be there to safeguard the bedrock values of the historically given society in which it is to operate, against materially identifiable conducts that

1 This is the concept of 'societal culture' elaborated by the Canadian philosopher Will Kymlicka. See Kymlicka, 1995.

cause actual damage to interests worth protecting. The content of the provisions of criminal law, then, is the direct expression of the values underlying the majority culture. Culturally 'different' subjects may act under cultural conditioning, which pertains to those values, but which works differently from the culture of the host legal system. In this case, the problem is raised of establishing whether, and how, to the effects of criminal law, relevance can or must be attributed to the cultural factor.

It bears noting that the issue of 'culturally motivated crimes' (de Maglie, 2010: 30; Van Broeck, 2001: 1 ff) takes on special interest in the discourse on 'gender and migration'. Judicial practice in fact shows that conducts of relevance under criminal law that are orientated by a cultural motivation are prevalently held to be to the detriment of 'weak' subjects, such as women (often minors) and children: domestic violence (abuse and kidnappings); honour crimes (understood as family or group honour, sexual honour, or personal honour); crimes of reduction into slavery; crimes against sexual freedom committed in denial of the victim's self-determination; genital mutilation and ornamental scarring; and crimes connected with parents' refusal to allow their children to attend mandatory schooling (Basile, 2008: 149–212).

In this regard, it has been observed that 'albeit in different ways, and at different stages of evolution, *all* social groups, *all* human societies have a gender structure, which normally entails the hierarchical subordination of women' (Brunelli, 2008: 204). This state of affairs must be carefully assessed when taking into consideration the role that women and children play in defining and perpetuating community identity with regard to the need of immigrant groups to preserve their cultural minority identity. Indeed,

> the opening of a group, its culture, and those belonging to it to overpowering outside forces and to the suggestions they release *intra moenia* lays upon certain subjects in particular burdens of imposed resistance, whose likelihood for success depends a great deal on how solid the bonds of faithfulness are and on the instruments for preserving them: the perpetuation of the community bond rests inevitably upon those who transmit those constraints, by virtue of their position as biological and cultural carriers of collective membership. (Olivito, 2006: 147)

In this sense, 'women and children are, on the one hand, the linchpin of cultural developments – as they are respectively the guardians and the recipients of cultural transmission – while, on the other hand, they struggle to be active protagonists thereof' (Olivito 2006: 135).

In this way, women and children end up being the main recipients of those minority-group claims that Kymlicka (1995: 65 ff) defines as 'internal restrictions'. As is known, 'internal restrictions' refer to intra-group relations. They are distinguished from 'external protections', which are claims made by the group against the dominant society and, therefore, inherent to inter-group relations.

Through internal restrictions, 'a minority group aims to limit its own members' freedom in the name of group solidarity, cultural purity, religious orthodoxy, and preservation of traditions' (Basile, 2007: 1320).

The issue of the relationships between multiculturalism and criminal law in the perspective of 'gender and migration' thus means raising the following question: what are, for the host legal system, the limits of tolerance or – *de jure condendo* – of tolerability of the internal restrictions that operate with regard to female members of immigrant communities, and that appear likely to compress or deny the exercise of fundamental human rights? The response offered to this question by Italian lawmakers takes shape – as we shall see – in the (legal) solution produced to deal with the phenomenon of female genital mutilation. We shall examine this solution, ascertaining its compatibility with the principles of the Italian constitution operating directly or indirectly in the matter of criminal law. This is also in order to verify the existence of possible valid alternatives that are (for the most part) consistent with the dictates of a welfare state under the rule of law, as ours is.

Cultural Pluralism and Criminal Law: Possible Criminal Law Policy Options in Light of Constitutional Principles

In this field, the validity of the assertion that law is policy, and that policy choices find in legal provisions their concrete realization, is even more evident (Moccia, 1992: 21 ff). Indeed, the options chosen in criminal proceedings can only be the reflection and, at the same time, one of the main expressions of policy's orientation towards an assimilationist or, rather, a multiculturalist or pluralist model. The former, of course, consists of assigning no relevance to the 'cultural diversity' of certain subjects. They too, then, are required to observe the traditions and lifestyle typical of the locally majority culture. The latter model is aimed at recognizing and upholding different cultural identities. It tends to show respect for or, at least, tolerance of culturally conditioned behaviours, even if they stand in a dialectic relationship with the locally prevalent culture (Bernardi, 2010: 7 ff).[2]

The first model, founded upon an essentially 'formal' idea of equality, gives rise, in a criminal-law setting, to an attitude oscillating between indifference towards and intolerance of culturally motivated behaviours: indifference is shown by choosing not to differentiate judgments in light of the typical nature (*tipicità*), the unlawfulness of the crime and the offender's liability for crimes committed under cultural conditioning; intolerance is shown in the tendency to harshen the response by the criminal law depending precisely on the cultural factor that may underlie the conduct maintained by the offender belonging to a minority group.

The pluralist or multiculturalist model derives from a criterion of equality understood in a truly 'substantial' sense. It gives rise to criminal law's orientation

2 For further classifications, inside the two basic models see de Maglie (2010: 32 ff).

towards taking due consideration of the effects that the cultural conditioning can have on whether certain crimes can be punished, at the various levels of the structure of the crime or outside it (Bernardi, 2010: 9 ff).

In the actual situation of the legal systems in force, the two theoretical models described above are not impermeable to one another, but end up alternating and overlapping: albeit while tending to recognize the prevailing political trends,[3] most European countries adopt policies 'half way' between the assimilationist and the multiculturalist models (Bernardi, 2010: 74; Bernardi, 2006: 65 ff), with the result that

> legislative responses in different directions often clash within the same national criminal law system and even in the same historical moment, on the basis of options of criminal law policy that at times are truly in opposition and at times only in apparent disharmony, since they regard situations incomparable with one another. The same may be said for the responses of the judges, which is moreover generally characterized by a still greater rate of variability. (Bernardi, 2010: 9–10)

To distinguish between what criminal law is and what it must be, in the conviction that what exists is not simply to be declared legitimate as such, we must ask ourselves which of the two models briefly described appears most consistent with the principles of criminal law policy as laid down by the Italian constitution, and then see whether or not the choices made thus far by lawmakers in this area fit the pattern.

In this regard, we need first to refer to the principles of pluralism (articles 3 and 21 of the constitution) and secularity (articles 2, 3, 7, 8, 19 and 20 of the constitution) which are characteristic of Italy's constitutional system (Canestrari, 2006: 139 ff).

Of relevance, then, is a need for equality (article 3 of the constitution), whose substantial aspects the constitution itself requires upholding; to be truly equal, equality must take differences into account, in accordance with the now-obvious criterion that requires equal treatment for the equal, and dissimilar treatment of dissimilar cases. In assessing criminal liability, equality is also relevant in terms of proportion. It is an essential limit which preserves the punitive action, because it anchors the punishment to the overall disvalue of the individual crime committed. In this way, the individual cannot be made an instrument of criminal law policy (Moccia, 1992: 88 ff), which might correspond with repressive or deterrent choices connected with the needs of social defence. The purposes under criminal law policy that the function of the punishment identifies with may operate only

3 For example, British policy (Basile, 2010: 60 ff), like those in the United States (Basile, 2010: 262 ff; de Maglie, 2010: 73 ff) and Canada (Olivito, 2006: 54 ff), is usually deemed orientated towards multiculturalism; French policy, on the other hand, is traditionally assimilationist (Basile, 2010: 57 ff; Bernardi, 2006: 63 ff; Olivito, 2006: 45 ff).

within and upon the assumption of the fundamental standard of proportionality. In this regard, however, it is necessary to gain understanding as to the purposes that the punishment may legitimately pursue in our system.

The constitutional function of the punishment is identified in social integration, understood as re-socializing – or not further de-socializing – the convicted person. This solution is reached through the systematic interpretation of constitutional provisions: article 27, paragraph 3, of the constitution, which enshrines the principle of the re-educational purpose of the punishment; articles 2, 3 (paragraph 1), 19 and 21 of the constitution – in part already referred to – which grant the individual autonomy and dignity, in accordance with the dictates of the state under the rule of law; and articles 3 (paragraph 2), 4 and 34 of the constitution, which express the solidarity typical of the welfare state.

> Through criminal penalty, it is actually necessary to offer the convicted person the possibility of orienting his or her own existence towards respecting the existence of others. This does not mean pursuing coercive adaptation towards heteronomous behavioural standards or therefore justifying an attempt at undue personality manipulations, in order to effect a true change in individual identity *ab externo*. Rather, with all the guarantees of the welfare State under the rule of law, the aim must be to foster the subject's true integration, to be obtained by carrying out a programme of (re)integration based upon social education and individual emancipation, which is achieved through the performance of effective forms of cultural support. … The focal point of the issue regards the actual identification of the individual treatment of rehabilitation and its actual modes of application. (Moccia, 1992: 104)

Therefore, a merely retributive punishment (Moccia, 1992: 85 ff), as well as the negative aspects of general and of special prevention – founded upon the idea that the threat and infliction of punishment must work as a general and specific deterrent to the future commission of crimes – cannot be the punishment's ultimate end; in fact, in light of constitutional provisions, the effect of intimidation is legitimate only insofar as it is physiologically connected with the criminal law's statement and its enforceability (Moccia, 1992: 109).

And, yet, a criminal law policy that expresses indifference or intolerance towards the cultural factor is based upon a preventive or repressive function of the punishment. In it, the negative aspects of general and special prevention prevail, against the background of ethical assessments based on retribution (Grandi, 2007: 347 ff).

In this vein, it has been rightly stressed that

> some point out how the fact that cultural crimes are carried out by types of offender particularly inclined to commit the aforementioned crimes, and thus in particular need of energetic punitive "counter-thrusts", might not be without repercussions in terms of the punishment choices made by lawmakers.

> Likewise, the fact that these persons, who almost always come from countries characterized by very harsh systems of punishment, would in all likelihood be inclined to be intimidated by the mere promise of harsh punishments, may impact those clauses that threaten penalty. (Bernardi, 2010: 91)[4]

These views are, however, in clear conflict with the postulates of fact-orientated criminal law, as ours should be, and show dangerous affinities with a logic of offender-orientated criminal law.

It has been maintained that 'exemplary' punishment of cultural crimes has the purpose of 'placating the collective need for punishment', with the result of 'reaffirming "by the sword" the imperative nature of the positive order, and … the supremacy of the values of the majority over those of the minorities' (Bernardi, 2010: 92–3, footnote 138). This opinion distorts the idea of positive general prevention – which is to say, the idea according to which the punishment must have a function of cultural orientation and reinforce its members' agreement with the legal system's values. As far as the necessary respect for principles is concerned, this opinion cannot be shared. In fact, the provision, infliction and enforcement of 'exemplary' punishments conflict with the principle of proportionality, as well as with the principles of the inviolability of human dignity, of personal criminal liability and of the re-educational purpose of punishment. Moreover, excessive or disproportionate punishments cannot give rise to any cultural orientation so much as to results of disaffection with and rebellion against a system felt to be unjust. Finally, the punishment cannot be given purposes of social stabilization, because this would undeniably mean to manipulate the individual subjected to it (Bernardi, 2010: 93; Fornasari, 2008: 194).

The above political and criminal principles contained in the Italian constitution are binding upon the criminal lawmaker. They inevitably encourage rejecting an assimilationist model, which cannot be held compatible with a secular and pluralist system based upon the value of a substantial equality between individuals and upon the re-socializing function of punishment. In light of these principles, greater legitimacy is certainly enjoyed by a multiculturalist model, in the context of which the cultural conditioning undergone by those who commit unlawful acts is taken into consideration from a perspective of recognition.

The Choices of Italian Lawmakers in Pursuit of a 'Discriminatory Assimilationist' Orientation

The Italian legal system has been defined as one 'straddling the two models' (Basile, 2010: 63). Actually, there has been no dearth of signals politically favourable to recognizing cultural diversity. However, these have mostly been 'weak' signals: mere programmatic declarations, such as the Charter of the Values of Citizenship

4 The author subsequently criticizes such arguments.

and of Integration, adopted with a decree of the Ministry of the Interior in 2007, or legislative provisions of little significance from the standpoint of criminal law policy, such as the one permitting butchery in accordance with Islamic tradition by way of derogation from the criminal-law provisions put in place for the protection of animals (article 5 of Legislative Decree no. 333/1998) (Basile, 2010: 64).

For the purposes of identifying the politically prevailing orientation in the matter of cultural diversity, the legislative choices made in recent years precisely in the area of criminal law – with the introduction, respectively in 2006 and 2009, of the crimes of female genital mutilation (article 583 *bis* of the criminal code) and of the use of minors for begging (article 600 *octies* of the criminal code) – appear far more important.

The aforementioned provisions, introduced rather recently into the criminal code, are particularly symptomatic of Italian lawmakers' responses to the question from which this analysis began: what limit is there on the tolerability of restrictions within immigrant communities that are capable of undermining the fundamental rights of the persons they address, which is to say, mainly such vulnerable subjects as women and children?

With respect to the latter, the need has been rightly pointed out for the choices in the matter of multicultural conflicts to take two factors into account. On the one hand are the claims for recognition originating from minority groups, aimed at preserving their identity. On the other are the majority–minority and dominant–dominated relationships within the minority group. The multiculturalist 'remedies' must be kept from turning out to the detriment of those subjects who are doubly disadvantaged, above all because they belong to the minority and also because, within that setting, they are in a condition of particular weakness (Olivito, 2006: 131 ff. See also Bernardi, Pastore and Pugiotto, 2008: 25 ff; Grandi, 2007: 350).

In our legal system, the comprehensible and by all means worthy concern for safeguarding the rights of those subjects was, however, translated into gravely intolerant punitive choices (Bernardi, 2010: 14 ff), in which the cultural matrix of the conduct was clearly placed as virtually the only basis for a considerably harshened punitive response.

This is particularly evident with reference to the case of female genital mutilation (article 583 *bis* of the criminal code) – to be discussed shortly – but also as regards the crime provided for by article 600 *octies* of the criminal code (*Impiego di minori nell'accattonaggio*) (Scalia, 2009: 1207–22; Scoletta, 2009: 123–32; Valsecchi, 2009: 275–82). This crime is due to the 2009 'security package',[5] marked by the now-usual scaremongering and a clearly discriminatory

5 The 2009 'security package' is composed of Law no. 94/2009 and Decree Law no. 11/2009, converted with modifications in Law no. 38/2009. It is part of the last years' decrees and legislative measures directed to ensure public safety. From the political–criminal point of view, the 'security packages' are orientated to deterrence and they sacrifice individual

logic. This logic may be seen in the following actions: the transformation into felony of the violation earlier in force, contained in the abrogated article 671 of the criminal code and already virtually fallen into disuse; the provision of a more severe punishment; and the categorization of the new crime among those against the person. The importance of the legal interest protected by article 600 *octies* of the criminal code, specified as the 'inviolability of the "right of the child"' (de Maglie, 2010: 51), cannot be denied. However, the regulatory action briefly described betrays the intent to criminalize a behaviour corresponding to a custom deeply rooted in Roma culture through the symbolic introduction of an *ad hoc* provision. This poses significant problems of systematic coordination with crimes of domestic violence (article 572 of the criminal code) and of reducing to or maintaining in slavery or servitude (article 600 of the criminal code).

Recent immigration policies have shown Italian lawmakers' clearly intolerant orientation. Consider, in particular, the introduction, with the 2008 'security package', of the so-called aggravating circumstance of clandestinity (article 61, no. 11 *bis*, of the criminal code),[6] as well as the 2009 provision of the disputed crime of illegal entry and stay in state territory.[7]

We may then understand why the Italian model has been effectively qualified as a 'discriminatory assimilationist' model (de Maglie, 2010: 35).[8] It therefore clashes with the criminal law policy principles of a welfare state under the rule of law, grounded in the constitution which, as explained above, should inform lawmakers' use of the criminal law instrument in this area as well.

The Special Case of Female Genital Mutilation (Article 583 *bis* of the Criminal Code)

The practice of female genital mutilation is, by virtually unanimous opinion, the typical example of a culturally motivated crime (de Maglie, 2010: 37 ff). It is in fact a set of behaviours[9] carried out by members of a minority group – in

guarantees. On the inadequacy of the 'security' concept as a legal interest to protect with the criminal law, see Moccia, 2007: 117 ff; Cavaliere, 2009: 43 ff.

6 Later declared illegitimate by the Constitutional Court with judgment no. 249/2010 (Bernardi, 2010: 77–8).

7 The Parliament, with Law no. 67/2014, has recently delegated the government to abrogate (and to convert in administrative infringement) this crime, which Law no. 94/2009 had introduced in article 10 *bis* of Legislative Decree no. 286/1998. The legislative delegation has not been implemented yet.

8 For a criminological criticism on the Italian model, see Pavarini, 2006: 176–8.

9 On the subject, see the classification elaborated by the World Health Organization and published in World Health Organization, *Female Genital Mutilation Report of WHO Technical Working Group Geneva*, June 2000.

particular, to the extent of interest here, by immigrants[10] – in keeping with the traditions of the culture to which they belong. These behaviours, however, are disapproved of by the host legal system because they are susceptible to harming the fundamental interests of the women who undergo it: their individual safety and, where mutilation is a tool of control over female sexuality, their personal dignity as well. If performed on minors, genital mutilation then impacts the minor's right to a harmonious development of her own personality (Basile, 2007: 1339; Canestrari, 2006: 153; Mantovani, 2011: 159; Longobardo, 2011: 128).

To combat this phenomenon, Italian lawmakers issued Law no. 7/2006, establishing 'provisions concerning prevention and prohibition of female genital mutilation'. The law introduced into the criminal code article 583 *bis*, which punishes these practices, and article 583 *ter*, which provides for the accessory sanction of excluding healthcare professionals from the profession – for three to ten years – if convicted of that crime.[11]

Article 583 *bis* of the criminal code provides for two distinct crimes. The first paragraph speaks of 'anyone, in the absence of therapeutic needs, who causes a mutilation of the female genital organs' and is punishable with four to twelve years' imprisonment. The provision also provides a definition of the sanctioned practices, specifying that '[f]or the purposes of this article, the term "female genital organ mutilation practices" shall be understood as clitoridectomy, excision, infibulation, and any other practice that causes effects of this type'; the closing clause, as it is open to similar cases, inevitably undermines the determinacy of the crime (Mantovani, 2011: 158; Fornasari, 2008: 187). This is a common and freeform offence which can be committed by anyone with any form of conduct. The state of mind (*mens rea*) is basic intent, given that consciousness of and will to commit the crime established by the provision is sufficient. There is possible omissive liability borne by the holder of a custodial position (for example, the parent that does not prevent the mutilation performed by others on his or her own daughter) (Longobardo, 2011: 129). For this crime, the absence of therapeutic needs constitutes a negative assumption of the conduct (Fornasari, 2008: 187).

The second paragraph, covering those cases where the first paragraph does not apply, provides as follows:

> Anyone who, in the absence of therapeutic needs, causes, for the purposes of impairing sexual function, injuries to the female genital organs other than those indicated in the first paragraph, giving rise to illness of the body or mind, shall be punished with three to six years' imprisonment. The punishment is diminished by up to two thirds if the injury is slight.

10 This practice is diffused in different countries of sub-Saharan Africa, in Egypt and in some Asiatic regions. See Basile, 2007: 1337.

11 This sanction is an automatic consequence of the principal one.

The text specifically requires the purpose of impairing sexual functions. This would appear to correspond to the requirement of a specific intent, which would end up thwarting the regulation's applicability. Indeed, in most cases, the practice is performed for other socio-cultural purposes, such as, for example, improving the woman's personal and social status, also with a view to acquiring the role of spouse and mother (Fiandaca and Musco, 2007: 5. For a different opinion: Mantovani, 2011: 156).[12]

The second paragraph establishes a mitigating factor, operative in the event of slight injury. It refers to the sole case regulated therein (Longobardo, 2011: 131; Gentilomo, Piga and Kustermann, 2008: 23). The third paragraph, on the other hand, provides for an aggravating factor, applicable to both crimes under the previous paragraphs, if committed against a minor or if the offence is driven by profit.

The fourth paragraph establishes accessory punishments of the withdrawal of parental authority, and the permanent disqualification from administering support, protection or care of minors, if the offence is committed, respectively, by the parent or by the guardian.

Lastly, the final paragraph establishes the prosecution of the crime when it 'is committed abroad by an Italian citizen or by a foreign national residing in Italy, or against an Italian citizen or a foreign national residing in Italy. In this case, the offender is punished upon request of the Minister of Justice' (Fornasari, 2008: 191).

Rather than making a critical interpretation of the provisions just mentioned,[13] our aim here is to draw attention to the significance, in terms of criminal law policy, of the choices they express, clearly orientated – as was already underlined – towards intolerance of 'cultural diversity'. In this regard, there has been discussion of an ethnocentric attitude (Longobardo, 2011: 132), aimed at 'the rigid re-affirmation of civilization's undisputable superiority over barbarism, with no openness to understanding the reasons behind what is different' (Fornasari, 2008: 193).

To be sure, it is absolutely necessary to recognize the need to protect under criminal law legal interests of fundamental importance, such as those undermined by the practice of female genital mutilation. However, the provisions introduced for this purpose by Italian lawmakers are marked by sterile symbolism and unfair

12 It is no accident that article 583 *bis* of the criminal code has been applied only one time. In fact, since 2006, only a woman has been condemned for being guilty of violating article 583 *bis*, paragraph 2: Court of Verona, 14 April 2010. See Pecorella, 2011: 838 ff, Bernardi, 2006: 81 ff; Basile, 2008: 188; Fornasari, 2008: 192–3. As to the question whether the puncture of the clitoris, as a harmless and symbolic alternative to female genital mutilation, is prohibited by the Italian Law no. 7/2006, see Di Pietro, Teleman and Faggioni, 2012: 1–3.

13 For a detailed comment of article 583 *bis* of the criminal code, see also Basile, 2006: 678–92; Cesqui, 2005: 749–59; de Maglie, 2010: 36 ff, 49 ff.

repressive rigor, with all that follows in terms of systematic inconsistency and potential ineffectiveness.

The needs of protection arising from the phenomenon of female genital mutilation would not have required introducing *ad hoc* crimes into our legal system. The provisions regarding personal injury, already in force, would be enough to ensure a sufficiently severe punitive response to these behaviours (de Maglie, 2010: 41). The punishment actually to be inflicted might then be mitigated on the basis of a fair consideration of the actor's cultural motivation, if that could be capable of reducing his liability. In this regard, it has been convincingly affirmed that

> if the need were truly felt to guarantee, without a doubt, protection from genital mutilation actions, … the fact that they rose to the already existing crime of serious injury could have been specified in art. 583, with an express addition to the cases already contained in the provision; but the impression is precisely that this was not felt to be sufficient, and there was the desire to pursue further, symbolic ends. (Fornasari, 2008: 195)

The symbolism of the introduction into the criminal code of article 583 *bis*, with its heightened deterrence function, is confirmed by the particular severity of the punishment or treatment provided for therein: female genital mutilations are punished more severely than any other injury of similar seriousness. However, this unequal treatment is not based on the greater social damage they result in, coinciding entirely with personal injury, unless out of cultural motivation. Clearly, it is this latter element against which the lawmakers intended to strike a blow in a perspective of offender-orientated, rather than fact-orientated, criminal law.[14]

It cannot be denied that every person's right to his or her own cultural identity cannot entail sacrificing (others') fundamental rights. However, the response to culturally orientated crimes by a fact-orientated criminal law cannot be exclusively founded upon or aggravated on the basis of the cultural factor. Otherwise, the general principles of criminal law – such as fragmentation and subsidiarity, materiality, offensiveness, personality of criminal liability and social integration – would be violated. In other words, cultural conditioning may be an element of speciality with respect to facts that would have at any rate been of relevance under criminal law even in its absence. This takes place, for example, in the relationship between female genital mutilation and personal injury. In these cases, the cultural factor cannot legitimately be the basis for aggravating the punishment or treatment in comparison with the corresponding culturally 'neutral'

14 See Grande, 2009–2010: 15–31, who suggests that only a comprehensive approach towards all modifications of sexual organs (for example, female and male circumcision, breast augmentation), using a single, not a double, standard will make the human rights discourse on sexual organs' modifications less imperialistic, more effective and less assimilating.

crime, unless this impacts the offensive content of the crime (Grandi, 2007: 351 ff). However, the latter hypothesis appears unlikely: 'the "cultural factor" underlying the offender's action does not appear able to significantly impact the extent of the damage, which tends to remain such regardless of the motivation underlying the injury event, and regardless perhaps of the objective "cultural characteristic" of the event in question' (Bernardi, 2010, 84–5). Lacking this unlikely impact of cultural conditioning on the objective level of the crime, the provision of a more severe punishment ends up being based solely on the offender's inner attitude, on 'the subject's motives connected with his cultural background, an element of no small importance in evaluating the fact, but too intangible on the one hand, and surreptitiously discriminatory on the other' (Fornasari, 2009: 181).

However, one thus ends up assigning to criminal law a promotional or pedagogical function that does not belong to it (Fornasari, 2008: 194) and compromising the rationality and consistency of the criminal law system. In this regard, it has rightly been observed that, given the regulations in force,

> whoever performs a cliteridectomy on a fifteen-year-old girl, in line with the traditions imposed by the culture of her ethnic group, risks sixteen years' imprisonment; whoever, with no criminal record, in order to take revenge on his girlfriend who cheated on him and derided him in public, kicks her in the abdomen and causes a laceration to the uterus that will keep her from procreating, risks at most three years! (de Maglie, 2010: 42)

Also, in terms of effectiveness, it must be recognized that the symbolic use of the criminal law instrument is unable to actually protect the rights in play, and women's health above all, because excision is a practice for which 'the restrictive force of community sanction has thus far been shown to prevail over the deterrent function of the criminal penalty' (Olivito, 2006: 165) and, moreover, because

> both the legislative provision of autonomous crime and the judicial prosecution of the intervention risk provoking isolation of the community that practises it; outside action might be perceived as discriminatory and an imposition of assimilatory attitudes, because it is conducted unilaterally, which is to say without the necessary dialogue with the interested parties and groups. (Olivito, 2006: 166)

On the other hand, in view of the legitimate aims of positive prevention and compliance with the principle of subsidiarity of the criminal law intervention, it would be desirable to see 'thoughtful education and information campaigns on the physical and psychic consequences of excision, non-arrogant initiatives raising awareness of its negative repercussions, and, above all, appropriate actions to eliminate the socioeconomic obstacles that provide the context in which they take place' (Olivito, 2006: 166). From this standpoint, Law no. 7/2006 was a missed opportunity because, although it contained provisions in this sense (Turillazzi and Fineschi, 2007: 98–101), it did not establish adequate financial coverage to make them truly enforceable (Fornasari, 2008: 192), nor did it prepare suitable specific measures to protect the women and children who are the victims of genital mutilation.[15]

Towards a Possible (Fair) Categorization of the Cultural Factor in the Structure of the Crime

What importance must then be given to the 'cultural factor' in criminal law's assessments of the three elements of the crime – typical nature (*tipicità*), unlawfulness and liability – for it to be possible to deem the corresponding choices of criminal law policy to be constitutional?

To respond briefly to this question (Masarone, 2014), we shall say that, especially when fundamental interests are in play, the place where the impact of culture in criminal law can more properly be considered – with a view to tolerance or recognition, in line with a legal system of a welfare state under the rule of law – appears to be the third element of the crime: criminal liability (Moccia, 1992: 92). A fundamental role, then, must be ascribed to the judgment of the punishment fitting the crime in actual terms (sentencing).

Indeed, in terms of the typical nature, the need for the criminal law to intervene cannot be denied in cases where committing culturally conditioned behaviours really endangers or offends legal interests worthy of protection under criminal law. As concerns unlawfulness, justifications should operate in relation to culturally conditioned crimes no differently from what takes place for every other type of crime of relevance under criminal law. The balance of interests that these justifications create should, as always, be connected to the individualism/solidarity perspective typical of our constitutional system, and to the interests safeguarded in it (Moccia, 1989: 1012).

In assessing the offender's personal liability, cultural conditioning may take on importance above all where the cultural diversity of the offender has influenced awareness of the unlawfulness of the act, thus placing him or her in a condition of mistake (or ignorance) of (criminal) law (article 5 of the criminal code) which, as is known, is a defence when it is inevitable (Constitutional Court judgment no. 364/1988). The inevitability of error or of ignorance, which excludes being able to punish the offender or hold him or her liable, must be ascertained in actual terms. Objective or objective/subjective factors impact this assessment in accordance with the known recommendations provided by the Constitutional Court in judgment no. 364/1988. These factors must refer specifically to the situation and the offender in question. Of importance in this regard are

15 For instance, recognition of refugee status to women who aim to escape or to deliver minor daughters from the risk of suffering the practices in question (Brunelli, 2008: 219).

> cases in which the fact was committed by an offender who, for instance, has come to our country only very recently, or still has little or no knowledge of the language, or has no autonomy from his/her own ethnic group, and for these or other similar reasons is unacquainted with the rule and has yet to acquire the tools to learn it or to become aware of its existence. (Fornasari, 2008: 198)[16]

At times, the culturally conditioned subject is aware of the unlawful nature of his or her own conduct, yet puts the rule – ethical, religious, social, and cultural in the broad sense – before the prohibition or before the order established by the legal system locally in force. In these cases, the question to be resolved, on the level of personal liability, regards the limits of excusability of a crime of this kind. This is done in the presence of a conflict between duties imposed by different kind of regulations binding to various degrees.

In this case, it is necessary to take into account the grounding of personal liability in criminal law policy. Moreover, the conflict in question produces inevitable effects on the offender's motivational process and therefore on his or her need for punishment – to be understood as the secular need for re-education. Therefore, reliance upon the category of the 'non-demandability' (*inesigibilità*) (Fornasari, 1990) of lawful alternative behaviour appears entirely consistent. This might result in a graduation of the offender's liability and thus in a mitigation of the punishment to which the offender will be subjected in actual terms. The committed crime would still remain complete in its structure.[17]

In this sense, even aside from introducing an *ad hoc* provision (or provisions) that, variously qualified from the dogmatic standpoint, provides adequate recognition of the cultural conditioning the offender may have undergone,[18] *de jure condito* the institution of judicial commensuration of the punishment (article 133 of the criminal code) takes on importance (Fornasari, 2008: 199–200).

References

Basile, F. (2006). La nuova incriminazione delle pratiche di mutilazione degli organi genitali femminili. Il commento. *Diritto penale e processo*, 678–92.

16 See for example Court of Cassation (*Cassazione Penale*), section VI, judgment no. 43646/2011, with remarks by D'Ippolito, 2012: 3711–20.

17 About the employment of the 'non-demandability' category in multicultural conflicts, see, among others, Bernardi, 2006: 94; Fornasari, 2009: 186; de Maglie, 2010: 229 ff; Basile, 2010: 417 ff; De Francesco, 2006: 143 ff.

18 See, particularly, de Maglie, 2010: 253 ff. She proposes to introduce a 'cultural' not-punishment cause, operating with reference to crimes that don't injure the 'basic immunities', when the offence is committed among adult, consenting and able-to-consent subjects.

Basile, F. (2007). Società multiculturali, immigrazione e reati culturalmente motivati (comprese le mutilazioni genitali femminili). *Rivista italiana di diritto e procedura penale*, 1296–345.

Basile, F. (2008). Premesse per uno studio sui rapporti tra diritto penale e società multiculturale. Uno sguardo alla giurisprudenza europea sui c.d. reati culturalmente motivati. *Rivista italiana di diritto e procedura penale*, 149–212.

Basile, F. (2010). *Immigrazione e reati culturalmente motivati. Il diritto penale nelle società multiculturali*. Milano: Giuffrè.

Bernardi, A. (2006). Società multiculturale e 'reati culturali'. Spunti per una riflessione. In Dolcini, E. and Paliero, C.E. (eds) *Studi in onore di Giorgio Marinucci*, I, *Teoria del diritto penale criminologia e politica criminale*, 45–98. Milano: Giuffrè.

Bernardi, A., Pastore, B. and Pugiotto, A. (2008). Legalità penale: tre atti di una crisi. In Bernardi, A., Pastore, B. and Pugiotto, A. (eds) *Legalità penale e crisi del diritto, oggi. Un percorso interdisciplinare*, 3–27. Milano: Giuffrè.

Bernardi, A. (2010). *Il 'fattore culturale' nel sistema penale*. Torino: Giappichelli.

Brunelli, G. (2008). Prevenzione e divieto delle mutilazioni genitali femminili: genealogia (e limiti) di una legge. In Bernardi, A., Pastore, B. and Pugiotto, A. (eds) *Legalità penale e crisi del diritto, oggi. Un percorso interdisciplinare*, 203–30.

Canestrari, S. (2006). *Laicità e diritto penale nelle democrazie costituzionali*. In Dolcini, E. and Paliero, C.E. (eds) *Studi in onore di Giorgio Marinucci*, I, *Teoria del diritto penale criminologia e politica criminale*, 139–67.

Cavaliere, A. (2009). Può la 'sicurezza' costituire un bene giuridico o una funzione del diritto penale? *Critica del diritto*, 43–63.

Cesqui, E. (2005). Le mutilazioni genitali femminili e la legge. *Questione giustizia*, 749–59.

De Francesco, G. (2006). Multiculturalismo e diritto penale nazionale. In Bernardi, A. (ed.) *Multiculturalismo, diritti umani e pena*, 137–63. Milano: Giuffrè.

de Maglie, C. (2010). *I reati culturalmente motivati. Ideologie e modelli penali*. Pisa: ETS.

Di Pietro, M.L., Teleman, A.A. and Faggioni, M.P. (2012) Female genital mutilation of minors in Italy: Is a harmless and symbolic alternative justified? *Italian Journal of Public Health*, 9(3), 1–3.

D'Ippolito, E. (2012). *Kulturnormen* ed inevitabilità dell'errore sul divieto: la Corte di Cassazione riconosce l'errore determinato da 'fattori culturali' come causa di esclusione della colpevolezza. *Cassazione penale*, 3711–20.

Fiandaca, G. and Musco, E. (2007). *Diritto penale. Parte speciale*, II(I), 2nd edn, *Addenda*. Bologna: Zanichelli.

Fornasari, G. (1990). *Il principio di inesigibilità nel diritto penale*. Padova: Cedam.

Fornasari, G. (2008). Mutilazioni genitali femminili e multiculturalismo: premesse per un discorso giuspenalistico. In Bernardi, A., Pastore, B. and Pugiotto, A. (eds) *Legalità penale e crisi del diritto, oggi. Un percorso interdisciplinare*, 179–202.

Fornasari, G. (2009). Le categorie dogmatiche del diritto penale davanti alla sfida del multiculturalismo. In Hassemer, W., Kempf, E. and Moccia, S. (eds) *In dubio pro libertate. Festschrift für Klaus Volk zum 65.Geburtstag*, 177–91. München: C.H. Beck.

Gentilomo, A., Piga, A. and Kustermann, A. (2008). Mutilazioni genitali femminili: la risposta giudiziaria. *Rivista italiana di medicina legale*, 13–33.

Grande, E. (2009–2010). Hegemonic Human Rights: the Case of Female Circumcision. *Archivio antropologico mediterraneo* on line, XII/XIII, 12(2), 15–31.

Grandi, C. (2007). Diritto penale e società multiculturali: stato dell'arte e prospettive *de iure condendo*. In De Francesco, G., Piemontese, C. and Venafro, E. (eds) *Religione e religioni: prospettive di tutela, tutela della libertà*, 327–71. Torino: Giappichelli.

Kymlicka, W. (1995). *Multicultural Citizenship*. New York: Oxford University Press Inc.

Longobardo, C. (2011). Le mutilazioni genitali femminili. In Cilardo, A. (ed.) *La tutela dei minori di cultura islamica nell'area mediterranea. Aspetti sociali, giuridici e medici*, 117–33. Napoli: Edizioni Scientifiche Italiane.

Mantovani, F. (2011). *Diritto penale. Parte speciale*, I, *I delitti contro la persona*. Padova: Cedam.

Masarone, V. (2014). L'incidenza del fattore culturale sul sistema penale tra scelte politico-criminali ed implicazioni dommatiche. Diritto penale e processo, 1237–50.

Moccia, S. (1989). Sui principi normativi di riferimento per un sistema penale teleologicamente orientato. *Rivista italiana di diritto e procedura penale*, 1006–24.

Moccia, S. (1992). *Il diritto penale tra essere e valore. Funzione della pena e sistematica teleologica*. Napoli: Edizioni Scientifiche Italiane.

Moccia, S. (2007). Alcune riflessioni su sicurezza e controllo penale, in Bevere, A. (ed.) *Questione meridionale e questione criminale. Non solo emergenze*, 117–33. Napoli: Edizioni Scientifiche Italiane.

Olivito, E. (2006). *Minoranze culturali e identità multiple. I diritti dei soggetti vulnerabili*. Roma: Aracne.

Pavarini, M. (2006). Criminalità e pena nella società multiculturale. In Bernardi, A. (ed.) *Multiculturalismo, diritti umani e pena*, 165–78.

Pecorella, C. (2011). Mutilazioni genitali femminili: la prima sentenza di condanna. *Rivista italiana di diritto e procedura penale*, 838–66.

Scalia, M.E. (2009). Le modifiche in materia di tutela dei minori. *Diritto penale e processo*, 1207–22.

Scoletta, M. (2009). Nuovo delitto di impiego di minori nell'accattonaggio. In Corbetta, S., Della Bella, A. and Gatta, G.L. (eds) *Sistema penale e 'sicurezza pubblica': le riforme del 2009. L. 15 luglio 2009, n. 94 e d.l. 23 febbraio 2009, n. 11, conv., con modif., dalla L. 23 aprile 2009, n. 38*, 123–32. Milanofiori, Assago: IPSOA.

Turillazzi, E. and Fineschi, V. (2007). Female genital mutilation: The ethical impact of the new Italian law. *Journal of Medical Ethics*, 33(2), 98–101.
Valsecchi, A. (2009). Due ulteriori delitti a tutela della vittima minorenne. In Mazza, O. and Viganò, F. (eds) *Il 'pacchetto sicurezza' 2009. (Commento al d.l. 23 febbraio 2009, n. 11 conv. in legge 23 aprile 2009, n. 38 e alla legge 15 luglio 2009, n. 94)*, 275–82. Torino: Giappichelli.
Van Broeck, J. (2001). Cultural Defence and Culturally Motivated Crimes (Cultural Offences). *European Journal of Crime, Criminal Law and Criminal Justice*, 9(1), 1–32.

Chapter 8
From Culture to Patriarchy: Recent Changes in Judicial Reasoning and in Normative Classifications of Multicultural Conflicts

Ilenia Ruggiu

Using Culture, Using Gender

Postmodernism has introduced to the philosophical debate the idea that everything is 'discourse'. According to postmodernism, the perception of reality we have does not rest on any ontological certainty but is a narrative construct, a web of words in which we are immersed and which forges our sense of reality. Shifting from one discourse to another can change completely how we interpret the same facts, as reality does not exist *per se*, but is created through words and concepts.

Having this philosophical framework in mind, this chapter explores what happens in the law when a different discourse emerges. Specifically, this chapter aims to explore the emergence of gender discourse in the context of what are commonly called multicultural conflicts or multicultural litigation, and how this discourse is prevailing over culture as a category to interpret a given behaviour. In summary, cultural conflicts are being re-scripted as gender conflict by judges and legislatures in Italy and comparatively.

It appears necessary to take a step back to better understand how the law deals with the different discourses that, in the twentieth century, shaped social dynamics.

With Marxism, class was the main category for reading social life, and social conflicts were cast as class conflicts, determined by what Marx called 'economic structure'. With the introduction of social rights, post-Second World War constitutions reflected how the class narrative was incorporated by the law.

The discourse of class was slowly abandoned in Western societies after the collapse of communist ideology, symbolically marked by the fall of the Berlin Wall in 1989. Another category emerged to explain social life and conflicts: culture. The battle of proletarian and subaltern classes to obtain access to economic resources became, in post-materialist societies (Inglehart, 1977), a battle for the symbolic recognition of a different way of seeing the world (Eisenberg and Kymlicka, 2011). This change, along with demographic changes in Western societies,[1] led scholars

1 This demographic change is due to immigration and globalization, which have increased the transnational movements of people.

to a new paradigm and narrative: culture. Some scholars entered with a pessimistic approach, using culture to explain a new clash of civilizations (Hungtington, 1996) or maintaining that culture was a modern-day substitute for race (Balibar, 1991); other scholars linked the new cultural trend to a more optimistic approach, seeing multiculturalism as a way to revitalize social life and to enlarge constitutional pluralism (Kymlicka, 1995). Again, the law was sensitive to this change of paradigm and started incorporating cultural rights and multicultural clauses. First recognized internationally in 1966,[2] cultural rights began to appear in constitutions on the national level. Nowadays, around 50 constitutions of the 193 existing in the world recognize cultural rights, and about 30 recognize a principle of cultural diversity or have a multicultural clause.

But when culture seemed to have conquered all the social narratives, another category began to emerge on the social and legal landscape. While first it was class, then culture, is it gender's time now? Actually, gender is not a completely new narrative. In fact, even when class was the unquestioned category for reading social life, feminism cast into doubt the idea that class oppression was the structural one (Eisenstein, 1977). According to Carla Lonzi, one of the most influential Italian feminists, the oldest and most structural oppression was gender oppression: 'the oppression of women is the result of centuries: capitalism inherited rather than created it' (Lonzi, 1982). According to this view, and in line with international feminism (Firestone, 1970; Mitchell, 1973), patriarchy was far more structured and oppressive than capitalism, as capitalism was just one of its by-products.

This intuition, that feminism has had since the 1970s, seems to be having an impact in the present legal context. In fact, the category of gender is increasingly consolidating its influence in the legal system. One proof of this is the shift from culture to gender, noticeable in the context of multicultural law and jurisprudence, which this chapter aims to explore with special regard to the Italian setting (for the international one, see Rao, 1995). My reflection focuses on the emergence of the gender discourse within multiculturalism, but this trend is part of a broader context that shows the law's increasing attention to the existence of a structural oppression of women: patriarchy. The appearance of what I call 'anti-patriarchal legislation' and 'anti-patriarchal jurisprudence' is the most evident proof of the law's aim to combat this structural oppression that concerns women. To provide just a few examples of what I mean by the terms anti-patriarchal legislation or jurisprudence, we may consider the recent legislation enacted in Italy on the killing of women. To deal with the rising rate of women being killed by their partners in acts of domestic violence, Italian Law no. 119/2013 created a new kind of killing, called

2 International Covenant on Civil and Political Rights, G.A. 2200A (XXI), articles 27 and 21 UN GAOR, Supp. No. 16, at 52, UN Doc. A/6316 (16 December 1966): 'In those States in which ethnic, religious or linguistic minorities exist, persons belonging to such minorities shall not be denied the right, in community with the other members of their group, to enjoy their own culture, to profess and practise their own religion, or to use their own language'.

femminicidio ('femicide', term invented by Caputi and Russell, 1990), with stiffer punishments for those guilty of committing it.

Another example of anti-patriarchal legislation is the criminal prosecution of stalking. First introduced in California in 1990, laws punishing stalkers have spread to several legal systems. Italy joined the list in 2009 with the introduction of article 612 *bis* in the Italian criminal code (by Decree Law no. 11 of 23 February 2009).

Moving from legislation to case-law, an example of anti-patriarchal jurisprudence may be found in that concerning battered woman syndrome. First theorized in the context of psychology (Walker, 1979), battered woman syndrome began to be used by judges in the United States several decades later (Dalton and Schneider, 2001). In several cases in which a woman had killed her partner fearing she would be battered to the point that her life was in danger, judges recognized a self-defence justification, acquitting the woman. Although Italian judges have never recognized battered woman syndrome as a defence, they did invoke it to mitigate the crime. In 2000, the *Santa Morina* case was brought to court: a woman had spent 23 years with a violent husband, whom she killed. Although the public prosecutor had asked for 24 years' imprisonment, the trial judge sentenced the woman to 11 years. The Court of Appeal of Catania in Sicily sentenced the woman to 14 years, which was confirmed by the Italian Supreme Court. More recently, the judges' attitude seems to be much more benevolent, as they have begun to recognize the particular position of women in a context of systemic violence. To quote just one of the more recent judgments, the Court of Appeal of Rome, on 22 April 2014, acquitted on the grounds of legitimate self-defence a woman who stabbed her husband and threw his body into the Tiber after suffering 10 years of physical attacks and having risked being suffocated by him.

Within this broader context, multicultural law is a very effective case to be studied in order to test the emergence of the gender narrative and its translation by legislation and judgments into gender arguments.

Since the appearance of the famous argument sustained by Susan Okin in her article *Is multiculturalism bad for women?* (Okin, 1999), the category of gender has appeared to be in potential conflict with that of culture. In fact, Okin questioned the 'progressive' nature of multiculturalism with the main argument that most cultural practices were, in fact, patriarchal practices. This position suggests that when social conflicts run along the lines of culture, and women are involved, we should also pay attention to another dimension: gender.

Okin's thesis polarized the debate of feminism versus multiculturalism. Scholars started to see in gender equality a limit upon cultural recognition (Volpp, 2001; Phillips, 2003; Song, 2007; Kukathas, 2001; Shachar, 2001) and to look at women as minorities within minorities (Eisenberg and Spinner-Halev, 2005). Again, the law remained not insensitive to this change of paradigm. Some constitutions have made gender an explicit limit upon cultural rights, such as section 35 of the Canadian Constitution Act, 1982, which, although willing to recognize aboriginal rights, is ready to obstruct their interpretation if it goes against gender equality.[3] Furthermore, many courts began refusing to recognize cultural practices where they affected women's rights.

The shift from class to culture to gender produces enormous differences in the social perception of a behaviour and consequently in the legal framework. For instance, if we use class to read the case of female genital mutilation, this practice appears to be a sign of the structural oppression that African countries suffered during colonization, an oppression which kept them from entering modernity and which fostered the conservation of tribal practices. In accepting this discourse, the action of the law should be – instead of simply criminalize female genital mutilation – to use the tools of redistributive justice to fill the economic gap that created the situation of ignorance, making it difficult to abolish the phenomenon.

On the contrary, if we enter another narrative using the category of culture, female genital mutilation may be seen as a set of rituals to establish sex and fertility rituals, and may be regarded with anthropological relativism. In accepting this discourse, the law should generally permit the practices as part of the group's cultural identity, intervening only in those more difficult cases (infibulation) in which other rights are involved.

Moving from a cultural narrative to one of gender, female genital mutilation appears as a practice expressing the will to exercise control over women's bodies. Within this discourse, it is perfectly sensible to maintain the differentiation between the legal treatments of male and female circumcision, as male circumcision appears to be an act of empowerment of the male baby.[4] A complete ban even of the milder practices is also reasonable, as they violate a specific juridical interest: the woman's dignity.

These three very different classifications influence the law, leading to very different legal results in the treatment of a single fact.

In the following paragraphs, I will analyse how in the legal language, and particularly in multicultural case-law, there has been a shift from culture to gender when a woman is involved. I will focus on the cases of female genital mutilation, honour killing, use of the burqa, and polygamy, using a comparative methodology, while also paying attention to the treatment of those practices chiefly in the Italian legal context.

---

3 After stating in subsection 1 'The existing aboriginal and treaty rights of the aboriginal peoples of Canada are hereby recognized and affirmed', subsection 4 of article 35 states: 'Notwithstanding any other provision of this Act, the aboriginal and treaty rights referred to in subsection 1 are guaranteed equally to male and female persons'.

4 As intersectional theory shows, several categories and discourses can often be applied to read the same fact and it is correct to have them all in mind when interpreting it. Generally, however, the law does not consider all the discourses at once and tends to embrace just one, drawing different legal consequences from it.

Female Genital Mutilation

The strongest example of the shifting of discourses from culture to gender emerges in the debate around female genital mutilation (FGM). With this name, Western democracies label a set of very diverse practices, all characterized by involving an alteration of the genitals. According to the World Health Organization, there are four kinds of FGM: infibulation, excision (of the labia minora and the clitoris), circumcision (of the clitoris) and a fourth type, including milder forms, such as extracting one or two drops of blood from the clitoris.

Although female genital mutilation was until recently perceived by the law as an age-old cultural practice, it is starting to be classified more often as a patriarchal practice, with entirely different legal consequences.

When the first cases of female genital mutilation began to appear in Italy in the 1990s, Italian judges tended to act as anthropologists, giving much consideration to the practice's cultural dimension. Sometimes they acquitted the parents and sometimes they mitigated their sentence.[5]

The legislature took action against this trend in the judiciary, which was considered too mild and too oblivious to the oppression of women that FGM implied. Italian Law no. 7/2006 introduced a new crime to article 583 *bis* of the criminal code. This article sentences people carrying out any kind of FGM to six to twelve years' imprisonment and to the loss of parental rights.

The new criminal provision received both praise (long detention was seen as a way to eradicate the practice) and criticism (over its establishment of an unreasonable detention time). In this regard, many scholars stressed the disproportion of article 583 *bis* with respect to article 582 of the criminal code, which punishes other violations of bodily integrity: the paradox is that if someone, motivated, say, by hate, were to cut off a person's leg or arm, he or she may be sentenced to a maximum of eight years' imprisonment, while an excision of the clitoris motivated by culture may result in a 12-year sentence (Brunelli, 2008). But other scholars affirmed that the high penalty was justified because the law was protecting a new constitutional interest: women's dignity (Fattibene, 2012). The aim of the practice (sexual control over women), and the fact that it was practised on women, was, according to this position, enough to justify the disproportion. What happened next seems to confirm this position.

Indeed, the UN resolution adopted on 20 December 2012,[6] which contains a blanket ban of any kind of FGM, based this ban on two arguments: the 'gender/patriarchal argument', according to which any FGM is an oppressive practice against women and girls, and the 'harm argument', according to which FGM causes irreversible and irreparable harm to a woman's health, both physically and psychologically. The resolution never mentions FGM as a cultural practice.

5 Juvenile Court of Turin (Tribunale dei minori di Torino), 17 July 1997.

6 A/Res/67/146, *Intensifying global efforts for the elimination of female genital mutilation*, adopted by the 67th Section of the General Assembly.

FGM is defined as a 'harmful practice' five times and a form of gender 'violence' nine times.

This new classification had immediate consequences on the Italian legal system. Following this new approach, Italian judges in 2013 began to classify FGM as 'gender violence', abandoning their previous classification as a cultural practice.

Under the resolution's influence, Italian judges began to accept asylum applications from women at risk of undergoing FGM procedures, using the 'gender/anti-patriarchal argument'. The following judicial reasonings are good examples of this.

According to the Court of Appeal of Catania,[7] a woman should obtain asylum in Italy:

> having suffered persecutory acts connected with her belonging to the female gender … FGMs are a form of moral and material violence, gender discriminatory violence based on belonging to the female gender … FGMs are inflicted upon women and girls because they are of the female gender, in order to assert power over them and to control their sexuality. The practice, then, is part of a broader model of discrimination against women and girls in a certain society … Recently, the question has been examined by the Third Commission of the UN General Assembly, which adopted the Resolution *Intensifying global efforts for the elimination of female genital mutilation.* The final adoption of the document will be by the General Assembly in its section on 20 December.

According to the Court of Appeal of Cagliari: 'acts of female genital mutilation are persecutory acts motivated by belonging to a given social group'.[8]

Both the UN resolution and the more recent Italian judgments make no mention of the custom's cultural dimension. Applying Marx's idea of structure and superstructure to gender, it appears that the discovery of the 'base' or 'structure' (patriarchy) aims to consider culture merely as a 'superstructure', and therefore cases of women experiencing FGM as an empowering ritual are to be considered cases of 'false conscience'.

This method of using the 'gender argument' raises an interesting question as to how judges are supposed to classify a multicultural conflict and the role culture plays in explaining the reasons for a behaviour.

A similar shift in discourse (from culture to gender) is occurring, in Italy and comparatively, with regard to cases of honour killing.

7 Judgment of 27 November 2012.

8 Order of 3 April 2013.

Honour Killing/Feminicide

A second shift we are observing in judicial reasoning on the gender discourse regards the killing of women for reasons of honour.

When, in 1980–90, judges in the US began to raise the cultural defence (Dundes Renteln, 2004), there were several cases in which culture was used in order to mitigate the punishment. The most famous case[9] is that of Dong Lu Chen, a Chinese man who killed his wife following her infidelity. Mr Chen was sentenced to only five years' probation as the judge decided to take into account the cultural explanation provided by an anthropologist, Dr Pasternak, heard as an expert witness in Chinese culture during the trial. Dr Pasternak explained the strong blow to honour caused by a woman's infidelity.

Judgments like this were sharply criticized and scholarship analysed the differences 'on whether to analyse "honour crimes" as gender-based violence, or as cultural tradition' (Reddy, 2008; Coomaraswamy, 2005; Sen, 2005).[10]

Italian judges never granted any mitigation of punishment in honour killing cases. Despite their cultural dimension often invoked by lawyers, Italian judges have tended to deny the existence of any cultural reason for them and to follow another classification instead: the patriarchal one. The most famous honour killing case in Italy confirms this.

In the summer of 2006, in Sarezzo, near Brescia, Mohammed Saleem invited his 20 year-old daughter Hina to her family home and, aided by a cousin and by his brother-in-law, killed her. Several days later, he confessed: 'It was me. I acted in a moment of rage. I didn't want her to become like the girls here. I asked her to change her lifestyle, but she refused'. Hina's mother confirmed her husband's thinking: 'My daughter wasn't a good Muslim'.[11] Hina's misdeed, to her family's values, was to live unmarried with an Italian man and follow an Italian or Western lifestyle.

While the media and public opinion presented the case as an example of a 'culture clash', Italian feminists stressed that 'Hina's death is not an Islamic crime, but rather a patriarchal one' (Dominijanni, 2006). This discourse was shared by the three courts that judged Mr Saleem.

His lawyer attempted to mount a cultural defence, but to no avail. The first court refused it, applying the 'reasonable Pakistani' standard: 'even taking into account the cultural reason for the killing … in the Pakistani community itself the crime

9 *The People v. Chen* (N.Y. Sup. Ct. 2 December 1988).

10 On the other side, there were also cases in which honour was not used against the woman. Another famous case was *The People v. Metallides* (1974). Mr Metallides killed his daughter's rapist and his defence was based on the Greek rule of revenge: 'the law of the old country (Greece) is that you do not wait for the police if your daughter has been raped'. This reasoning seems to be incorporated in the patriarchal protection of the woman.

11 È tornata la madre di Hina 'Mohammed ha fatto giustizia', in *La Repubblica*, 21 August 2006. Available at www.repubblica.it.

appeared to be totally unreasonable and the motivation absolutely insufficient to cause (a father to) to have such a reaction'.[12]

The Court of Appeal[13] added two further arguments: time of residence in the host country and the patriarchal argument. According to the judge, in this case the cultural defence:

> is misleading ... because such a crime is not justified in Pakistan, because Saleem has been living in Italy since 1989 and has had time to learn our national customs and rules, and lastly because using the cultural explanation is tantamount to concealing what is simply the attitude of a patriarchal father (padre-padrone) who wishes to avenge the great offence caused by his daughter, as could happen to any subject with the same character and inclination, whatever ethnic group or culture he belongs to.

The Italian Supreme Court, confirming the 30-year prison sentence handed down in the previous two levels of prosecution, stated: 'the absorbing input for the defendant's action was caused by a pathological and deranged sense of parental possession'.[14]

All three judgments embodied the position expressed by several Italian feminists following the case. After the killing, Italian public opinion began a descent towards populist sentiment. But, according to feminist thought, Hina's death was not an 'Islamic killing' due to Pakistani culture, but a 'patriarchal killing' caused by the superstructure that conditions both traditional and modern societies; as proof of this, women in Europe and Italy are killed by their partners at a rate similar to that of women killed in Pakistan for reasons of honour. The two phenomena belong to the same structure of oppression. Other judgments that followed a similar reasoning,[15] and the introduction of the law 119/2013 that condemns "femicide" as a plague of Italian society are the proof of the capacity of gender/patriarchy discourse to overcome the cultural discourse.

---

12 Trial Judge of Brescia (Tribunale di Brescia), 19 January 2008.

13 Court of Appeal of Brescia (Corte d'Appello di Brescia), 5 December 2008.

14 Italian Supreme Court (Corte di Cassazione), Criminal Section I, no. 6587/2010.

15 See the Lashni case decided by Trial Judge of Padua (Tribunale penale di Padova), judgment 9th June 2005, no. 446 in which the judge refused to grant any mitigating circumstance to Mr. Mohammed Lashni, who beated to death his daughter Kaoutar, stating: "he is a person of Muslim culture, that with the pretext of an apparent legitimation coming from Islamic religion, adhere to styles of life in which there is a disparity of treatment between man and woman, being the last by custom, according to archaic rules, subjected to the will of the patriarchal tribal family that disposes of her as a property and does not consider her as a person". In this case culture and patriarchy are intermingled. See also Italian Supreme Court (Corte di Cassazione), Criminal Section I, no. 35496/2012, in which the Court states that given the time of residence in Italy Mr D., another father who killed his daughter, should have had "extricate himself from the aberrant dominance o the man over the woman in his culture of origin".

The Burqa

Gender discourse and the idea of protecting women from the patriarchal structure have been strongly present in the debate on the burqa and the banning of the Islamic veil in Italy; in this case, however, the cultural/religious argument has prevailed – at least so far.

While, on the one hand, Italian lawmakers periodically debate plans to explicitly ban the burqa, and even the Islamic veil, Italian judges have shown a sensitivity to the cultural dimension and permit it.

The Italian administrative judge[16] removed the administrative fine levied upon a woman for having refused to remove her veil. The fine was assessed on the basis of article 5 of Law no. 152/1975, which forbids people to wear 'a mask in a public space', or to 'cover their face by any means, unless there is a justifying reason'. The law makes some of those reasons explicit, such as covering one's face in order to practise sports.

The Italian administrative judge stated that the law is not applicable to Muslim women, using a cultural argument:

> with reference to the "veil covering the face", and in particular the *burqa*, its use is not generally directed towards avoiding recognition, but towards acknowledging a tradition of some people and cultures.

The cultural dimension of the practice satisfies, according to the judge, the 'justifying reason' required by the law. Furthermore, the judge considered that the aim of the law was to punish a dangerous situation caused by people who wish to avoid being recognized. Article 5 was in fact devised in the 1970s: the Italian context at the time was characterized by domestic terrorism in the struggle between the communist Red Brigades (*Brigate Rosse*) and fascist terrorist groups. But the situation is quite different today and the law cannot apply to Muslim immigrants.

Although the gender argument is occasionally made by some Member of Parliament when they propose bills banning the burqa, this is likely to become rare after the European Court of Human Rights judgment of 1 July 2014, *S.A.S. v. France*. Indeed, the ECHR refuted this argument, recognizing the agency of women. According to the court, 'a State Party cannot invoke gender equality in order to ban a practice that is defended by women – such as the applicant' (paragraph 119).

The court also rejected the argument made by the French government based on the idea that the 'wearing of the full-face veil by certain women shocked the majority of the French population because it infringed upon the principle of gender equality as generally accepted in France' (paragraph 119). In this regard, the European Court of Human Rights stated that gender equality should not be

---

16 Administrative Supreme Court (Consiglio di Stato), sez. VI, 19 June 2008, no. 3076.

measured using the French parameter, but, to the contrary, should be measured by opening the concept to cultural relativism:

> The Court is aware that the clothing in question is perceived as strange by many of those who observe it. It would point out, however, that it is the expression of a cultural identity which contributes to the pluralism that is inherent in democracy. It notes in this connection the variability of the notions of virtuousness and decency that are applied to the uncovering of the human body. Moreover, it does not have any evidence capable of leading it to consider that women who wear the full-face veil seek to express a form of contempt against those they encounter or otherwise to offend against the dignity of others.

The ECHR confirmed the validity of the French ban with respect to the Convention, using the argument of 'living together', but refused the gender argument along with the security argument, the human dignity argument and the secularity of the state argument.

Nowadays only France and Belgium prohibit the burqa, while all the other 45 members of the Council of Europe admit it. Should those 45 wish to prohibit it, they would have to demonstrate having a principle of fraternity and 'living together' similar to that used by France, as they can no longer rely on the gender argument.

Polygamy

Another controversial cultural practice has begun to be read through the lens of gender instead of through that of culture: polygamy. Italy has yet to see cases in which the gender argument has been used against polygamy, that is by the way banned by criminal law, but from the comparative standpoint a judgment that shows the gender dimension involved in polygamy is the decision rendered by the Supreme Court of British Columbia in 2011.[17] Called upon to ascertain whether the clause of British Columbia's criminal code denying the possibility of polygamy was contrary to the Charter of Freedom and Rights, the court stated that polygamy is a practice harmful to women: 'I have concluded that this case is essentially about harm; more specifically, Parliament's reasoned apprehension of harm arising out of the practice of polygamy. This includes harm to women, to children, to society and to the institution of monogamous marriage.'

The harm to women is specified by the judge as follows:

> Women in polygamous relationships are at an elevated risk of physical and psychological harm. They face higher rates of domestic violence and abuse, including sexual abuse. Competition for material and emotional access to a shared husband can lead to fractious co-wife relationships. These factors

17 *Section 293 of the Criminal Code of Canada* [2011] BCSC 1588.

> contribute to the higher rates of depressive disorders and other mental health issues that women in polygamous relationships face. They have more children, are more likely to die in childbirth and live shorter lives than their monogamous counterparts. They tend to have less autonomy, and report higher rates of marital dissatisfaction and lower levels of self-esteem. They also fare worse economically, as resources may be inequitably divided or simply insufficient.

Despite the fact that the judge used data strictly referring to a specific polygamous community – the Bountiful Mormon community, which was characterized by several socio-pathologies – the judge applied his reflections without distinction to all classes and types of polygamous relationships, everywhere in the world. The pattern of the court's reasoning is similar to the other cases examined with regard to Italy: a predominant classification of the practice as patriarchal and oppressive towards women, which obscures its cultural or religious dimension.

At this point in my analysis, we now move from the portion describing what is taking place in multicultural case-law and legislation, to the assessment portion, examining whether this shift in discourse is persuasive and whether it makes the demands of legal feminism stronger.

Conclusions: The Risks Connected with the Use of the Gender/Patriarchal Argument

The above paragraphs have shown the emergence of a sort of anti-patriarchal law, both in Italy and comparatively, composed of legislation and judgments attempting to combat what is perceived as a structural form of oppression of women. While this attitude may generally be perceived as progressive and as a sign that the law is translating into norms a new social view aimed at gender equality, there are also some risks that should be taken into account when using patriarchy to forbid a cultural practice. They may be summarized as follows: (1) the risk of adopting a restricted notion of patriarchy limited to women, while patriarchy is a more complex system of control including that of parents over children, older women over younger women (Gruenbaum, 2001); (2) the risk of the judge remaining blind to the cultural dimension of a practice; (3) the risk of adopting an abstract notion of patriarchy that keeps women from bargaining with it (Kandiyoti, 1988) or from adopting strategies of passive resistance which end up making their situation worse; and (4) the risk of concealing the majority's patriarchal practices by projecting patriarchy only upon the minority and removing similar practices in the majority (Mancini, 2012; Braunmühl, 2012).

I will try to analyse those four risks with respect to each of the examples mentioned in the previous paragraphs.

Female genital mutilation is an interesting case that demonstrates the first risk of adopting a restricted notion of patriarchy limited to women.

In my opinion, the patriarchal argument as used lately by Italian judges, and by the 2012 UN resolution in the case of FGM, is not completely persuasive. In fact, to limit the effects of patriarchy merely to the subjugation of women is to conceal other forms of domination that are equally significant. The introduction of the gender argument legitimates the completely different legal treatment of female circumcision and male circumcision in Italy and in many of the Western democracies: as shown, while any kind of FGM is forbidden in Italy, male circumcision in perfectly admitted. According to the gender argument, FGM is an oppressive practice of sexual control over girls, while male circumcision is an act of empowerment of the baby, who is then recognized as part of the community. Nevertheless, we have to consider that patriarchy is a very complex power structure that is not limited to control by men over women; one of its chief characteristics is the idea of the child as property (Gruenbaum, 2001).[18] In this sense, male circumcision could also be read under the category of patriarchy: it may express the absolute control by the parent over his son's body.

In Italy, male circumcision has been discussed since 1989, when the National Bioethics Committee submitted an opinion stating that it was admissible, despite being a permanent alteration of the body's integrity. The Bioethics Committee stated that, in balancing the parents' freedom of religion with the child's right to health and integrity, the former should prevail. In fact, unlike female genital mutilation, male circumcision results in no alteration of the 'functions of the body', as the sexual and reproductive functions of the penis are not compromised. This opinion has been quoted by several judges in acquitting parents and practitioners brought to court, generally by hospitals and doctors who treated bleeding and complications suffered by children after male circumcision.

In my opinion, judges (and lawmakers) should not focus on the reasons that create the practice (empowerment versus humiliation or subjugation), but on other factors. No matter which criterion the law chooses – for instance, it could be the choice criterion, the harm criterion, the religious criterion or the patriarchal criterion – what is not admissible is the present discriminatory treatment of facts that are similar.

In the case of genital alteration performed on a child, if the law were to choose the child's freedom of choice over his or her own body, any kind of genital alteration, perpetuated over male or female children, even Jewish and Islamic circumcision, would be forbidden.

---

18 Ellen Gruenbaum notes: 'patriarchy is not simply a system of rules by males over females, but a more complex set of relationships that result in domination by older men over both younger men and females. But there is other domination and authority here as well: females over children, older women over younger women, older children over younger children, boys as they grow up increasingly asserting themselves over girls, even older sisters who used to have authority, and so on. Even in the most strongly male-dominated culture, where women might be said to be very subordinated, young men often do not feel that they have power' (2001: 41).

If the law were to consider the 'harm' criterion and the functionality of the body, both male circumcision and the milder forms of FGM (now all forbidden by the 2012 UN resolution) would be admitted. In Italy, this is not the case, because the criterion developed by the Bioethics Committee in 1989 is not equally applied to the milder forms of FGM, which are all condemned as violations of the woman's dignity by article 583 *bis* of the criminal code.

Were the law to consider adopting the patriarchal argument, I think both male and female circumcision would be forbidden because, taken together, they are an expression of parental control over children. What I would like to stress with this reflection is that, once the law chooses one criterion, it should apply it consistently to any practice, because I think there is currently discrimination in the different treatment of male and female circumcision.

The second risk of using patriarchy as the main discourse for reading some facts is that of judges remaining completely blind to the cultural dimension of a practice. In the case of honour killing or of domestic maltreatment, classification under patriarchy may obscure a cultural dimension that is present and that can be used to better appreciate the conduct. By this, I do not mean that the defendant should be acquitted in this case, or that he or she should benefit from mitigating circumstances, but there may admittedly be cultural reasons that can influence the conduct, which are taken into account in other cultural defences not involving women as victims. A possible way to avoid this risk might be that of using different discourses simultaneously, as the intersectionality movement has taught us (Crenshaw, 1991).

The third risk I would like to focus on is that of adopting an abstract notion of patriarchy that keeps women from bargaining with it by, for instance, adopting strategies of passive resistance. Since patriarchy has a multiple and heterogeneous nature, Deniz Kandiyoti has attempted to oppose the ontological 'abstract notion of patriarchy encountered in contemporary feminist theory' with a more concrete vision of patriarchal phenomenology, in which 'women strategize within a set of concrete constraints' (Kandiyoti, 1988). In this context, according to this scholar, 'different forms of patriarchy present women with distinct "rules of the game" and call for different strategies to maximize security and optimize life options with varying potential for active or passive resistance in the face of oppression'. The burqa affair analysed earlier is a good example of this possible risk. During the *S.A.S. v. France* case, decided on 1 July 2014, some feminist movements opposed to the French law banning the burqa stressed the following: even assuming that the burqa is a patriarchal practice, wearing a burqa can provide women with a certain degree of security and protection and be the lesser evil in a context of broader oppression. The burqa is a patriarchal practice, but should not be prohibited, because it offers some advantages to women: for instance, the possibility of leaving the home unaccompanied, something which might be prohibited if they were not allowed to wear it. The fact that many women defended it could be seen as a strategy of 'bargaining with patriarchy'.

The fourth risk raised is that of concealing patriarchal practice in a majority, thereby projecting patriarchy only on the minority. This risk was raised by Susanna Mancini with regard to the burqa[19] and it emerges, in my opinion, in the polygamy case as well. In fact, in asserting that the practice is a patriarchal one, the majority assumes that its own marriage practices are not. There is something ironic about this assertion: in fact, it is well-known that much of feminism has denounced the institution of monogamous marriage as one of the first expressions of patriarchy. In this way, using a gender argument, the judge reinforces an institution – monogamic marriage – that is the very essence of patriarchy (Engels, 1884; Gough, 1975). Furthermore, classifying polygamy as gender oppression closes the door on a possible revolution in the conception of the modern family and of male–female relations. In fact, from a cultural and anthropological point of view, Western societies already practice a sort of *de facto* polygamy: when the crime of adultery was decriminalized (in Italy, this took place with the Constitutional Court's judgment no. 126 of 1968), the behaviour of having a lover during another relationship became legal. The introduction of divorce was a way to legalize serial monogamy, which is to say, not polygamy in a single setting, but over time. Not to mention counter-culture movements such as polyamory, that challenges at its very root the institution of monogamy as entirely oppressive.

In conclusion, while the opening to patriarchy could be considered an advance in recasting the law towards a more gender-sensitive legal system, we should pay attention to what Michel Foucault called the 'microphysics of power' (Foucault, 1977). In fact, patriarchy might just be regenerating itself, hiding its face behind anti-patriarchal legislation and case-law.

References

Balibar, E. (1991). Is there a 'Neo-Racism'? In: Balibar, E. and Wallerstein, I.M. (eds) *Race, Nation, Class, Ambiguous Identities*, 17–28. London: Verso.

Braunmühl, C. (2012). *Colonial Discourse and Gender in U.S. Criminal Courts: Cultural Defenses and Prosecutions*. New York: Routledge.

Brunelli, G. (2008). Prevenzione e divieto delle mutilazioni genitali femminili: genealogia (e limiti) di una legge. In: Bernardi, A., Pastore, B. and Pugiotto, A. (eds) *Legalità penale e crisi del diritto, oggi. Un percorso interdisciplinare*, 203–220. Milano: Giuffrè.

Caputi, J. and Russell, D. (1990). 'Femicide': Speaking the unspeakable. *MS* Sept. Oct., 1, 2, 34–7.

Coomaraswamy, R. (2005). Violence against women and 'crimes of honour'. In: Welchman, L. and Hossain, S. (eds) *'Honour': Crimes, Paradigms and Violence Against Women*, xi–xiv. London: Zed Books.

19 Mancini (2012) stressed that creating the Islam as the 'patriarchal other' removes the patriarchal aspects of Western societies.

Crenshaw, K. (1991). Mapping the margins: Intersectionality, identity politics, and violence against women of color. *Stanford Law Review*, 43(6), 1241–99.

Dalton, C. and Schneider, E.M. (2001), *Battered Women and the Law*. New York: Foundation Press, Thomson West.

Dominijanni, I. (2006), Patriarcati trasversali. *Il Manifesto*, 22 August.

Dundes Renteln, A. (2004). *Cultural Defence*. Oxford: Oxford University Press.

Eisenberg, A. and Spinner-Halev, J. (eds) (2005). *Minorities within Minorities. Equality, Rights and Diversity*. Cambridge: Cambridge University Press.

Eisenberg, A. and Kymlicka, W. (eds) (2011). *Identity Politics in the Public Realm. Bringing Institutions Back In*. Toronto/Vancouver: UBC Press.

Eisenstein, Z. (1977). Constructing a Theory of Capitalist Patriarchy and Socialist Feminism. *Insurgent Sociologist* (Summer), 3–17.

Engels, F. (1884). *The Origin of the Family, Private Property, and the State*. Chicago: Kerr 1902.

Fattibene, R. (2012). Verso una Risoluzione dell'Onu per l'abolizione delle mutilazioni genitali femminili a livello mondiale. il trattamento giuridico di questa pratica tra atti internazionali, modelli culturali e normative nazionali. *Rivistaic*, 1–12. Available at www.rivistaic.it.

Firestone, S. (1970). *The Dialectic of Sex: The Case for Feminist Revolution*. New York: Morrow.

Foucault, M. (1977). *Microfisica del potere. Interventi politici*. Torino: Einaudi.

Gough, K. (1975). The origin of the family. In Reiter Rayana (ed.) *Toward an Anthropology of Women*. New York: Monthly Review Press, 51–76.

Gruenbaum, E. (2001). *The Female Circumcision Controversy. An Anthropological Perspective*. Philadelphia: University of Pennsylvania Press.

Hungtington, S. (1996). *The Clash of Civilizations and the Remaking of World Order*. New York: Simon & Schuster.

Inglehart, R.F. (1977). *The Silent Revolution*. Princeton: Princeton University Press.

Kandiyoti, D. (1988). Bargaining with patriarchy. *Gender and Society*, 2, 274–90.

Kukathas, C. (2001). Is feminism bad for multiculturalism? *Public Affairs Quarterly*, 15/2, 83–101.

Kymlicka, W. (1995). *Multicultural Citizenship: A Liberal Theory of Minority Rights*. Oxford: Oxford University Press.

Lonzi, C. (1982). *Sputiamo su Hegel, la donna clitoridea e la donna vaginale e altri scritti*. Milano: Gammalibri.

Mancini, S. (2012). *Patriarchy as the exclusive domain of the other: The veil controversy, false projection and cultural racism,* in *International Journal of Constitutional Law [ICON]*, 10(2), 411–28.

Mitchell, J. (1973). *Women's Estate*. New York: Vintage.

Okin, S.M. (1999). Is multiculturalism bad for women? In Cohen, J., Toward, M. and Nussbaum, M.C. (eds) *Is Multiculturalism Bad For Women? Susan Moller Okin With Respondents*. Princeton: Princeton University Press.

Phillips, A. (2003). When culture means gender: Issues of cultural defence in the English courts. *Modern Law Review*, 66(4), 510–31.

Rao, A. (1995). The politics of gender and culture in international human rights discourse. In Peters, J. and Wolper, A. (eds) *Women's Rights, Human Rights: International Feminist Perspectives*, 167–75. London: Routledge.

Reddy, R. (2008), Gender, culture and the law: Approaches to 'Honour Crimes' in the UK. *Feminist Legal Studies*, 16, 305–21.

Sen, P. (2005). 'Crimes of honour': Value and meaning. In Welchman, L. and Hossain, S. (eds) *'Honour': Crimes, Paradigms and Violence Against Women*, 42–63. London: Zed Books.

Shachar, A. (2001). *Multicultural Jurisdictions: Cultural Differences and Women's Rights*. Cambridge: Cambridge University Press.

Song, S. (2007). *Justice, Gender and The Politics Of Multiculturalism*. Cambridge: Cambridge University Press.

Volpp, L. (2001). Feminism versus multiculturalism. *Columbia Law Review*, 10, 1181–218.

Walker, L.E. (1979). *The Battered Woman Syndrome*. New York: Harper and Row.

Chapter 9

Gender and Religious Symbols in the European Public Sphere: Unveiling the Paradoxes of Italian Toleration

Susanna Mancini

Introduction: Culture, Identity and Gender in the Controversies over Religious Symbols in the European Public Sphere

The display of religious symbols in the public sphere typically raises two sets of conflicts. The first set of conflicts arises over the extent to which the right to wear religious symbols and clothes can be limited in the name of other rights and principles of equal constitutional value, such as state secularism. While there have been cases in which the contested symbol is a Christian one,[1] most controversies of this kind concern minority religions' symbols, such as the Muslim hidjab and niqab, the Sikh turban and the Jewish yarmulke.

The second type of conflict arises when a religious symbol, such as the crucifix, the Ten Commandments or the crèche, is displayed by state authorities in public places, typically state schools and courtrooms. In this case, unlike in the first type of conflict, the contested symbol represents the dominant religion and not that of minority groups.

The first set of conflicts has dramatically intensified in virtually all European countries during the last three decades, as the consequence of mass-scale migration and globalization. These phenomena have led to confrontations between newly arrived religions that are at significant odds with prevailing mores and well-entrenched religions established in the country of immigration. Moreover, the concurrent process of globalization and privatization has led to a blurring of the line between the public sphere and the private sphere. Religion, as famously maintained by sociologist José Casanova, has become 'deprivatized' (Casanova, 1994), and seeks a much-increased role in the public sphere and specifically in the

1 See, for example, European Court of Human Rights, 13 January 2013, *Eweida and Others v. The United Kingdom*, (App. No. 48420/10, 59842/10, 51671/10 and 36516/10), in which two of the applicants, Ms Eweida and Ms Chaplin, were Christians who believed that their faith required them to wear a small cross on a chain visibly around their neck. In both cases, the applicants' respective employers had refused to allow them to continue in their role unless they removed their cross.

political arena. Consequently, the reconciliation of constitutionalism and religion through adherence to traditional notions of secularism in the public place becomes increasingly difficult and contested.

European models for managing the relationship between the state and religion are deeply different from one another. Some states adhere to a strict neutrality, some have state churches. All systems, however, share a common feature, i.e. a degree of entanglement between national identity and the polity's Christian heritage. In Europe, the process of secularization and the transition to liberalism did result in a state model that no longer endorsed a conception of the good related to a particular religion, but it thereby raised a key question concerning the powers of integration of a secularized society. The nation-state, with its emphasis on a distinct national identity anchored in a common history, language, tradition and culture, came to displace religious belief as the source of integration of the polity. The explicit removal of religion as the glue that binds together did not, however, preclude its persistent survival as an implicit mainstay engrained in the secular nation's tradition and culture. And, because Europe had been overwhelmingly Christian, even after the state has removed all or most Christian religious vestiges, Christianity has endured by permeating the different European national cultures and traditions. 'As a consequence of these developments, religious tolerance [became] relegated from the level of religious beliefs to the level of merely religiously permeated national traditions that remain, albeit in different ways, infused with Christian values' (Augenstein, 2008: 7). Moreover, historically, secularization has implied a process of separation between the state and Christian churches, and hence it had naturally entailed the accommodation of the majority's (Christian) religion. Religious tolerance, thus, was bent on keeping religious diversity within the private sphere, while the public sphere was imbued in cultural Christianity. Today, however, the traditional model of tolerance for religious minorities in a religiously homogeneous Europe, characterized by a strict separation between 'private' and 'public', fails to meet the needs of what has become a less homogeneous continent, where the private and public spheres collapse into one another, and religious diversity can no longer be confined to the private one.

Religious symbols play an important role in these dynamics. As Seyla Benhabib puts it, '[o]ur contemporary condition is marked by the melting down of all naturalistic signifiers in the political and cultural realm and a desperate attempt to recreate them' (Benhabib, 1999: 336). Religious symbols, thanks to their capacity to evoke unquestioned belongings, allow for the construction of simplified and artificial identities, and thus provide clear-cut dividing lines. For example, the crucifix is often depicted as a symbol of a 'Christian cultural inheritance', shared as a common legacy by the West, irrespective of the fact that Christian unity broke up in the sixteenth century. By the same token, the 'veil' is depicted as 'Muslim', as if Islam were a monolithic structure, in which all adhere to the same set of values, and, as a consequence, to a given dress code. On the other hand, religious symbols 'mark' the public sphere. Their presence and their absence symbolize the power relations between different cultures. The display of a crucifix in state schools or courtrooms clearly identifies the 'official culture' with that of the majority, whereas the ban on the wearing of the veil in state schools unambiguously marks the marginalization of the culture the veil is supposed to represent. Moreover, religious symbols can easily turn into catalysers of aggression, to the extent that they mirror power inequalities and generate blind fixations and unquestioned belongings (Lombardi Vallauri, 2005). Religious symbols unite, but, at the same time, they divide and erect barriers between the self and the other.

> The more fluid the environment becomes, the more unpredictable and opaque it grows and the more we retreat into the walls of our certainties, into the markers of the familiar. Hence globalization is accompanied by demands for isolationism, for protectionism, for raising even higher and making even sturdier the walls that divide us and them. (Benhabib, 1999: 355)

Hence, the intensification of the struggles over the presence of religious symbols in public places testifies to a generalized European identity crisis and to an increasing difficulty in building 'accounts of individual and collective identity that do not fall into xenophobia, intolerance, paranoia, and aggression toward others' (Benhabib, 1999: 355). As Jose Casanova puts it,

> Europeans are not sure whether European civilization is to be defined by the particular historical legacy of Western "civilization", of which cultural Christianity, to be sure in an increasingly secularized form, remains a central component. Or, alternatively, whether European civilization ought to be defined by the cosmopolitan "civilization" of secular modernity, which Europe itself claims to have produced. (Casanova, 2006: 236)

Sex and gender play a crucial role in the definition of collective identities. Women 'make a critical contribution to the transmission of collective identity', since they reproduce future members of their group and, being children's primary caregivers, transmit the group's social norms, culture, and traditions to future generations (Shachar, 2002: 56–7). Thus, intercultural conflicts often focus on practices, such as veiling, genital cutting (FGM), polygamy and forced marriages, that involve women: their clothing, their bodies and their legal status (Benhabib, 2002: 83). In the past decades, as cultural diversity increased in European societies, much attention has been placed on the gender dimension of intercultural clashes by politicians, legislators, courts, scholars and the media. Many laws have been enacted in different European countries that target practices, such as FGM and veiling, that affect exclusively women belonging to cultural minorities.

Unsurprisingly, thus, the struggle concerning religious symbols in the public sphere has focused in Europe almost exclusively on the right of women to wear traditional Muslim attire.

The struggle against the Muslim headscarf started in France in 1989, when a handful of schoolgirls were suspended for wearing their hidjab in a state school in Creil, a suburb of Paris. 'Anti-veil' measures rapidly spread within and beyond France: between 1989 and 2010, Muslim traditional attire had become an issue in most European countries. Laws have been enacted prohibiting or limiting the right to wear various types of 'veils' in France, Belgium and Germany. Cases concerning the right of civil servants, pupils and teachers to wear the hidjab, the jibab or the niqab have been dealt with in most European jurisdictions, including Switzerland, Germany, Belgium, the Scandinavian countries and the United Kingdom. The European Court of Human Rights has also decided various 'veil cases' brought by applicants from Turkey, France and Switzerland. In the overwhelming majority of cases, and quite irrespective of the very divergent models of managing the relationship between religion and the state under which European countries operate, different types of veils have been associated with beliefs and behaviour that contradict the essential values that constitute the core of a liberal democracy. Hence, the display of Islamic symbols (or certain variants of them) has been legitimately restricted in many European countries because it is perceived as objectively violating the rights of others and/or endangering democratic values, and, particularly, secularism and gender equality. For example, in five German *Länder* (Baden-Württemberg,[2] Saarland,[3] Hesse,[4] Bavaria[5] and North Rhine-Westphalia[6]) laws have been enacted which prohibit Islamic symbols but specifically permit Christian ones in the public schools, including nuns' habits.[7]

2 Gesetz zur Änderung des Schulgesetzes, 1 April 2004, and Gesetz zur Änderung des Kindergartengesetzes, 14 February 2006.

3 Gesetz Nr. 1555 zur Änderung des Gesetzes zur Ordnung des Schulwesens im Saarland (Schulordnungsgesetz), 23 June 2004. In the explanation to the draft law, it is stated that the regulation is not limited to headscarves, however, the wearing of Christian and Jewish symbols remains possible.

4 Gesetz zur Sicherung der staatlichen Neutralität, 18 October 2004.

5 Gesetz zur Änderung des Bayerischen Gesetzes über das Erziehungs – und Unterrichtswesen, 23 November 2004.

6 Erstes Gesetz zur Änderung des Schulgesetzes für das Land Nordrhein – Westfalen, 13 June 2006. The law of North Rhine-Westphalia was challenged before the Federal Constitutional Court, which held that a general prohibition against teachers' wearing headscarves in public schools is unconstitutional under Article 4 (1) and (2) of the German Basic Law. According to the Court, the abstract possibility of endangering state neutrality or peace at school is not sufficient to justify a general ban on headscarves. While states legislatures can legitimately act in order to ensure peace at school and state neutrality, a state-wide prohibition of religious expression by outward appearance — wearing a headscarf — is disproportionate. Only a concrete danger would justify prohibiting the exercise of a binding religious command. Moreover, the Court held unconstitutional the privileging of Christian symbols and traditions over non-Christian ones, on the ground that if the display of religious messages by teachers is to be prohibited, such a prohibition must apply equally to all religions (1 BvR 471/10 and 1 BvR 1181/109).

7 These laws constitute a direct reaction to a Federal Constitutional Court judgment concerning the wearing of the veil by a teacher (Ludin, Bundesverfassungericht, 24 September 2003, 2BvR, 1436/02). The woman was refused a permanent civil servant post

As a Bavarian ministry official stated, unlike the nun's habit, the headscarf can be interpreted as a political symbol that denies the equality of women.[8] The British House of Lords in the *Begum* case of 2005,[9] accepted the arguments of a state-maintained school, according to which allowing a schoolgirl to wear the jilbab (which conceals the whole body but leaves the face and the hands uncovered) would have violated the religious freedom of others and made pupils and teachers feel 'uncomfortable' in the presence of clothes that are generally associated with fundamentalism. Baroness Hale added that

> Like it or not – she stated – this is a society committed, in principle and in law, to equal freedom for men and women to choose how they will lead their lives within the law. Young girls from ethnic, cultural or religious minorities growing up here face particularly difficult choices: how far to adopt or to distance themselves from the dominant culture. A good school will enable and support them.[10]

The European Court of Human Rights (ECtHR) in the case of *Dahlab v. Switzerland*,[11] emphasized: 'It must also be acknowledged that it is difficult to reconcile the wearing of a headscarf with the principle of gender equality, which is a fundamental value of our society enshrined in a specific provision of the Federal Constitution and must be taken into account by schools'.[12] The rationale of both the French and the Belgian laws prohibiting the wearing of the niqab heavily relies on the radical incompatibility between face-covering and the democratic process, as well as on assumptions relating to dignity concerning women's visibility.

In my previous work, I have argued that the mobilization of female symbols and feminist rhetoric in the fight against Muslim clothing is ill-founded and

---

as a teacher in a primary school in the conservative *Land* of Baden Württemberg because she insisted on wearing the veil, which prompted the conclusion that she had a 'lack of personal aptitude'. The Constitutional Court ruled that German *Länder* had the right to ban teachers from wearing the veil as long as they passed specific laws on the matter. As a result, the *Länder* with the strongest Catholic traditions adopted specific laws on the issue.

8 Human Rights Watch, 'Discrimination in the Name of Neutrality: Headscarf Bans for Teachers and Civil Servants in Germany' (2009), 26. Available at http://www.iiavnl/epublications//2009/Discrimination_in_the_Name_of_Neutrality.pdf (citing the explanatory comments in the Bavarian government draft law, Gesetzentwurf der Staatsregierung zur Änderung des Bayerischen Gesetzes über das Erziehungs – und Unterrichtswesen, Bavarian parliament, 15th election period, Drucksache 15/368, 18 February 2004).

9 *Regina (Shabina Begum) v. Governors of Denbigh High Sch.* [2006] UKHL 15, [2007] 1 AC 100 (HL) (appeal taken from Eng.).

10 *Regina (Shabina Begum) v. Governors of Denbigh High Sch.*

11 European Court of Human Rights, 15 February 2001, *Dahlab v. Switzerland* (App. no. 42393/98).

12 *Dahlab v. Switzerland* (quoting the Federal Court of Switzerland) (internal citations omitted).

actually counterproductive for the advancement of gender equality. I have posited that equating the veil to the subjection of women relies on an ambiguous confusion between gender equality and sexual openness, which reflects Western gender roles and gender hierarchies. Veiling is perceived as a woman's refusal to engage in the 'normal' protocol of interaction with the opposite sex and as a form of resistance to the public sexualization of women that is typical of contemporary Western cultures, and constitutes a patriarchal response to the emancipation of women (Mancini, 2012). Moreover, anti-veil measures can be interpreted according to the pattern of false projection. In the *Dialectic of Enlightenment*, Adorno and Horkheimer describe false projection as the phenomenon which enables majority cultures to project on minorities some features of their own which they seek to hide from themselves (Adorno and Horkheimer, 1944: 186 ff). In this light, Muslim women come to embody the projected visions of Islam as 'the' patriarchal 'other', which is a particularly useful device for the purpose of hiding an unresolved conflict within Western civilization (Mancini, 2012). Thus, the use of feminist arguments in anti-veil measures contributes to the strengthening of the (imagined) identitarian boundaries (Christian/occidental versus Muslim/oriental), as well as to the reinforcement of (real) gender oppression, by enabling a political use of women's bodies (Mancini, 2012). These two outcomes are strictly intertwined, as sex and gender play a key role in identity-related dynamics. As posited by Seyla Benhabib, the construction of the self and the other, the struggle over identity, is linked to sexual difference (Benhabib, 2002). In the veil struggle, sexual difference demarcates the line between the self-portrait offered by the self and the portrait that the latter offers of the other; that is, between the Western, gender-egalitarian self against the Oriental and patriarchal other.

Surprisingly, Italy has shown little interest in the debate concerning veiling and women's equality. In Italy, controversies concerning religious symbols in the public school have focused almost exclusively on the mandatory display of the crucifix in state schools and courtrooms. The crucifix has undergone a meticulous dissection process by Italian courts in order to justify its mandatory presence in otherwise secular schools and tribunals. Interestingly, this process of semantic disarticulation has never touched upon gender.

In the following pages, I will analyse 'Italian exceptionalism' in the context of the controversies over religious symbols in the public sphere, taking the gender dimension into account.

Italian Exceptionalism

The Italian legislature has enacted no law regulating the wearing of the headscarf and the full-face veil. Under the fourth Berlusconi government (2008–11), several bills prohibiting face-covering veils were introduced in the Italian Parliament but never adopted. The populist and xenophobic Northern League has failed to ignite a national debate on the necessity of criminalizing the wearing of the full-face veil.

Italian judges have refrained from charging Muslim attire of anti-feminist significances and have shown a remarkable degree of sensitiveness to the cultural dimension attached to veiling practices. In 2008, the High Administrative Court (*Consiglio di Stato*) upheld the annulment of a municipal ordinance that equated the full-face veil to masks and other items, such as full-face helmets, that have the purpose of preventing or hindering identification and cannot be worn in public places without a reasonable justification. The ordinance had been adopted by the Northern League mayor of a small municipality in the Friuli region. As a consequence, a women was fined for refusing to remove her facial veil in a courtroom, where she had accompanied a family member. The court reasoned that the rationale of the criminal provision (article 5 of Law no. 152/1975) forbidding people from covering their face in a public space is to protect public order, to avoid the potential danger posed by individuals who purposely hide their identity. This Law had been adopted during the 1970s as a consequence of the intensification of terrorist attacks; hence, according to the court, it cannot be understood as targeting Muslim individuals. 'Obviously the *burqa* is not a mask, but a traditional type of attire, that is used by certain peoples, also in connection with religious practices.' It follows that 'The wearing of the *burqa* is not intended to prevent or hinder identification, but rather to comply with a particular tradition that is shared by certain peoples and cultures.'[13]

In a similar line of reasoning, in 2012, the public prosecutor of the city of Turin decided to drop the accusations against an Egyptian woman, who had been sued by a private individual for wearing a full-face veil in a supermarket. The accuser claimed that her attire violated Law no. 152/1975, as it prevented her identification. The prosecutor, however, argued that 'the woman obviously did not wear her *burqa* to avoid being identified'. To the contrary, whenever asked to remove her face-veil for purpose of identification, she had always willingly complied. Wearing the full-face veil – concluded the public prosecutor – is a religious practice protected by the constitution, 'which guarantees the right to manifest one's faith and one's religious belonging, also though one's appearance'.[14] Hence, Law no. 152/1975 is not applicable in this case because its rationale is to protect public order, not to limit constitutional liberties.

There is no attempt, in these decisions, to try to decipher the actual significance of veiling practices, and, particularly, to decide on their compatibility or incompatibility with gender equality. The Italian judge and prosecutor take a subjective stance and look at the full-face veil as a practice that testifies to the plurality of cultural forms, without automatically channelling the difference between 'veiling' and 'not veiling' into the dialectic of the clash of civilizations. There is no judgmental attitude in the Italian decisions: the full-face veil is nothing but the mirror of a cultural tradition, which can be associated with a religious practice, and is thus protected by the constitution.

13 Italian High Administrative Court (VI Section), Judgment of 19 June 2008, no. 3076.

14 Procura di Torino, 2012.

The Italian cases resemble the decision of the Spanish Supreme Court, which quashed a judgment of the Catalonia High Court of Justice that had upheld a number of municipal provisions limiting or prohibiting access to various public places (including municipal areas and public transport) for persons wearing full-face veils, balaclavas, full-face helmets or other forms of clothing or accessories preventing or hindering identification and visual communication. The Supreme Court expressed its disagreement with the finding of the Catalonia High Court of Justice to the effect that, whether or not it was voluntary, it was hard to reconcile the wearing of the full-face veil with the principle of gender equality, which was one of the values of democratic societies. The Supreme Court took the view that the voluntary nature or otherwise of the wearing of the full-face veil was decisive, since it was not possible to restrict a constitutional freedom based on the supposition that the women who wore it did so under duress. It thus concluded that the limitations in question could not be regarded as necessary in a democratic society. Lastly, the court expressed its preoccupation that a ban on the wearing of the full-face veil would have the result of isolating the women concerned and would give rise to discrimination against them, and would thus be incompatible with the objective of ensuring the social integration of groups of immigrant origin.[15]

The contrast between these cases and those decided by the French and the Belgian courts, upholding the criminalization of the full-face veil in all public places, is striking. The French Constitutional Council declared Law no. 2010-1192, prohibiting the concealment of one's face in public places, compliant with the constitution, on the ground that

> Women who concealed their face, voluntarily or otherwise, were placed in a situation of exclusion and inferiority that was patently incompatible with the constitutional principles of liberty and equality. In passing the statutory provisions referred for review, the legislature thus complemented and generalised rules which were previously reserved for *ad hoc* situations for the purpose of protecting public order.[16]

A law 'to prohibit the wearing of any clothing entirely or substantially concealing the face' was also enacted in Belgium on 1 June 2011. Applications for the annulment of this law were lodged with the Constitutional Court on the basis, *inter alia*, of Article 9 of the European Convention on Human Rights (ECHR). The Belgian Constitutional Court dismissed the applications, on the ground that the law pursued three aims: public safety, gender equality and a certain conception of 'living together' in society. In particular, the court noted that:

---

15 Spanish Supreme Court, Judgment of 6 February 2013 (no. 693/2013, appeal no. 4118/2011).

16 French Constitutional Council, Decision of 7 October 2010 (no. 2010-613 DC), paragraph 4.

> Even where the wearing of the full-face veil is the result of a deliberate choice on the part of the woman, the principle of gender equality, which the legislature has rightly regarded as a fundamental value of democratic society, justifies the opposition by the State, in the public sphere, to the manifestation of a religious conviction by conduct that cannot be reconciled with this principle of gender equality … [T]he wearing of a full-face veil deprives women – to whom this requirement is solely applicable – of a fundamental element of their individuality which is indispensable for living in society and for the establishment of social contacts.[17]

One could be tempted to attribute Italy's (and Spain's) seeming lack of interest for Muslim attires mainly to the relatively limited number of Muslims in these countries, and to the recent nature of immigration waves, which has not yet allowed for much social mobility. Hence, veiled women are not commonly employed as teachers and white-collar workers. The reasons for 'Italian exceptionalism' are, however, multifaceted and ambiguous. They have to do with the complex and in many respects unresolved relationship between the state and the Catholic church, as well as with the role of Catholic doctrine and the influence of the church in shaping women's roles in Italian history and society.

Living Together (Under the Cross): The Italian Way

Unlike in the French case, secularism is not explicitly enshrined in the Italian constitution. The Constitutional Court, however, has declared that it is to be regarded as one of the fundamental principles of the Italian legal system. According to the Constitutional Court,[18] secularism (*laicità*) emerges from the combined interpretation of various constitutional provisions: article 2, which protects 'the inviolable rights of man, both as an individual and as a member of the social groups in which his personality finds expression'; article 3, which guarantees equality before the law; article 7, according to which the 'State and the Catholic Church are, each within their own sphere, independent and sovereign'; article 8, according to which '[a]ll religious denominations are equally free';[19] and article 19, which protects the freedom to profess and promote religious beliefs, individually or collectively. Consistent with this thesis, the Constitutional Court constructs secularism as a principle that has multiple constitutional referents,

17 Belgian Constitutional Court, Judgment of 6 December 2012.

18 Italian Constitutional Court, Decision no. 203/1989.

19 It is true that the Catholic church, whose relationship to the state is regulated by the Lateran pacts, enjoys certain privileges. Nevertheless, all religious denominations have the right to organize themselves according to their own creed (article 8, paragraph 2, of the constitution) and can make specific agreements (*intese*) with the state, which are regulated by law and which may confer a wide range of collective rights.

going well beyond the guarantee of freedom of religion. Freedom of religion and secularism are therefore two separate fundamental constitutional provisions, and all sources of law, to be legitimate, have to be consistent with both.

The Constitutional Court has been emphatic that the principle of secularism does not mean indifference towards religion, but instead the equidistance and impartiality towards different faiths, which it is necessary for the state to maintain in order to safeguard freedom of religion in a context of religious and cultural pluralism.[20] Accordingly, unlike the French concept of *laicité* (which has an undeniable anticlerical component), secularism in the Italian system does not imply neutrality, but a positive or welcoming attitude towards all religions and religious communities.

Some scholars have stressed that religious freedom is likely to be optimized across a range of systems characterized by this kind of state–church relationship. Cole Durham and Brett Scharffs distinguish 'secularism' from 'secularity'. They maintain that the first is an ideological position that is committed to promoting a secular order as an end in itself, while the latter can be described as a framework within which different comprehensive views – both religious and secular – can be held, an approach to religion–state relations that avoids the identification of the state with any particular religion or ideology (including secularism itself) and that provides a neutral framework capable of accommodating or co-operating with a broad range of religions and beliefs (Durham and Scharffs, 2010: 114 ff).

Thus, one could argue that Italy adopts the model of 'secularity', and is therefore more likely to provide a robust protection of minority religions than the French 'secular' model. To a certain extent this is true, especially if one compares the different treatment of Muslim symbols in the two countries. Undoubtedly, '[a] more flexible or open secularism … based on the protection of freedom of religion, even if this requires a relaxation of the principle of neutrality' is more accommodating than a militant secular system, because 'flexible' secularism conceives 'state neutrality towards religion and the separation of Church and State not as ends in themselves, but rather as the means to achieving the fundamental objectives of respect for religious and moral equality and freedom of conscience and religion' (Woehrling and Jukier, 2010: 185). Thus, in principle, the Italian flexible approach in managing the relationship between religion and the state provides a much wider space for the religious freedom of Muslim women than the French rigidly secular approach. Having said this, the Italian 'secularity' model is not as committed to 'religious and moral equality' as one could assume.

The notion of equidistance developed by the Italian Constitutional Court is increasingly contested. Not only the Vatican, but also leading political forces, suggest that Italy needs a 'new' understanding of secularism in order to respond to the relativistic wave that Western democracies are supposedly experiencing in the era of globalization and large scale migration. In this 'new' understanding,

20 Italian Constitutional Court, decisions no. 203/1989; no. 259/1990; no. 13/1991; no. 195/1993; no. 421/1993; no. 334/1996; no. 329/1997; no. 508/2000; no. 327/2002.

secularism should not place all denominations on an equal footing. Quite to the contrary, for the proponents of this new view, the state should recognize that the 'national religious inheritance' is not just one among several denominations, but rather a crucial component of civic cohesion (Zagrebelsky, 2008: 16). Accordingly, the historical national religion should enjoy preferential treatment. This results in a 'new form of alliance between religion and public power, where the ethical force of the first one upholds the political force of the latter and vice versa' (Zagrebelsky, 2008: 17). There is obviously nothing veritably 'new' about this understanding of the relationship between the church and the state. According to Gustavo Zagrebelsky, 'new' secularism is nothing but a 'pale reincarnation of the past, a sort of "semi-secularism" that represents what remains of the old dream of the Christian Republic, and is based on the opposite of the Westphalian principle: "*cuius religio, eius et region*"' (Zagrebelsky, 2008: 16).

This 'semi-secular' model is certainly the one envisioned by the Grand Chamber of the European Court of Human Rights in its decision in the case of *Lautsi v. Italy*.[21] In this decision, the ECtHR upheld the mandatory displacement of the crucifix in Italian public schools, on the ground that the crucifix, while conferring more visibility to Catholicism, does not constitute a tool of proselytism. Importantly, the Court added that:

> [I]taly opens up the school environment in parallel to other religions. The Government indicated in this connection that it was not forbidden for pupils to wear Islamic headscarves or other symbols or apparel having a religious connotation; alternative arrangements were possible to help schooling fit in with non-majority religious practices; the beginning and end of Ramadan were "often celebrated" in schools; and optional religious education could be organised in schools for "all recognised religious creeds". (para. 74)

Said differently, the display of the crucifix is legitimate as long as the wearing of the headscarf is also permitted. Obviously, this construction relies on a very light understanding of Italian secularism, as a principle that allows for the granting of privileges (other than those guaranteed by the Concordat) to the Catholic church in the name of its traditional (secularized) role in shaping Italian culture and identity.

Three years after *Lautsi*, in the case of *S.A.S. v. France*, the ECtHR upheld the French full-face veil ban.[22] The court rejected the argument that the ban was necessary to protect gender equality and public safety, but relied on a vague notion, that it was not listed among the justifications that states can legitimately invoke to place limitations on the rights listed in the Convention: the notion of 'living together'. According to the court: '[T]he impugned ban can be regarded as justified

21 European Court of Human Rights (GC) 18 March 2011, *Lautsi and Others v. Italy* (App. no. 30814/06).

22 European Court of Human Rights (GC) 1 July 2014, *S.A.S. v. France* (App. no. 43835/11).

in its principle solely in so far as it seeks to guarantee the conditions of "living together"' (paragraph 142). Taking into account that state parties enjoy a wide margin of appreciation in cases involving freedom of religion, 'the ban imposed by the Law of 11 October 2010 can be regarded as proportionate to the aim pursued, namely the preservation of the conditions of "living together" as an element of the "protection of the rights and freedoms of others"' (paragraph 157). The ban can thus be regarded as 'necessary in a democratic society' (paragraph 158).

Taken together, *Lautsi v. Italy* and *S.A.S. v. France* suggest that the ECtHR is willing to uphold very divergent understandings of 'living together' and to justify heavy limitations on fundamental rights stemming from such understandings. In the French case, 'living together' justifies the exclusion from the public sphere of women based on their dresses. In the Italian case, 'living together' means that Catholics and non-Catholics are equally free to exercise their religious rights under the cross.

Gender and Migration under the Cross

'Living together under the cross' affects gender models and gender norms in the context of Muslim immigration at a very deep level. Catholicism is commonly perceived as a universalistic religion. The Italian administrative courts have consistently upheld the constitutionality of the mandatory display of the crucifix in state schools on the ground of the 'universal' nature of Christianity. According to these administrative judges, inherent in Christianity are the ideas of tolerance, freedom of religion, reciprocal respect, acceptance of the other, human dignity, fundamental rights, solidarity and non-discrimination, which constitute the basis of a secular state in general and of the Italian state in particular, because secularism has been achieved in Italy thanks to – amongst other things – the founding Christian values.[23]

The Church also portrays itself as universalistic, as a world church where (at least after the Second Vatican Council) bishops of Asia, Africa, Latin America, and the Pacific Rim democratically act together with the pope as equals when articulating and deciding the theology of the Council.

As feminist theologian Elisabeth Schüssler Fiorenza notices, however, the church, while it was able to (partially) overcome its Eurocentrism, remains monolithically elite male-centred. According to Schüssler Fiorenza,

> The absence of women from the ranks of bishops is not just an historical accident but the result of systemic discrimination and legal exclusion. It is due to the structural sin of sexism and its theological rationalizations, and it has prevented the world-church from achieving full feminist catholicity. Today, the

23 Italian Regional Administrative Tribunal (TAR Veneto), decision of 17 March 2005, no. 1110, paragraph 11.7.

> lack of women's voices is even more obvious because other Christian churches have welcomed women as official ministers, priests and bishops and thereby practice the feminist catholicity which is lacking in the Roman Catholic church. (Schüssler Fiorenza, 2005)

Moreover, as Schüssler Fiorenza further stresses,

> [the] Hierarchy's discourses of "orthodox truth" are also highly gendered. They are full of references to the clergy as "sons and fathers", to the church as "mother and she", and to the people of God as "men of faith". Rome has categorically refused to change exclusive androcentric language and has overturned the recommendations of several bishops' conferences for the adoption of non-gendered liturgical language. Hence, androcentric language which linguistically excludes women is no longer conventional but deliberate. It maintains the status quo and limits our imagination. Moreover, the use of the feminine for the church serves to symbolically exclude and obliterate real women, since Christ and the church can be represented by men only. It reinforces the colonial discourses of domination in which the feminine serves to signify the subordination and exploitation not only of women but of all those who are non-persons: slaves, heathen savages, homosexuals and impoverished peoples, all of whom are seen and treated as "feminine" other. (Schüssler Fiorenza, 2005)

Under the pretences of universalism, the church has consistently upheld West-centric patriarchy and perpetuated gender and race hierarchies and patterns of domination.

It was a widespread assumptions among colonizers of Arab countries that, while Christianity 'elevated' women, Islam 'degraded' them (Ahmed, 1993). In the nineteenth and twentieth centuries, missionaries systematically relied on the depiction of Jesus as a liberator of women who broke out of the Jewish tradition, in their effort to convert Third-World women, by equating the subordination of women in their native tradition with the inferiority of their religion (PuiLan, 2005). Christian feminism in the 1970s and 1980s typically portrayed Judaism as 'the' patriarchic religion *par excellence*, and Christianity as a feminist corrective to it. According to Judith Plaskow, such assertions – based on a sloppy and ahistorical scholarship – by reducing the complex textual tradition of Judaism to a monolithic assertion of patriarchy and portraying Judaism as the religion that imposed domination over women, ultimately aimed at adding 'a new slant to the old theme of Christian superiority'. Projecting Christian patriarchy onto the Jewish 'other', in fact, enabled Christian feminism to perpetuate 'traditional Christianity's negative picture of Judaism by attributing sexist attitudes to Christianity's Jewish origins, at the same time maintaining that Christianity's distinctive contributions to the "woman question" are largely positive' (Plaskow, 2005: 89 and Heschel, 1990). Jesus is still represented as a liberator of women (from Jewish patriarchy) in contemporary Christian theology. In a book published in 2014, Michael Muonwe writes that:

> Jesus lived and taught the values of communion, inclusion and equal respect. Of special importance is our examination of his use of the theological anthropology of the creation narrative in the Book of Genesis to challenge the Jewish patriarchal and exploitative marriage institution, thus bringing to the fore the need to give women and the oppressed equal voice in the society. (Muonwe, 2014)

Clearly, the strategy of portraying Christianity as a 'women-elevating' tradition has been a successful one. When the European Court of Human Rights upheld the mandatory display of the crucifix in Italian schools, it did not view the crucifix as the symbol of the subordination of women, and of the superiority of the Christendom. Quite to the contrary, in *Lautsi* the ECtHR stated that, in a state school, the presence of the crucifix cannot be compared to the wearing of a headscarf by a teacher, on the account that the crucifix is a 'passive' symbol, and the veil a 'powerful religious one'. In this passage, the court referred to the case of *Dahlab v. Switzerland* (mentioned above), where the headscarf had been judged a 'powerful religious symbol which is difficult to reconcile with gender equality'. In the construction of the court, the subordination of women pertains exclusively to Islam. The 'passive' crucifix represents a secularized religious tradition that the court does not associate with gender inequality, with the subordination of women and/or with the reiteration of colonial discourses of domination.

In Western mainstream culture, veiling practices are associated with the seclusion and the subjugation of Oriental women within the private sphere. In the colonial context, the veil symbolized the resistance of local cultures to Western domination. Franz Fanon maintains that French colonizers attacked the veil in Algeria precisely in order to destroy the structure of the native colonial societies, together with their capacity for resistance. As women represent not only biological, but also cultural reproduction, 'conquering women', finding 'them behind the veil, where they hide themselves, and in the house where the men keep them out of sight' (Fanon, 1959: 164) constituted a crucial step in asserting the domination of the superior Western power. Today, this dynamic is perceivable in the French, Belgian, British and Swiss laws and cases regulating the wearing of Muslim attire, as well as in the 'veil jurisprudence' of the European Court of Human Rights, analysed above.

In Italy, however, there is no need to unveil Muslim women. 'Living together under the cross' suffices to reinforce the colonial discourses of domination in which the feminine serves to signify the subordination and exploitation of women and other inferior others. Veiled women are not perceived as challenging gender hierarchies and cultural patterns of domination in Italy, because the association of their appearance with the oriental desire to resist Western conquest is neutralized by the role of Catholicism in the public sphere. The crucifix in state schools represents the preferential treatment of Catholicism in its cultural (secularized) form, in the context of an alliance between religion and public power, where the ethical force of the first one upholds the political force of the latter and vice versa (Zagrebelsky, 2008). This context, under the pretences of universalism, substantially favours the crystallization of traditional gender roles, race relations and patterns of domination.

References

Ahmed, L. (1993). *Women and Gender in Islam. Historical Roots of a Modern Debate.* New Haven: Yale University Press.

Augenstein, D. (2008). *A European Culture of Religious Tolerance.* European University Institute Working Paper LAW 2008/04.

Benhabib, S. (1999). Sexual Difference and Collective Identities: The New Global Constellation. *Signs*, 24(2), 335–61.

Benhabib, S. (2002). *The Claims of Culture: Equality and Diversity in the Global Era*. Princeton: Princeton University Press.

Casanova, J. (1994). *Public Religions in the Modern World.* Chicago: Chicago University Press.

Casanova, J. (2006). The Long, Difficult, and Tortuous Journey of Turkey into Europe and the Dilemmas of European Civilization. *Constellations*, 13(2), 234–47.

Durham, W.C. Jr and Scharffs, B.J. (2010). *Law and Religion: National, International and Comparative Perspectives.* Austin, Boston, Chicago, New York, Aspen: Wolters Kluwer.

Fanon, F. (1959). Algeria Unveiled. In Oglesby, C. (ed.) *The New Left Reader*, 161–85. New York: Grove Press.

Heschel, S. (1990). Anti-Judaism in Christian Feminist Theology. *Tikkum*, 5(3), 25–9.

Adorno, T.W. and Horkheimer, M. (1944). *Dialectic of Enlightenment.* London: Verso.

Lombardi Vallauri, L. (2005). Simboli e Realizzazione. In Dieni, E., Ferrari, A. and Pacillo, V. (eds) *Symbolon/Diabolon: Simboli, religioni, diritti nell'Europa multiculturale*, 13–26. Bologna: Il Mulino.

Mancini, S. (2012). Patriarchy as the Exclusive Domain of the Other. The Veil Controversy, False Projection and Cultural Racism. *International Journal of Constitutional Law*, 10(2), 411–28.

Muonwe, M. (2014). *Challenging the Myths of Gender Equality – Theology and Feminism.* Bloomington: X Libris.

Plaskow, J. (2005). Christian Feminism and Anti-Judaism. In Plaskow, J. and Berman, D. (eds) *The Coming of Lilith. Essays on Feminism, Judaism and Sexual Ethics 1972–2003*, 89–93. Boston: Beacom Press.

PuiLan, K. (2005). *Post-Colonial Imagination and Feminist Theology.* Louisville: Westminster John Knox Press.

Schüssler Fiorenza, E. (1994). The Bible, the Global Context, and the Discipleship of Equals. In Choppand, R.S. and Lewish Taylor, M. (eds) *Reconstructing Christian Theology*. Minneapolis: Augsburg Fortress.

Schüssler Fiorenza, E. (2005). *We are Church – A Kindom of Priests*. Keynote Address delivered at the Women's Ordination Worldwide (WOW) Second International Conference, Breaking Silence, Breaking Bread: Christ Calls Women to Lead Ottawa, Canada July 22–24. Available at http://womensordinationworldwide.org/ottawa-2005/2014/2/2/elizabeth-schussler-fiorenza-we-are-a-church-a-kingdom-of-priests.

Shachar, A. (2002). *Multicultural Jurisdictions. Cultural Differences and Women's Rights*. Cambridge: Cambridge University Press.

Woehrling, J. and Jukier, R. (2010). Religion and the Secular State in Canada. In Martínez-Torrónand, J. and Durham, W.C. Jr, *Religion and the Secular State / La Religion et l'État laïque*. Interim National Reports Issued for the Occasion of the XVIIIth International Congress of Comparative Law. Provo: International Center for Law and Religion Studies.

Zagrebelsky, G. (2008). *Stato e Chiesa. Cittadini e cattolici. Passato e presente*, 73, 5–19.

PART IV: Citizenship and Second-Generation Migrant Women

Chapter 10
Second-Generation Migrant Women and the Acquisition of Italian Citizenship

Elena Paparella

Introduction: Immigration's Second Generation and the 'Rights Limbo'

This analysis pertains to some of the most salient themes linked to the constitutionally protected legal status of immigrants' children who, born in Italy or arriving in Italy at a tender age, have been educated in Italian schools and have grown up in that country's social context from their earliest years.

The problematic aspect lies in the fact that, once they attain their majority, second-generation young people regress to a condition that could be described as a 'rights limbo'. Indeed, while waiting to acquire Italian citizenship, while they have reached adulthood and the entitlements and guarantees they enjoyed as minors have come to an end, they do not automatically become entitled to other fundamental rights, including the right to vote.

The above mentioned effect is caused by the fact that the Italian legislation currently governing the acquisition of citizenship (Law no. 91/1992) is, to a large degree, inadequate in the face of recent developments. It has proved quite incapable of coping with the kinds of transformation currently characterizing the fabric of Italian society as a result of rising migration levels.

Despite the fact that a growing proportion of foreign citizens has succeeded in meeting the conditions for requesting Italian citizenship, and although a good part of the overall number of minors in Italy is of foreign origin, the general inadequacy of Law no. 91/1992 transforms the failure to acquire citizenship into an element of discrimination. This occurs especially *vis-à-vis* the exercise of fundamental rights and gives rise to a cause of further, not always 'just', inequalities for which there does not appear to be any immediately obvious, reasonable justification. Considering the importance of the fundamental rights being denied to young, second-generation immigrants, the argument in favour of a graduated recognition of rights relating to a variety of legal statuses generating different levels of inclusion (which would leave the formal acquisition of citizenship out of consideration) appears still less appropriate (Granaglia and Rigo, 2013; Sciortino, 2014).

Article 33 of the recent Decree Law no. 69/2013 (the so-called *Decreto del Fare*[1]) has resulted in a streamlining of procedures; this constitutes a small step

---

1 'Urgent Provisions for Re-launching the Economy'.

towards adapting the law governing citizenship to meet the expectations of young people of foreign origin. However, there are at present only a few signals that allow one to predict a full passage from the *jus sanguinis* principle to the *jus soli* one. This despite the fact that the *jus soli* principle is more than desirable in a situation where there is not only a growing sense of belonging to a multicultural social structure unforeseeable until a few decades ago (Olivito, 2006),[2] but also an increasing need, at an institutional level, to promote such demand: a situation that the new immigrant generations are helping to stabilize in a doubtlessly irreversible manner.

This contribution will examine the legislation currently governing the acquisition of citizenship by the children of foreigners, born in or outside Italy. It will also examine some of the implementing measures of a governmental nature that, during the last few years, have attenuated the legislation's restrictive nature. The most important judicial decisions will then be examined. This in order to highlight the evolution from a case-law grounded in administrative law and based on the principle of the administration's 'wide-ranging discretion' when evaluating and granting citizenship applications (in line with a formal, restrictive interpretation of the legislation) to a case-law grounded in ordinary civil law, which has proved decisive, being as it is directed at assessing the substantive, concrete existence of the conditions required for citizenship.

Finally, the work will examine the reform bills that have been introduced, beginning with those dating to the Fourteenth Parliament and ending with those introduced on the people's initiative in 2013. It will also consider the minimal legislative amendments already in force that, although not altering the framework founded on the *jus sanguinis* principle, do facilitate a simplification of the procedure for acquiring citizenship for foreigners born in Italy.

In this complex scenario, where a definitive result still appears to be a long way off, the intention is to proceed with a reading of the legislation and case-law on the acquisition of citizenship (as well as the related bills that have been introduced), so as to assess their adequacy and effects concerning the connection between concepts of identity and belonging and second-generation activism. Some attention will be paid, throughout, to the position of young women of foreign origin. For them, amongst the many existing and potential causes of hardship, the lack of voting rights (a devastating consequence of the difficulty in acquiring citizenship) translates, in fact, into their being denied the possibility of promoting or reinforcing particular interests stemming from their specific condition of being women. Such a fact results, daily, in their having to preserve a highly delicate balance, not only between different cultures, but also between such balance and the widest imaginable range of legitimate aspirations.

It is probably the combination of such dynamics that has resulted in this female component (a minority compared to a silent majority) developing a voice that is distinguishable for its specific 'gender notes'. This clearly appears through forms

2 As regards the idea of multiculturalism as a problem inevitably to be shared both by the minority groups and the majority culture, see Olivito (2007a and 2007b).

of participation[3] that are enriching the experiences of activism that the young second generation has, to a certain extent, already consolidated.[4]

The Legislation Governing Acquisition of Citizenship and the Regression of Rights

The inadequacy of the legislation currently governing the acquisition of citizenship is clearly the result of a 'squint-eyed' approach on the part of the government and Parliament. With Law no. 91/1992, Parliament took pains to protect Italian citizens residing abroad, granting them the right to vote despite their not living within the fabric of Italian society. Nevertheless, it took no account of the explosive population growth marking immigration's second – indeed, now third – generation (Paparella, 2011: 353; Capesciotti, 2014). Making the acquisition of citizenship difficult for the young sons and daughters of immigrants means denying the very foundations of the institution of citizenship (and its 'equalizing function' (Onida, 2009), first and foremost), since it takes its shape from the overall level of inclusion and the variety of the guarantees the legal order offers to those who acquire citizen status.[5]

The approach taken in Law no. 91/1992 is the result of a lack of prospective vision that would not, in fact, have been difficult to develop if attention had only been paid to the growing number of minors born to resident immigrants: 80,000 'foreigners' were born in Italy in 2012 alone and, if the children born to mixed couples are added to those having two foreign parents, the number having at least one foreign parent swells to 107,000, equalling 20.1 per cent of the total.[6] Furthermore, it was already possible, a few years ago, to calculate that the immigrants residing lawfully in Italy numbered roughly 5 million. Of these, approximately 900,000 were minors, including 560,000 born in Italy to foreign parents, to whom those arriving in Italy at a tender age must be added.[7]

---

3 See Associazione DG2 (Donne delle Seconde generazioni), *Seconde a chi? Giovanni donne di seconda generazione tra cittadinanza e poltica*, (Second-Generation Young Women between Citizenship and Politics). Available at www.donnedisecondagenerazione.it.

4 Amongst recent experiences, see the interview 'Minister Giannini says to Rete G2: Committed to including immigrants' children in the "*Buona Scuola*" ["The Good School"] programme and never again allowing foreigners to be excluded from public competitions', 20 October 2014. Available at www.secondegenerazioni.it.

5 As regards the distinction, as well as the passage from the status of 'subject' to that of citizen, see Zincone (1992, 2010 and 2011); as regards the various perspectives on citizenship issues, see Zolo (1994b).

6 See statistical updates at www.donnedisecondagenerazione.it, 8 June 2013.

7 Caritas Italiana, 2010. More recent data show that the numbers are still rising: as at 1 January 2013, the non-EU nationals with Italian citizenship numbered 3,764,236, of whom 49.3 per cent were women and 24.1 per cent were minors, equalling 907,181 persons present, see Caritas/Migrantes, 2014.

These data prove that migration levels in our country are moving in the direction of an apparently irreversible stabilization. Despite this fact, the legislative framework in force has been structured to conform to policy guidelines directed chiefly at containing immigration through emergency measures. These are inadequate in the face of transformations in the social fabric resulting from the ever-increasing presence of migrant workers and other immigrants but deriving, above all, from the specific component of the young second-generations. These latter are not only actively involved in the processes of integration at an institutional level, but also bring with them a complex heritage regarding identity, one that demands specific, systematic measures (Ricucci, 2010; Caponio and Schmoll, 2011).

What the law on the acquisition of citizenship currently offers immigrants' young adult children, born in Italy and wishing to become Italian citizens, is almost certainly a clash with complicated bureaucratic procedures that are nothing other than the reflection of inadequate legislation. Article 4(2) of Law no. 91/1992 requires both that applications for citizenship be made within one year of an applicant's eighteenth birthday and that demonstrations be made, with documentation relating to residence,[8] of the fact that the applicant has resided in Italy 'legally and without interruption' for 18 years. Throughout this period, the 'non-citizen' status of immigrants' children[9] does not prevent them, as minors, from exercising certain rights, such as the right or duty to receive education and the right to health care (in addition to the right to protection against forms of discrimination[10] that are punishable through the courts), regardless of their parents' status.[11] What happens is that these areas of protection guaranteed to minors tend to be gradually reduced until they dry up completely in relation to those who have attained their majority, resulting in a material 'regression' of the rights that these persons would enjoy.

Very often it emerges that, although the foreign parents were legally present in Italy, they failed to add the names of their children born in Italy onto their stay permit or to register them with the Central Registry Office, or did so out of time. The failure to comply with these requirements has frequently been the ground on which the competent authorities have denied citizenship, thus making its acquisition impossible.

For these reasons, the Ministry of the Interior has considered it appropriate to establish certain criteria for applying the legislation in a manner that might correspond better to immigrants' needs and their objective difficulties in

---

8 Article 3(4) of Decree of the President of the Republic no. 572/1993.

9 See data of the Ministry of Education, Universities and Research (MIUR), 22 November 2013, available at www.integrazionemigranti.gov.it.

10 Pursuant to article 43 of Legislative Decree no. 286/1998, the Immigration Consolidation Act.

11 See the Court of Milan's Order no. 2380, dated 11 February 2008, which refers to article 38(1) of Legislative Decree no. 286/1998.

becoming socially rooted. This 'for the purpose of preventing that the omissions or delays, relating to the ... duties incumbent on the persons exercising parental authority and not imputable to the minor, may cause the latter harm'.[12] Certain ministerial circulars and their implementing regulations[13] therefore introduced the principle that

> the late registration of a minor's birth with an Italian municipality shall not necessarily be considered prejudicial for the purposes of acquiring citizenship pursuant to article 4(2) of Law no. 91/1992, where there exists documentation capable of demonstrating the actual presence of the same in our country during the period preceding the regularization (vaccination certificates and medical certificates in general), [even] if during periods following the birth, brief interruptions in the possession of a stay permit were to be noted. For the purpose of fostering the possibility of demonstrating his/her continuing stay within the Italian territory, the interested party shall be entitled to produce integrating documentation such as school, medical or other certificates that testify to his/her presence in Italy.[14]

This substantial opening has nevertheless been frequently counterbalanced by the vast 'area of the administration's discretion in the procedure for granting Italian citizenship, which procedure provides for the foreigner's advance integration within the country's social fabric':[15] an integration sanctioned at the level of governmental policy-setting and also confirmed by the administrative courts in some cases.

In cases where the young, second-generation adults were born outside Italy and came to the country at a tender age, the acquisition of citizenship is governed by the residence requirement, i.e. that they demonstrate they have 'resided legally in the Republic's territory' for at least 10 years.[16] The legislation provides for the granting of citizenship: (a) to those who have parents or direct, second-degree ascendants who were citizens through birth; (b) to those who are adopted by Italian citizens and who reside legally in the Republic's territory for five years; (c) to those who work as employees of the State; (d) to those who are European citizens and have been residing for at least five years in Italy; and (e) to stateless

12 Ministry of the Interior Circular no. 22, dated 7 November 2007, issued by the Department for Civil Liberties and Immigration.

13 See Decree of the President of the Republic no. 572/1993.

14 Ministry of the Interior Circular no. 22, dated 7 November 2007, issued by the Department for Civil Liberties and Immigration, which refers to the Ministry of the Interior Circular no. K 69/89, dated 18 February 1997, concerning ways of overcoming certain omissions relating to the regularization of minors in Italy, such as registration of birth and uninterrupted residence, for the purposes of applying article 4(2) of Law no. 91/1992.

15 Ministry of the Interior Circular no. K 60.I, dated 5 January 2007.

16 Article 9(1)(f) of Law no. 91/1992.

persons who have been residing legally in Italy for at least five years (article 9(1) (a), (b), (c), (d) and (e) of Law no. 91/1992). Those who, on the other hand, are not covered by any of these legislative provisions have no other choice than to request citizenship on the basis of their – legal – residence for 10 years. Thus, no account is taken of the fact that the person aspiring to citizenship not only has been residing in Italy possibly for far longer than 10 years, but has also attended Italian schools and has obviously integrated into the Italian social structure to a far greater degree than someone who came to Italy as an adult.

The inadequacy of the law on citizenship and the fragmentary nature of the corrective interventions have fostered a reform project having various political and participatory origins, ranging from Parliament to the people's initiative and benefitting from the encouraging effect of the Head of State's support.[17] The effects of such drives for reform on the procedures currently governing the acquisition of citizenship would be minimal in comparison with the primary, *jus soli* objective and yet they are not wholly irrelevant. Partly as a result of the participatory action of those directly affected, an amendment was introduced in 2013 by way of the so-called 'Doing decree'. It provides that possible failures traceable to parents or to offices within the public administration shall not be imputed to the interested party, and it permits the latter to show that he or she possesses the requisites by way of every other appropriate form of documentation. It further puts the administration under a duty to provide information to potentially interested parties upon their eighteenth birthday.[18]

In such a context, it also appears indicative that the Ministry of the Interior is providing data on the number of citizenship-acquisition procedures that were concluded favourably on the basis of residence (equalling 22,844 in 2012, i.e. 38 per cent of the total),[19] but is not including in its statistics the data concerning applications and grants relating to persons who, upon attaining their majority, declare that they wish to become Italian citizens. In other words, it appears indicative that no information is provided about the 'grant' of citizenship.

The Evolution of Judicial Decisions

As far as judicial intervention regarding the acquisition of citizenship is concerned, two distinct phases may be noted. A first phase, relating to the grant of citizenship not limited to second-generation young people but extending to all categories of immigrant applicants, essentially involved the administrative courts. In this

17 President Giorgio Napolitano, 22 November 2012: Rete G2 press release, 'We Italians with a stay permit thank you, Mr President'. Available at www.secondegenerazioni.it.

18 Decree Law no. 69 of 21 June 2013, article 33, 'Simplification of the procedure for acquiring citizenship for foreigners born in Italy'.

19 See www.interno.gov.it.

context, administrative justice has frequently resulted in citizenship being denied[20] in cases that have confirmed and, at the same time, consolidated certain guidelines of government policy directed at increasing the administration's exercise of its discretion in procedures for the granting of citizenship.[21]

A second, more recent phase has been marked, on the other hand, by the intervention of the ordinary civil courts in the specific context of proceedings relating to citizenship applications made by second-generation young people. The main line of argument supporting appeals and contained in judgments has shifted from the public-law context of the unlawfulness of administrative acts denying citizenship, to the private-law one of individual responsibility for performing duties and the actual requirements for acquiring citizen status. All this has resulted in a U-turn in the case-law, and one in favour of minors applying for citizenship. In other words, in applications against measures denying citizenship, the ordinary courts have sanctioned a principle of removing responsibility from the minor (or newly adult child of foreigners) for failures and/or omissions attributable to other parties such as parents or public officials. Therefore, they have made use of alternative documentation provided by schools, or health certification, as proof of the interested party's actual and uninterrupted residence in Italy. In so doing, the ordinary courts have themselves, too, implemented certain specific government directives aimed at softening the effect of the legislation on the proof of legal and uninterrupted residence.[22]

Five decisions following that line of interpretation may be found during the period 2012–13.[23] Of these, one was a decision of the Court of Appeal in Naples issued in April 2012. Deciding an appeal against the denial of citizenship, the court emphasized the importance of

> a situation of actual (and, therefore, legal) residence on the part of the minor, to be shown, as was shown in the case under examination, by significant facts

---

20 See the Lazio Regional Administrative Court (Second Section, Fourth Subsection), judgment no. 37926/2010; Lazio Regional Administrative Court (Second Section, Fourth Subsection), judgment no. 11771/2009; Council of State, Sixth Section, judgment no. 1788/2009; Lazio Regional Administrative Court (Second Section, Fourth Subsection), judgment no. 5360/2008, and the Veneto Regional Administrative Court (Third Section), judgment no. 1958/2008.

21 Council of State (Fourth Section), judgment no. 1474 of 16 September 1999. Council of State (Sixth Section), ruling no. 52/2011 of 10 January 2011.

22 See article 3(4) of Decree of the President of the Republic no. 572/1993 and article 4(2) of Law no. 91/1992.

23 Judgment no. 1486 issued by the Naples Court of Appeal on 13 April 2012; Decree no. 1295 of 11 September 2012, issued by the Court of Imperia; Decree issued on 31 January 2013 by the First Civil Division of the Court of Reggio Emilia, in Proceeding No. 6448/2012; judgment issued by the Second Civil Division of the Court of Lecce on 11 March 2013 and the Decree issued by the First Civil Division of the Court of Florence on 5 April 2013.

> proving a lasting and stable stay within the territory from birth and integration within the socio-cultural context (for example, progressive cycles of schooling).[24]

In 2013, the Court of Lecce also confirmed the line removing responsibility from the minor (in foster care, in this case) for failures not attributable to him, that must not have 'negative repercussions' on him 'by precluding the possibility of fruitfully making a declaration pursuant to article 4(2) of Law no. 91/1992 for the purposes of applying for citizenship'.[25]

A parallel trend may be observed in the administration and in the courts as they both move from a lesser to a greater interpretive openness to the granting of citizenship. In any event, these recent developments allow one to deduce that the case-law has, in this case too, proved crucial for protecting individual rights that the legislation, on the other hand, fails to protect.

Reform Bills and the Second-Generations' Intervention

A proper perception of how the foreign presence would have grown and become an established part of the Italian demography was totally absent at an institutional level at the beginning of the 1990s. In reaffirming the *jus sanguinis* principle as the only source of citizenship, Law no. 91/1992 is clearly the product of such a lacuna, as well as the expression of a general will to preserve the *status quo*, a will that was totally anachronistic considering Italy's unequivocal mutation from an emigration country to a destination for migrants. The inversion of migratory flows has made the pre-eminence of the *jus sanguinis* principle over the *jus soli* one increasingly inappropriate and out of keeping with reality. Heavily weighted in favour of protecting descent, Law no. 91/1992 has, by now, been largely discredited in its original rationale of protecting Italian emigrants. In the face of a strong (and, one could add, quite natural) desire for integration on the part of foreign immigrants in Italy, the law is profoundly hostile, above all, towards foreign children who were born and/or raised and educated in Italy.[26]

For these reasons, reforming the law on the acquisition of citizenship has, albeit somewhat patchily over the last few years, become a matter of institutional

24 Judgment no. 1486, issued by the Naples Court of Appeal on 13 April 2012.

25 Court of Lecce (Second Civil Division), 11 March 2013.

26 See Zolo (1994b: 43–44), who reflects on the need for a 'consistent theory of citizenship' capable of 'supporting a 'fight for rights' that does not turn into generic and rhetorical slogans', as well as 'a table of legislative demands directed against the growing risks of discrimination towards which citizens who are not members of the big political, professional, trade-union and religious interest-groups are heading'. On the topic of a multi-dimensional citizenship complying with multi-dimensional societies and individuals, see, of course, Marshall (1950); for a constitutional lawyer's approach to this issue, see Azzariti (2013).

urgency, and the lack of continuity in political interventions has not prevented the proliferation of numerous bills connoting different conceptions both of the institution of citizenship and of possible ways of transforming it. They may all, essentially, be traced back to two predominant visions: the first, more restrictive one sees the recognition of citizen status as the result of a concessionary process that accords citizenship the value of a prize, whilst the second, better-suited to the changing social reality, takes note of the stabilization of migrants within the territory and promotes citizenship as a vehicle for integration insofar, as it is the expression not only of the 'nexus between the enjoyment of certain rights and the belonging to a political group' but also of a 'politico-legal status' and a 'tie through which one is part of a particular community' (Baccelli, 1994: 130).

The 'nation of citizens' is, in fact, that in which the chance demographic composition of the population is continually redefining 'the horizon of the value orientations on which the cultural battles and the self-clarifying ethical-political discourses take place. If we modify citizenship's social composition then we also modify this 'values horizon' (Habermas, 1998: 157).

During the period 2009–10, under the centre-right government, bills presented by the majority and the opposition corresponded, respectively, to the two conceptions of citizenship recalled above (one 'concessionary/prize-like' and the other 'integrationist'). To a certain extent, these found a degree of convergence in the bipartisan 'Granata-Sarubbi' Bill (Chamber Document no. 2670/2008). In the period May-June 2010, a series of bills introduced over the two preceding years (Chamber Document no. 103 and connected bills[27]) gave rise to a parliamentary investigation that directly involved some of the second-generations young people representing Rete G2.[28] Although the latter had already been committed members of associations for some years,[29] from this moment onwards they really became active participants in the process of reforming the law on citizenship, arousing a widespread consensus on the need to revise the criteria governing its attribution.

Subsequently, during the course of 2012, a bill was introduced into Parliament on the people's initiative. Supported by 200,000 signatures, it was the fruit of a national campaign entitled *L'Italia sono anch'io* ('I, too, am Italy') which

27 See Chamber of Deputies, Sixteenth Parliament, Report by the First Standing Committee (for Constitutional Affairs and those relating to the Presidency of the Council of Ministers and the Interior) on Bill nos. 103, 104, 457, 566, 718, 995, 1048, 1592, 2006, 2035, 2431, 2670, 2684, 2904 and 2910-A, 17 December 2009, which envisaged, inter alia, reducing the stay period in Italy for those seeking citizenship from ten to five years, ascertaining the foreigner's real linguistic and social integration, reducing the degree of discretion involved in the granting of citizenship and extending the attribution of citizenship to the second generations. See Fumicelli (2013: 3, 15).

28 Chamber of Deputies, Sixteenth Parliament, *Indagine conoscitiva nell'ambito dell'esame delle proposte di legge c. 103 e abbinate, recanti nuove norme in materia di cittadinanza*, 11 June 2010. See Paparella (2011: 359–60).

29 The Rete–G2 Association has been active in many Italian cities since 2005: see www.secondegenerazioni.it.

was promoted on the occasion of the 150th anniversary of Italy's unification by numerous civil society organizations.[30] Like the bills introduced before it, this bill failed to produce any legislation but, thanks to the broad consensus behind it, it contributed to inaugurating a parliamentary debate. The most significant element of both the campaign and the popular initiative is the attempt to extend the *jus soli* principle's sphere of application, with the aim of redirecting immigration policies from a public order context to action truly geared to integration. In the specific case, the bill introduces the '*jus culturae*' criterion, i.e. the possibility of acquiring citizenship at the request of the parents in cases where a minor has frequented primary school, secondary school or professional training courses.[31]

Between June and July 2013 (during the XVII Parliament), the Constitutional Affairs Committee at the Chamber of Deputies embarked upon a consideration of numerous bills[32] that not only reconfirmed a trend in favour of affirming the *jus soli*[33] principle but also referred to the *jus culturae* one. The latter strongly reconnects the acquisition of citizenship to schooling, albeit with some differences regarding the years of attendance required[34] in addition to the type of studies.[35] Finally, some bills introduce the right to citizenship founded on a *jus domicilii*, in cases where a minor, who is the child of foreign parents and was either born in Italy or entered Italy before his or her tenth birthday, can demonstrate that he or she has stayed legally[36] – or 'regularly' – in Italy until attainment of his or her majority[37] or has resided there

30 See www.litaliasonoanchio.it.

31 Bill introduced on the people's initiative ('Amendments to Law no. 91/1992, entitled 'New Rules on Citizenship'). Available at www.litaliasonoanchio.it.

32 See Chamber of Deputies, Studies Service, Department for Institutions, *Rules for Citizenship – Chamber Document no. 9 and Connected Documents, Documentation for the Consideration of Bills*, no. 37, 26 June 2013; Chamber of Deputies, Studies Service, Department for Institutions, Second edition, 24 May 2014.

33 Amongst the various hypotheses, one can detect a reference both to the German model, by virtue of which citizenship through birth may be acquired by those born of foreign parents of whom at least one has stayed legally for an established period, and to the French model of 'double *jus soli*', which provides for the acquisition of citizenship by those born within the territory of foreign parents of whom at least one was born. The bills therefore also differ as regards the length of the legal stay-period required (ranging from one to five years) and the type of stay required of the parent (which ranges from a regular stay to legal residence or a long-term stay permit). As regards these specific themes, see Fumicelli (2013: 17–18).

34 Just attendance, Chamber Doc. nos. 250 (Vendola), 273 (Bressa), 274 (Bressa), 369 (Zampa), 463 (Bersani), 707 (Gozi: 8 years) and 349 (Pes); completion of the course of studies, Chamber Doc. no. 525 (Marazziti).

35 Chamber Document nos. 463 (Bersani) and 273 (Bressa). More recently see bill S. 271, on *jus soli* and *jus culturae*, which is now being examined in the Senate.

36 Chamber Document no. 9, introduced on the people's initiative.

37 Chamber Document no. 250 (Vendola).

legally.[38] As one can see, both the *jus culturae* criterion and the *jus domicilii* one contribute to the definition of a 'European style' *jus soli* that differs from the 'American' one because it requires a journey in education and a certain rootedness on the part of the young child's immigrant family of origin (Zincone, 2013).

Second-Generations between Solidarity and Deliberative Actions: G2 Women Activism

The difficulties of the legislative and judiciary evolution concerning the acquisition of citizenship and the attempts to reform the related legislation have to be observed also in the perspective of political activism and of the ever-growing crucial role played by young second-generations, who triggered transformations both in the legal-ruling system and in the overall social structure. The analysis of the legal status of the young G2[39] crucially highlights two aspects: the peculiar relationship with the institutions and the growing role played by young women of foreign origins in the construction of a complex identity.

The young G2 deprived of Italian citizenship find themselves in a condition of 'institutional inferiority' due to a very uncertain legal-constitutional status. Betraying any expectation concerning the fulfilment of equality of opportunities, the missed acquisition of the citizenship converts itself in a substantial juridical inequality, in other words in a status of minority, if not actually of exclusion from the enjoyment of fundamental individual rights.[40] The constitutional lawyer should keep questioning himself on the rationality of this betrayal, despite the strong and well-established acknowledgement by the Constitutional Court.[41]

For those reasons, young G2 perform deliberative actions, in the broad sense of participation in actions that are socially necessary and are not performed by public institutions. In this way, they lay out the foundations for the construction and the realization of their own 'constitutional program' of future citizens,[42] whose basis may be represented precisely by that principle of 'political, economic and social solidarity' stated in article 2 of the constitution.[43] In fact, among the various public actions of the G2,[44] the stress put on 'constitutional duties' can be taken as a deeply

38 Chamber Document nos. 200, 273, 274, 249, 494, 525, 647, 707 and 1204: see Chamber of Deputies, Studies Service, Department for Institutions, *Rules for Citizenship – Chamber Doc. No. 9 and Connected Documents, Documentation for the Consideration of Bills*, no. 37, second edition, 24 May 2014.

39 'Young G2' meaning immigration's second-generation young people.

40 In constitutional law, see Azzariti (2013) and Manetti (2014).

41 The first ruling on this matter is Constitutional Court judgment no. 120/1967.

42 Rodotà (2014: 51–67), on the idea of solidarity according to article 2 of the Constitution as citizenship's characterization.

43 See Bascherini (2014: 534–41 and 2007: 126). On the topic of the constitutional duties in the previous constitutional legal thought, see Lombardi (1967).

44 www.secondegenearzioni.it.

meaningful indicator of a process towards a new identity, where that has also been enhanced in compliance with the principle of solidarity (Giubboni, 2012).[45] In fact, all the associations that have been established everywhere in the country meet the profound demand of self-identification and of a substantial lack of attention by the competent institutions, at least until very recently.[46]

On the specific topic of the citizenship legislation reform, the proposal that was the result of the *L'Italia sono anch'io* campaign takes on a crucial significance for second-generation young people. This could be connected to a self-identification process to which the activation of participation processes largely contributes. The advocacy of direct democracy procedures such as the people's legislative initiative, could be included in a more extended 'experiment of new democracy', actually launched by those who suffer from a non-existent, or very narrow, guarantee of institutional representation (Prandini, 2013: 9). Therefore, although it has been channelled into the ordinary legislative procedure through the people's legislative initiative, the 'public discourse' launched by the G2 could be related to the dynamics of the 'deliberative democracy',[47] according to which the promoters of specific demands are also potentially concerned with the final decisions that follow the deliberative process (Bifulco, 2011: 271; Martì, 2006: 28).

In the case of the G2's activism, the 'deliberative actions' are imposed by the need to fill the flaws of the representative democracy procedures; indeed, they are founded on premises and principles that are different from those of the traditional dynamics of negotiations and vote from which the majority of second-generation young people are excluded. Therefore, differently from what occurs in a society characterized by a common culture, a common ethic and a common feeling of belonging, the deliberative solution could be considered crucial in a multicultural society in which multiculturalism is a pluralism of different cultures within the same political society (Viola, 2003: 11, 33–71).

Very often it is asked whether the deliberative processes have to be considered a method that simply gives support to representative processes or, quite the opposite, they are themselves the cause and the result of the actual evolution of representative democracy. This question is actually a difficult theoretical conundrum for constitutional lawyers. What appears to be extremely clear,

---

45 Furthermore, on the principle of solidarity related to European citizenship, see Ross (2011: 283).

46 www.integrazionemigranti.gov.it, 'Filo diretto con le seconde generazioni Il nostro manifesto in 10 punti'.

47 The definition of 'deliberative democracy' – recalled from Bessette (1980) – indicates that theory according to which the processes of public decision are steered by two principles: a previous public debate and the intervention of those who are potentially interested by the final decision (Bifulco, 2011: 271). The theoretical basis of deliberative democracy, as it is well known, can brought back both to Habermas (2008) and to Rawls (1996). The importance of the 'public discourse' as an instrument for democracy was also the focus of the American pragmatic tradition (Spadafora, 2003). In the tradition of Italian public lawyers, see Mortati (1971).

independently from the chosen perspective, is that the common element to any theoretical approach related to the deliberative democracy processes is the shifting of the focus from the state's sphere – i.e. representative institutions – and from political parties to civil society. As far as the relationship between the state and the 'public sphere' is concerned, the most important issue, both in the theory and in the practice of deliberative processes, is how to provide an 'institutional mediation' between the substantially procedural nature of the deliberative dynamics, on the one hand, and the political institutions, in charge of the final decision and ruled by constitutional provisions, on the other (Mastropaolo, 2001: 1625).

In this scenario, the young G2 experiment offers us the opportunity to investigate a concrete experience, even though 'decentralized'. In the specific case the necessity of a relationship with the institutions was confirmed, even if in the negative. In fact, the reason of the only partial success of the debate that led to the people's legislative initiative of the *L'Italia sono anch'io* campaign could be considered the lack of solutions to the 'institutional mediation' problem, which revealed itself right at the moment of meeting with the institutions. If one considers the inevitable, but at the same time desirable, expansion of the deliberative process towards representative institutions and political decisions' actors, what seems to be missing is exactly an element of institutional support. More explicitly, what is needed and missing is constitutional legitimacy in the form, for example, of support in the Parliament by the majority or a political group. The risk – not a light one, indeed – is that social demands are directly addressed to constitutional bodies and brought before the general legislation, in the absence of intermediate institutions.

This 'public discourse' is growing according to a dynamic process that appears not easy to reverse; however, a central question is whether the distinct demand of acknowledgment and, therefore, of access to Italian citizenship by the feminine component of immigration's young generation is sufficiently highlighted and supported.

Indeed, if one of the reasons why citizenship as an 'ideal' is still recommended (despite the well-known crisis of classical theories on democracy) is its capacity of associating the topic of individual rights with that of pre-juridical reasons of belonging and political exclusion (Zolo, 1994a: IX–X), the issue of a potential 'feminine citizenship' (Saraceno, 2008) looks more than justified, even if hard to achieve (Siim, 2000).

Obviously this issue should not be confined to a strictly formal level; on the contrary, the solution to the dilemma between reaching a condition of full equality, in the meaning of the equalizing function of citizenship, and promoting the differences related to women's conditions should be searched for at a substantive level.

In fact, a well-established trend all over Europe is that second-generation immigrant women are rapidly becoming key players in political issues.[48] This occurs despite the fact that their identity problems, arising from the multiplicity of

48 See, in particular, Muslim women's experience (Moors and Salih, 2009: 375–8).

their cultural origins, are very often amplified by their specific gender condition which, in turn, has further peculiarities according to ethnic groups and cultures.

Data concerning women's different origins and respective ethnic groups are scanty; nonetheless, they allow us to get a picture of the diverse experience of second-generation women in Italy, ranging from the extremely fragile condition of the little gypsy girls, to the integration and education of girls coming from a foreign background and studying in secondary schools or attending university courses. According to the last MIUR-ISMU Report on *Alunni con cittadinanza non italiana* ('Students with Non-Italian Citizenship'), the drop-out of gypsy students occurs, for the greatest part, between primary and secondary high school; more precisely, the percentage of girls attending the school before finalizing their education decreases as they move to higher-level schools (Gubbini, 2014). The number of girls in secondary high school coming from a foreign familiar background is quite high; we also know that they have different orientations compared to their Italian peers.[49]

Unfortunately, the data supplied by the Italian government do not provide information about the different origins of those girls, nor do they make a distinction between boys and girls not having Italian citizenship who have achieved the school-leaving certificate and have enrolled in a three-year university programme.[50] Beyond these aseptic data, there are interesting realities that some recent studies have brought to the surface. Among them, we recall the case of Muslim women in Italy facing difficulties deriving from a hierarchical ranking of Christianity and Islam that has recently re-emerged and that has not been mitigated by political choices. Nonetheless, it does not prevent various forms of activism through the GMI (*Giovani Musulmani Italiani*: 'Young Italian Muslims') association and the *Consulta giovanile per il pluralismo culturale e religioso* ('Youth Council for Religious and Cultural Pluralism'). These experiences contribute to what has been defined as '*de facto* secularism' of the Islamic component in Italy and, above all, to a redefinition of the Islamic identity that comes very close to a complex 'public

---

49 MIUR-ISMU, *Alunni con cittadinanza non italiana. L'eterogeneità dei percorsi scolastici* ('Students with Non-Italian Citizenship. The Heterogeneity of the study courses'), National Report 2012/2013, 65: among girls from with a foreign background, choosing high school remains limited (27.9 per cent) compared with choosing professional or technical secondary school (33.3 per cent and 34.8 per cent respectively), whereas 54 per cent of Italian girls choose high schools, compared with technical secondary schools (23.1 per cent) and professional secondary schools (16.7 per cent).

50 The ISTAT-MIUR database highlights that in the academic year 2012–13, among 216.497 enrolled in a three-year university programme, 11,796 (5.4 per cent) do not have Italian citizenship; 6,691 of these latter achieved the school-leaving certificate in Italy, equal to 56.7 per cent of the non-Italian students and to 3.1 per cent of the total number of the students enrolled; see MIUR-ISMU, *Alunni con cittadinanza non italiana. L'eterogeneità dei percorsi scolastici* ('Students with Non-Italian Citizenship. The Heterogeneity of the study courses'), National Report 2012/2013, 66.

sphere', within which women are in many circumstances key players (Salih, 2009; Pojmann, 2010; Saint-Blancat, 2015).

In fact, this is proved by the peculiar forms of women's aggregation, which claim a distinction from that of men (Khachi, 2014). Furthermore, other specific forms of activism concerning matters related to the political participation of women with foreign origins are arising in connection to the broader and very general issue of women's participation in politics,[51] apart from a permanent careful consideration of the problematic theme of citizenship (Frisina, 2014).

Final Remarks

The main object of this chapter is not to present final solutions to the problem of the acquisition of Italian citizenship for 'immigration's second generation'. In this respect, some essential proposals already exist; they actually are those concerning the reform of citizenship's law, which at the moment are buried and forgotten in Parliament. Among them is the one worked out by young G2.

The aim is, rather, to analyse the experience of the immigration of second-generations in Italy from the point of view of the deficiencies in the legal-constitutional status of those young men and women due to their difficult access to citizenship. In this scenario, many second-generation women, instead of citizenship, are gradually acquiring an awareness that is affecting the process through which they develop more articulated identities. Indeed they are less and less slavishly conforming to their cultural traditions while, with several difficulties along the way, they are gaining space in a complex society such as the Italian one (Khachi, 2014).

The automatic acquisition of citizenship on the basis of the *jus soli* principle would represent for the young G2 a decisive step towards the implementation of the equality principle. The exercise of their right to vote would allow them to access the sphere of representative democracy. This would not guarantee, however, full democratic participation. Indeed, this is demonstrated by the difficulties that citizens from many generations encounter in finding a proper channel of transmission of specific needs, individual or collective, through the right to vote. These considerations lead us to the problem of democratic representation and to the crisis of political parties (Manin, 2010: 218).

Observed from the point of view of immigration, those phenomena look even more serious and in urgent need of solutions more suitable for all the transformations under way. In the search for new solutions, it could be useful to consider the resources of the deliberative democracy actions, both as a possible remedy to

51 See *Giovani donne di seconda generazione tra cittadinanza e politica* ('Second-generation young women between citizenship and politics'), which is part of the European 'More Women in European Politics 2012–2014' project, launched by the European Commission, DG Justice, Fundamental Rights and Citizenship.

the crisis of political representation and as an instrument for the development of a more fruitful relationship between society and state. This is not to say that in the new setting there should be no final institutional outcome, with its regulatory underpinnings; much to the contrary, in the specific case of immigration's second generation, such an outcome appears necessary in order to restore a relationship with the institutions which actually broke up from the beginning.

For several years Italian scholars have been questioning the exclusion of such a remarkable and still-growing component of Italian society from the full enjoyment of fundamental individual rights (Paparella, 2011: 363). The question is not losing its importance as time goes by and, also, the awareness of the problems seems not to decline;[52] on the other hand, the potential of reaction to this *status quo* by directly interested people is getting stronger and it will likely be addressed to the acquisition of a status that would allow them to be equal even if they are 'different'.[53]

References

Azzariti, G. (2013). La cittadinanza: appartenenza, partecipazione, diritti della persona. In *Costituzione, economia, globalizzazione: liber amicorum in onore di Carlo Amirante*, 25–41. Napoli: Edizioni Scientifiche Italiane.

Baccelli, L. (1994). Cittadinanza e appartenenza. In Zolo, D. (ed.) *La cittadinanza. Appartenenza, identità, diritti*, 129–65. Roma-Bari: Laterza.

Bascherini, G. (2007). I doveri costituzionali degli immigrati. In Balduzzi, R., Cavino, M., Grosso, E. and Luther, J. (eds) *I doveri costituzionali: la prospettiva del Giudice delle leggi*, 86–139. Torino: Giappichelli.

Bascherini, G. (2014). Il servizio civile tra Stato e Regioni, i doveri di solidarietà, la cittadinanza. *Giurisprudenza costituzionale*, 1, 534–41.

Bessette, J. (1980). Deliberative Democracy: The Majority Principle in Republican Government. In Goldwin, R.A. and Schambra, W.A. (eds) *How Democratic is Constitution?*, 102–16. Washington: American Enterprise Institute for Public Policy Research.

Bifulco, R. (2011). Democrazia deliberativa. *Enciclopedia del Diritto. Annali IV*, 271–94.

Capesciotti, M. (2014). Su alcune novità legislative e giurisprudenziali in tema di seconde generazioni dell'immigrazione. *Associazione Italiana dei Costituzionalisti* – Rivistaic.it, 1, 1–11.

Caponio, T. and Schmoll, C. (2011). Lo studio delle seconde generazioni in Francia e in Italia: tra transnazionalismo e nazionalismo metodologico. In Barbagli, M. and Schmoll, C. (eds) *Stranieri in Italia. La generazione dopo*, 103–46. Bologna: Il Mulino.

52 For a critique of a '*jure sanguinis* democracy' see Onida (2009).

53 Touraine (2012: 66).

Caritas Italiana (2010). *Dossier statistico immigrazione Caritas-Migrantes 2010.* Roma: Caritas.

Caritas/Migrantes (2014). *XXIII Rapporto immigrazione 2013. Tra crisi e diritti umani*. Todi: Tau.

Frisina, A. (2014). *Vocabolario minimo sulla cittadinanza italiana. Una prospettiva generazionale*. Available at www.donnedisecondagenerazione.it, 15/01/2014.

Fumicelli, D. (2013). Spunti di riflessione in tema di cittadinanza: l'azione di integrazione degli stranieri extracomuniatri tra profili comparatistici, progetti in discussione e *best practices*. Costituzionalismo.it, 3, 1–49.

Granaglia, E. and Rigo, E. (2013). Eccesso di disuguaglianze? In Saraceno, C., Sartor, N. and Sciortino, G. (eds) *Stranieri e disuguali. Le disuguaglianze nei diritti e nelle condizioni di vita degli immigrati*, 339–64. Bologna: Il Mulino.

Giubboni, S. (2012). Solidarietà. *Politica del diritto*, 4, 525–53.

Gubbini, C. (2014). Miur: rapporto sugli alunni non italiani. 'Stranieri' fino a quando? Available at www.cronachediordinariorazzismo.org, 15/03/2014.

Habermas, J. (1998). *Between Facts and Norms: Contribution to a Discourse Theory of Law and Democracy*. Cambridge: The MIT Press.

Habermas, J. (2008). *L'inclusione dell'altro. Studi di teoria politica*. It. translation by Ceppa, L. (ed.) Milano: Feltrinelli (German edn 1996. *Die Einbeziehung des Anderen. Studien zur politischen Theorie*, Frankfurt am Main: Suhrkamp).

Istat (2013), *Report Statistiche, Anno 2012 – Natalità e fecondità della popolazione residente*. 27 November 2013, 1–16. Available at http://www.istat.it/it/archivio/104818.

Khachi, F. (2014). I marocchini non pagano più il conto dell'associazionismo al cous cous. Available at www.Yallaitalia.it, 1/12/2014.

Lombardi, G. (1967). *Contributo allo studio dei doveri costituzionali*. Milano: Giuffré.

Manetti, M. (2014). Profili costituzionali in materia di diritto alla cittadinanza degli immigrati. *Rassegna parlamentare: rivista mensile di studi costituzionali e di documentazione legislativa*, 515–34.

Manin, B. (2010). *Principi del governo rappresentativo*. Bologna: Il Mulino.

Marshall, T.H. (1950). *Citizenship and Social Class and Other Essays*. Cambridge: Cambridge University Press.

Martì, E. (2006). The epistemic conception of deliberative democracy defended. Reasons, rightness and equal political autonomy. In Besson, S. and Martì, J.L. (eds) *Deliberative Democracy and its discontent*. London: Ashgate.

Mastropaolo, A. (2001). Democrazia, neodemocrazia, postdemocrazia: tre paradigmi a confronto. *Diritto pubblico comparato ed europeo*, 3–4, 1613–35.

Mortati, C. (1971). *La persona, lo Stato e le comunità intermedie*. Torino: Eri.

Moors, A. and Salih, R. (2009). Muslim Women in Europe: Secular Normativities, bodily performances and multiples publics. *Social Anthropology-Antropologie Sociale*, 17, 375–8.

Olivito, E. (2006). *Minoranze culturali e identità multiple. I diritti dei soggetti vulnerabili*. Roma: Aracne.

Olivito, E. (2007a). Primi spunti di riflessione su multiculturalismo e identità culturali nella prospettiva della vulnerabilità. *Politica del Diritto*, 1, 71–109.

Olivito, E. (2007b). Lo spazio della cittadinanza: teorie di inclusione, pratiche di esclusione. *Rivista critica del diritto privato*, 3, 517–34.

Onida, V. (2009). *Lo statuto costituzionale del non cittadino. Relazione introduttiva*, Annual conference held by the Italian Association of Constitutionalists, 16–17 October 2009. Available at http://archivio.rivistaaic.it/materiali/convegni/aic 200910/index.html.

Paparella, E. (2011). Accesso alla cittadinanza e seconde generazioni dell'immigrazione. In Angelini, F., Benvenuti, M. and Schillaci, A. (eds) *Le nuove frontiere del diritto dell'immigrazione*, 353–66. Napoli: Jovene.

Pojmann, W. (2010). *Donne immigrate e femminismo in Italia*. Italian translation by Meloni, M. (ed.) Roma: Aracne. (US edn 2006. *Immigrant Women and Feminism in Italy*. Aldershot: Ashgate).

Prandini, R. (2013). Esperimenti di (nuova) democrazia: come salvare l'esperienza democratica nell'epoca della sua crisi. In Prandini, R. (eds) *Sabel, C.F., Esperimenti di* nuova *democrazia. Tra globalizzazione e localizzazione*, 7–40. Roma: Armando Editore.

Ricucci, R. (2010). *Italiani a metà. Giovani stranieri crescono*, 66–71. Bologna: Il Mulino.

Rawls, J. (1996). *Political liberalism*. New York: Columbia University Press.

Rodotà, S. (2014). *Solidarietà. Un'utopia necessaria*. Roma–Bari: Laterza.

Ross, M. (2011). The Struggle for EU Citizenship: Why Solidarity Matters. In Arnull, A., Barnard, C., Dougan, M. and Spaventa, E. (eds) *A Constitutional Order of States?: Essays In EU Law in Honour of Alan Dashwood*, 283–300. London: Bloomsbury Publishing.

Saint-Blancat, C. (2015). 'Italy'. In Cesari, J. (ed.) *The Oxford Handbook of European Islam*, 265–310. Oxford: Oxford University Press.

Salih, R. (2009). Muslim women, fragmented secularism and the construction of interconnected <publics> in Italy. *Social Anthropology/Anthropologie Sociale* 17(4), 409–23.

Saraceno, C. (2008). Tra uguaglianza e differenza: il dilemma irrisolto della cittadinanza femminile. *Il Mulino*, 4, 603–14.

Sciortino, G. (2014). A European Sociology of Migration? Not Yet, not Quite. In Koniordos, S. (ed.) *Routledge Handbook of European Sociology*, 252–67. London: Routledge.

Siim, B. (2000). *Gender and Citizenship. Politics and Agency in France, Britain and Denmark*, Cambridge: Cambridge University Press.

Spadafora, G. (ed.) (2003). *John Dewey: una nuova democrazia per il 21 secolo*. Roma: Anicia.

Touraine A. (2012). *Dopo la crisi. Una nuova società possibile*. Italian translation by Antimo, L.F. and Toscano, E. (eds). Roma: Armando Editore. (First French edn 2010. *Après la crise*. Paris: Edition du Seuil).

Viola, F. (2003). La democrazia deliberativa tra costituzionalismo e multiculturalismo. *Ragion pratica*, 11, 33–71.
Zincone, G. (1992). *Da suddito a cittadino*. Bologna: Il Mulino.
Zincone, G. (2010). *L'immigrazione e l'incerta cittadinanza*. Bologna: Il Mulino.
Zincone, G. (2011). Citizenship Policy Making in Mediterranean EU States: Italy. Available at http://eudo-citizenship.eu.
Zincone, G. (2013). La controversia dello *jus soli* in Italia: Risposta a Giovanni Sartori, 21 June 2013, Available at *http://eudo-citizenship.eu.*
Zolo, D. (1994a). Prefazione. In Zolo, D. (ed.) *La cittadinanza. Appartenenza, identità, diritti*, VII-XIX. Roma-Bari: Laterza.
Zolo, D. (1994b). La strategia della cittadinanza. In Zolo, D. (ed.) *La cittadinanza. Appartenenza, identità, diritti*, 3–45. Roma-Bari: Laterza.

Chapter 11
Translating Cultural Identities, Permeating Boundaries: Autobiographical and Testimonial Narratives of Second-Generation Immigrant Women

Cristina Greco

Introduction

In a study of gender identity and immigration there must be a specific analysis of the role played by migrants' daughters in generating pathways of construction and reconstruction of collective identities. In this chapter I'll try to deal with the key points of this issue and how it could be approached in relation to the Italian context and in connection with second-generation migrants. These issues are implied in deeper concerns typical of contemporary scenarios, especially in the Italian case, regarding the relationship between immigrants and natives, where the attention is focused on the status of women and on the emerging conflict between old and new generations. This has a lot to do with the phenomenon of globalization, not meant as flattening and standardization, but as a process of deepening differences and drawing boundaries: although these are sometimes invisible ones, they're far from destined to disappear (Sassen, 1999). In this sense, our study considers the idea of territoriality, and therefore the conception of a culture that rewrites places according to mutable elements and boundary lines that don't correspond to national borders; it also reflects on the movement of cultural material, which leads to a phenomenon of interchangeability of behaviours in cultural styles (Appadurai, 1990). It's a tension between the idea of globalization as a cultural homogenization and the idea of it as a cultural heterogeneization: the substantial difference between these concepts lies in the lack of the evaluation of the translation process, whereby – following Jurij M. Lotman's line of reasoning and his concept of 'semiosphere' – when an element is migrating from one cultural context to another, one never stays the same, because in entering another's territory it generates a sense, changes the existing information and creates new ones (1985). In this perspective, the process of identity-development lies on the border, meant as a porous and permeable membrane, the sum of the semiotic filters of translation, in an uninterrupted and articulate dialogue between various cultural entities. Such a mechanism interlaces narratives, where culture, intended as a set of texts, determines its own typological characterization depending on the way it defines itself (Lotman, 1973). Listening to others, to the self-narrating voices, sets in motion the identity-construction (Arendt, 1978); in building a dialogue, migrant women's autobiographical and testimony-narrations function as a passkey to a point of view that may affect the stereotypical concept of differences.

This study is built around testimonies taken from short stories or novels. The textual corpus consists of texts that analyse gender and cultural belonging, and individual and collective identity from an unusual point of view, the one of second-generation migrant women. Among the texts considered representative in relation to the hypotheses proposed, we mention some short stories extracted from the collection *Pecore nere* ('Black Sheep')[1] and the autobiographical novels *Un'italiana non italiana* ('A non-Italian Italian') and *La mia casa è dove sono* ('My home is where I am'); this textual corpus is based on a comparison between narrations, correlating the imaginative dimension to the facts that actually occurred. By doing so we emphasize the importance of considering the intertwining of discourses and therefore the concept of a multidiscursiveness that deploys within the semiophere and generates new areas of meaning. We use a methodology proper of the structural semiotics that, based on the paradigm of cultural semiotics, is attentive to the cultural impact of certain phenomena. This perspective allows us to understand some social, cultural and political transformations and acts like a critical analysis of social phenomena, even when the object of study is recalcitrant, as in this case, and even where the transformation processes can't be easily observed.

The look on second-generation migrant women is orientated to the understanding of the discourses on identity and migration mediated by texts. This paper is therefore an effort of contamination, not only between concepts, but also between discourses; a work that not only is based on the concepts of translation and border, but that also tries to translate the testimonies of second-generation migrant women, drawing attention to a little-known point of view in the Italian context.

From Otherness to Otherness: New Citizens between Memory and Resistance

Based on these assumptions, before proceeding it's necessary to dwell on the meaning of 'second-generations', with particular reference to the phenomenon of migration. This term, recently coined, acknowledges in Italian youth a character of mixture, identified by multiculturalism, and therefore by a heterogeneous reality consisting in both Italians of Italian origin and Italians of foreign origin.

1 *Pecore nere* is an anthology of eight short stories written by Gabriella Kuruvilla, Ingy Mubiayi, Igiaba Scego and Laila Wadia, and edited by Emanuele Coen and Flavia Capitani.

Based on the reflection about this phenomenon, which some researches called cross generation,[2] we can make two remarks: first of all, it can be an instrument to organize and preserve the culture inherited from immigrants' parents and, secondly, it can project into the future a generation that is unprecedented in the Italian context. This line of reasoning inevitably leads us to think that culture is the 'non-hereditary memory of the community' (Lotman and Uspenskij, 1975) and that some identities function as borders in translation and self-determination processes within the semiosphere[3] (i.e. the total semiotic space in which communication processes can be realized, developing new information). Therefore, when speaking of second generations or new citizens, we don't mean to imply a form of finished life, but we acknowledge the multiple differences that distinguish this category in comparison both with tradition and with the two cultures, the one of origin and the one of the home country or the country where the subject lives. As a result, this heterogeneity affects in a deeper or shallower way values, behaviours and interpretations of our culture, but also of others' cultures. We're not exclusively talking about *a priori* differences, but we're dealing with dissimilarities that exist and, last but not least, express themselves through the texts. This also implies the overthrow of some concepts trapped in the idea of monoculture, mono-ethnic and mono-religious dimensions, first of all the notion of citizenship, constantly called into question by women and men born and raised in Italy.

The efforts to draw a new concept of citizenship aim to redefine national and transnational borders, not only geographical but also cultural ones, using expressions like 'cultural citizenship' (Turner, 1994) and 'post-national citizenship' (Soysal, 1994). This raises a fundamental question: is it possible to create a new idea of identity and recognition? In this perspective, the solution of dual citizenship, which combines the *jus sanguinis* to the *jus soli*, would be the answer to the need for change claimed by the contemporary world. So, if on the one hand stands the idea of a society committed to preserving its culture, and therefore to defining its identity, on the other hand arises a system that leads us to imagine an interruption of that fixed idea of self-retreat and self-designation, a phenomenon that Lévi-Strauss called 'ethnocentrism' (1973).[4] In this direction, society has to choose between preserving its culture and imagining a path on the

---

2 See Visconti and Napolitano, 2009.

3 Lotman develops the concept of semiosphere, borrowing it from Vernadskij's biosphere, a biological term he used in 1926 to describe the set of living organisms. The semiosphere, instead, is an abstract and concluded system, a semiotic space in which the different signs relate to each other and in which it's not possible to consider the elements individually.

4 In *Race et histoire* (1973), Lévi-Strauss calls ethnocentric the prejudice that makes a group think that humanity will end at the borders of their own village, naming themselves as good people and naming the outsiders bad, evil and so on. Meanwhile, the cooperation between men could lead to a homogenization of identity, undermining the process of self-determination.

side of those who actually compose today's society, for example privileging second-generation migrants instead of Italian citizens residing abroad who now belong just marginally to the society they left behind. The search for an identity given by self-retreat has to be replaced by an identity built on a relational perspective, where the other is a constitutive part of identity (Levi-Strauss, 1977). Therefore, we can find a connection to Lotman's idea that the process of translation is a gesture that moves from otherness to otherness (1985) and that, starting from listening to the other, leads to a mutual transformation.[5] This shift is radical in second-generation migrant women, since they fulfil the experience of translatability, regarding not only the linguistic universes, through bilingualism, but also regarding cultural codes, for example gender ones, according to which translation happens on the border between two cultures, but also within their own tradition.

Therefore, reducing the debate about gender and second-generation migrant women to 10 pages and to the Italian context is not doable, since the issues and the theoretical matters cover different fields of knowledge and produce a variety of texts, not only scientific texts (gender studies, postcolonial studies, etc.), but also cultural expressions. Let's take, for example, the prolific work of the so-called postcolonial and migrant literature, or the significant contribution that, in recent years, has come from the internet, which is a fundamental resource for the study of strategies for identity-construction of migrant and, obviously, of second-generation migrants. Once again, these phenomena reflect themselves in associative organizations which create connections between collective memory and individual creativity. A good example is the Archive of Migrant Memories (AMM),[6] which gathers together contributions from writers, directors and researchers, migrant and non-migrant. We are dealing with areas of valorization of national and transnational collective memory, where selection of memory acts like a form of resistance to forgetfulness and where first and second generations of migrants and natives are put into dialogue.

Narrations by Second Generation Migrant Women between Identity and Difference

This research tries to investigate the strategies of identity-construction that we can find in the narrations made by second generations; we have to look into the narratives to see where and how the issue of translation and creolization of identity surfaces. It's intriguing, in this sense, the attempt to describe the differences underlying

5 Lotmanian theory is all focused on the dialogue between self and other and on the strategies that convey the difference, essential to a culture to define itself in relation to an out-of-self. For more details, see Lotman, 1985.

6 http://www.archiviomemoriemigranti.net/. For the question of second-generation immigrants in Italy, see also http://www.secondegenerazioni.it/about/ and http://www.yallaitalia.it.

the production and therefore the reception of cultural meanings that, like in this case, define gender together with dominated cultures. Not always have second-generation migrant women been objects of attention: media attention often includes them in a discussion generically related to migrants, often resulting in the common idea that they are a problem that needs to be resolved. In addition, in the Italian case, this unifying vision derives also from totally ineffective integration policies. Therefore, narrations allow to destabilize aspects of the Italian culture considered immutable, since the appearance of the other is upsetting and never definitive and, by its own nature, helps to deconstruct the existing situation. We're dealing with realities that appear adamant, but that actually are continually renegotiated.

So, narration represents still an ideal opportunity for subjectivity-construction and self-determination which, in the case of second-generation migrants, establish the dialectic between identity and difference. If narrating the self means building a place where not only facts could surface, but also an inner thought, for a woman – even more when it comes to second-generation migrants – means the possibility to draw paths of life imbued with passion, testifying also to some kind of denial of the historical models of femininity derived from the culture of origin and the one of destination.

The autobiographical narrations analysed in this study lay bare the border role of second-generation migrant women: as 'keepers of tradition', they are aware of the customs and they can take on the role of the encoder between different parties, establishing the cultural model of memory exchange. Like their parents, second-generation migrant women help to preserve the memory of the culture of origin, just like their mothers – who also bear the burden of something problematic, often a trauma – preserve the traces of the female identity of their families, but at the same time they develop a point of view that rarely reaches its recipient through other means and that stands at the crossroads between past and present, between transformation and conservation. As already said, this has to do with the issue of the weakening of the borders and with the notion of creolization.

The concept of culture is so inextricably tied to the narration of self, starting from a personal history that is inscribed in the history of the community of reference, intended as a prerequisite of both individual and collective identity.

Considering an object of analysis such as autobiographical and testimony-narrations made by second-generation migrants, we can recognize its specificity, primarily due to the work of deconstruction and construction that continually occur in these texts, but also due to the constant effort in reducing disparities and dissonances mediated by this generation.

The Reconsideration of Roles and the Issue of Belonging

The semiotic study of narrations, from the perspective of Algirdas Julien Greimas's generative semiotics, allows us to highlight a variety of elements, such as enunciative strategies, values, themes and passions, able to create an effect of sense[7] of involvement in the recipient. It's here that the transition takes place from what is visible to what is invisible, implicit and unspoken. The regulatory mechanism of this passage is the narrative grammar,[8] which ensures the congruence of meaning that the reader is invited to enter. Let's see some of the extracts I consider the most representative for this subject. As we'll see, in some of these narrations we can notice the surfacing of a subjectivity that on the one hand seeks the detachment from the stereotypes attributed to immigrants in the restraining context of Italian culture, while on the other hand re-elaborates the status of women within the family, especially regarding the tensive relationship between parent and child.

The meanings within translation stand opposite to the fixity of the gender category, redefining the borders of discourse, but also the semiotic forms that regulate the processes of identification and cultural affiliation.

> Not because I'm black I have to be actively involved. Instead, my sister is like that. Because she was a teenager, she had to have the turmoil and do all the crap that went through her head. Because she was black, she had to attend all the meetings, all the assemblies, all the migrant associations, she had to go to all the festivals of all communities and consume shoes and vocal cords in every demonstration, in every pit of Italy (for the happiness of my mother, who gave vent to her concerns on me).

In this passage, extracted from the short story by Ingy Mubiayi Kakese entitled *Concorso* ('Contest'),[9] included in the anthology *Pecore nere* (Kuruvilla et al., 2005), the reconsideration of roles arises from the need of the narrating subject to answer to highly stereotyped models, denying their familiarity to define its own identity. The narrator-self is built on a strong passionate component, from which surfaces the dysphoric term when talking about the rejection of other's expectations ('Not because I'm black I have to be actively involved') and a state of agitation always attributed to the other ('gave vent to her concerns on me'), and in which the subject appears modalized[10] according to a not-wanting-to-be.

The narrator's strategy, which corresponds with the simulacrum of the author inscribed in the enunciate, consists in showing a personal transformation that

7 The words 'effect of sense', that Greimas and Courtés (1982) drew on from G. Guillame, refer to an impression of reality that our senses generate when they get in contact with the sense. See Pezzini, 2007.

8 In the conceptual design proposed by Greimas, semiotic and narrative grammar is placed at the most abstract level of the generative path of sense. For more details, see 'Generative path' in Greimas and Courtés, 1982.

9 Ingy Mubiayi Kakese was born in Cairo to an Egyptian mother and a Zairian father; when she was just a little girl her family moved to Rome, where she still lives.

10 We can consider the modalization as the production of a model utterance, that overdetermines a descriptive one (Greimas and Courtés, 1982).

already occurred: see the detachment from certain values and from a political framework, where the other's action ('Because she was black, then she had to attend all the meetings …') is negatively sanctioned and coincides with the rejection of the collective ideology here associated with black pride and, therefore, with a preservation of its own origins.

Another thematic isotopy frequent in autobiographical second-generation narrations is the relationship between belonging to the culture in which one is born or in which one has lived since childhood, and the adherence, or its attempt, to their fathers' and mothers' religion, as often happens with young Muslim women.

> So, we are Muslim. Born and raised in Rome (except my mother). But always Muslim. My mother came here very young, but in Cairo she had been taught the basic notions of obedience to Allah and His Prophet (at this point I should say that peace be upon him, but I take it for granted) and the Five Pillars … (*Concorso* in Kuruvilla et al., 2005)

If on the one hand we recognize the denial of an ideological, cultural and political belonging, of the stereotype of the black person actively involved in politics, on the other hand, as we can clearly see from the extract above, we identify the acknowledgement of a religious affiliation and, therefore, a sharp distinction of the borders. This is also due to the transition from a determination of the 'self', who was in contrast with the other, to the appearance of a 'we'. Religion, in this sense, is perceived, regardless of whether one refuses it or not, as an element to define identity, both cultural and religious.

In many narrations made by second-generation migrants we can observe a tendency in avoiding to stress out one belonging to the detriment of another one, according to a principle of non-exclusion, which would see on the one hand migrants as fully integrated subjects, while on the other hand as subjects placed outside the context of growth. In fact, these narrations don't show an attempt of self-definition of the subject as a migrant, since often it wouldn't be correct, but neither do they show a self-definition of the subject as exclusively Italian.

The Passionate Subject and the Never-Lost Identity

The final sequence of *Ruben* (Kuruvilla et al., 2005), a short story written by Gabriella Kuruvilla, born in Milan to an Indian father and a Milanese mother, describes the experience of a woman who struggles with an unexpected pregnancy. In connection with other texts part of the corpus, this story helps us to define the co-ordinates of the feminine narrations we are dealing with, because it describes a difficult personal experience and explores the theme of the dialogue between three distinct generations: the one of the immigrant father, the one of the daughter, born in Milan, and the one of the child she is expecting, as a joining link with lost origins.

The story also allows us to deepen our considerations about identity-construction.

> Perhaps you, next generation, will be able to approach more spontaneously and naturally your Indian quarter. Mathematically it already weighs less, it's diluted. But probably the black kids will look at you and will point their finger at you again, and more. Still laughing. They won't be able to recognize you as a brother, but instead I hope that you could do it.

The search of the subject is narrated by an 'I' who talks to a 'you', showing the syncretism between the narrator and the subject of doing, the one who performs the action. In the transition from the first to the second extract, we can see a shift from a 'you' to an 'I': while the first makes a future-tense speech, the second one makes a past-tense speech.

> I had just made friends with my black half, I was hoping to be able to excite me in a frenzy of africanitude. India wasn't enough for me anymore. Because India, a country unknown to me, for me was always just one of the many Countries in the Third World. Whereof, in Italy, I could see emigrants. The marginalized. Their, identical, situation. So India, South America or Africa: the difference didn't exist.

These two parts of the story are meaningful because they are based on a twin-narrative program that involves the discovery of the self and the other: in the first case it's referred to as a pragmatic relationship between the self and the other, while in the second case it's first of all referred to as a cognitive doing of the subject in relation to another one, which is part of the self ('I had just made friends with my black half …'). These passages recall the diaristic-epistolary communication, which finds its highest expression in the parental relationship. The subject configures itself both as epistolary and passionate subject. The epistolary discourse is introduced by the dialogic subject based on an inter-subjective isotopy 'Perhaps you'; 'but instead I hope that you could do it'. At the same time, the subject makes a passionate path, which intensifies in the latter extract: first the fear of rejection ('But probably the blacks kids will look at you and will point their finger at you again …'), then the faith ('I hope that you could do it'); at last, a euphoric state of desire for a reunification with its origins ('I had just made friends with my black half, I was hoping to be able to excite me in a frenzy of africanitude'), but then its denial, a dysphoric state where the subject is modalized according to a not-knowing and not-being.

It's here that the analysis allows us to reason about the idea of identity-construction and reconstruction. Precisely, the expression 'my black half' is a starting point for this reflection. To examine it in depth we compare it with another exemplar text. It's the autobiographical novel *Un'italiana non italiana* by Nima Sharmahd (2011), a researcher and author of Iranian origin.

The novel tells the adventures of a young Iranian woman, born in England – because her parents wanted to assure her European citizenship – and raised in Italy since she was three months old, just like the author describes herself. Since the allograph preface (Genette, 1987) by Anna Vanzan, Iranologist and Islamologist, we can locate the thematic–figurative isotopy[11] of identity-denial.

> With relief and increasing pleasure I immersed myself in her story, almost Kafkaesque, but narrated with great irony and grace.

While on the one hand the preface acts as a reading guide, on the other hand the presence of enunciation marks ('I') identifies the narrator as witness of the narrated events.

> We can "label" Nima as Second Generation or New Italian, although Nima is just a young woman who should be considered Italian to all intents and purposes …

In addition, following Genette's reasoning, this text presents itself as a preface-manifesto, because it's an attack on 'bureaucracy, insipience and lack of foresight of the [Italian] immigration policy' and an adhesion to the cause. She also activates a veridictive[12] mechanism at the moment when she declares the adherence of the novel to autobiography, an issue that presents us with the problem of reality effect and already outlines the profile of a potential reader. In doing so, she attests the plausibility of the events that will be narrated and puts the reader in a wanting-to-know position, stimulating his desire to read.

> Actually, more than one "DOC Italian" reader, who comes close to this brief autobiography, would think that he had to overcome similar misfortunes to obtain a document at the Land Registry, a municipal certificate, a change of phone company … only that, for the 'foreigners' like Nima, things can be more complicated and painful.

A work like this requires us to consider something that Genette calls 'peritext', i.e. all the elements that we can find in the volume space, as the author's name, the preface, the epigraph and so on. These are verbal-visual strategies which relate to the effectiveness of the text. In fact, if we take a look at the title *Un'italiana non italiana*, we can find from the very beginning an attempt to connect worlds

11 The term isotopy indicates the occurrences of classemes, but also of semic, thematic and figurative categories. It's like a *fil rouge* that passes through the discourse-enunciation and that is able to disambiguate its sense (Greimas and Courtés, 1982).

12 This term refers to veridiction and to discourses that aren't true, but produce the effect of sense of 'truth'. For more details, see Greimas and Courtés, 1982.

that seem distant and to emphasize the status of 'identity crisis'. And this global isotopy is confirmed by the narration, creating an internal reference.[13]

> My first eighteen years passed like this, in the back of a stationer's shop, our house often invaded by friends who came from all over, the school and the unawareness of the quarrels that a foreign citizen living in Italy have to face at full age. Yes, I knew that my mother every year had to struggle with offices, residence permit to be renewed, expired insurance cards, but it didn't affect me that much, it was faraway, and I had other things to think about. But my nineteenth birthday woke me up from numbness. At full age, in fact, my residence permit couldn't be included in my mother's one and I had to have one of my own, and mine alone. And so began my odyssey, an adventure in common with all foreigners in Italy, unless they are connected or unless they won some Olympic medals.

Identity and Difference

It's here that the debate I already anticipated about the strategies of identity-construction allows us to take a step forward, talking not only about identity but also about identification, i.e. an identity in process. Keeping this in mind, we can find a comparison in the concept of 'sliding identities', that Stuart Hall utilizes to understand the continuous transformations of the self: 'such positional identities are narratives … they are stories we tell ourselves about ourselves. They are necessarily fictional' (1995: 63–9). This concept means that individual and collective identities are never defined, stable, immutable; instead, they are constantly changing. In close connection with the subject of this investigation, he asserts that identities come from many places and they are first of all stories, indicating this process of transformation with the expression 'radical historicization'. This idea is perfectly captured by Hall's concept of 'ethnicity', i.e. a form of national identity that isn't exclusive, but open, and it's the place where history, language and culture participate in the construction of subjectivity and identity. Even more relevant is the consideration of the 'cultures of hybridity', on which Hall elaborates in a study on the origins of the third-generation young black men who live in England (Hall, 1992). It appears that, though knowing their origins and recognizing being English, these young people don't want to choose a belonging in a neat way.

The theme of the border once again becomes a key element to understand the identity developments which, in crossing physical, cultural and generational borders, upset the existing set-up, conserving traces of their own past, thus

13 This expression refers to the fact that every discourse builds an internal reference capable of supporting other levels of discourse. For an analysis of external reference and its overcoming, see Greimas and Courtés, 1982; Eco, 1975 and 1997.

rewriting their identity positions. They're unprecedented configurations, which don't confine their origins to oblivion but conserve their perceived fragments. The subjects involved in various ways bear in their biographies the signs of the cultures of origin, of their traditions and languages, things that make even more imperative a study of autobiographical narrations. All of this confirms the fact that identity and difference are inextricably tied: individuality is built from different antagonisms, which are ethnic, cultural, gender, social and so on. Based on this conception, the conduct of the 'dominant' culture, generalizing in calling everyone 'immigrant' or 'second-generation', tends to look at such categories as if there were no differences between them. On the contrary, they often have nothing in common and are deeply disconnected due to different cultural translation.

The fragmentary nature of the subject, this suspended and floating identity, emerges prominently in *Un'italiana non italiana* (Sharmahd, 2011), especially in the steps that the subject narrator (also the subject of doing) makes becoming the subject of the wanting-to-be:

> I looked away from the optical shop and I looked around. The coming and going of the people was the usual, but it seemed to me to discover it for the first time. Some were going to work, some were taking a break, some were taking a walk with their child. I recognized a few faces, I stopped to watch them and I realized that I wanted to be like them, an Italian on paper. It had never happened to me before.

> The entire house was imbued with the smell of Iranian food mixed with my mum's cigarette smoke, and it seeped through my clothes and my soul. Knick-knacks, paintings, books, colors, carpets, fabrics. Everywhere. Everyone who entered the house, found it cozy, warm, alive. That house, instead, weighed on me for its diversity, its intrusiveness, its chaos. Only now I can love it and make it part of me. Back then I was ashamed of it.

Here the imaginary is orientated to the past thanks to the pronouns, the past tense, on the track of a specific memory. In fact, in this particular passage, the details play a fundamental role ('Knick-knacks, paintings, books, colors, carpets, fabrics'): they create an effect of reality (Barthes, 1984) through the medium of the description itself that would appear insignificant at first sight. On the contrary, those minute fragments aren't there to reproduce reality, but to mean it.

In this direction, the individual memory seems to require a cultural and social reference frame within which to share the memories and the experience of a self who, as in this case, splits from itself.

> Now, this bureaucratic journey that I was obliged to make in my Italian *foreignitude* showed in broad daylight all my contradictions, all the riches, the divisions and the fragments of me that I'd have wanted to sew together to fully inhabit myself (Sharmahd, 2011).

That framework is the recognition of her being Italian, against the dominant will that would want to flatten to a single dimension and simplify subjectivities, which varies depending on the bilingualism, on their parents' migratory history and on the life context.

Passional Dimension and Ironic Discourse between Knowledge and Belief

Another interesting perspective on which I wish to dwell is the epistemic assumption concerning the relationship between knowledge and belief and the passional discourse (Greimas, 1987; Greimas and Fontanille, 1993).

> The moments spent on those mountains are some of the dearest memories that I carry in my soul. They were beautiful. They were tremendous. Those were the years when I was trying to find a place in the world among the many contradictions that cross the desire to be myself and to please others at the same time. Often it was me who surrendered, ending up looking like I thought others wanted me to be. So I dressed like a boy, always with pants and oversize sweaters, afraid of betraying that wild pact that I felt I had secretly made in our group of adventurers. It took some time before I learned that the opposites that animate me could coexist inside me. It took some time before I opened the doors to my femininity. (Sharmahd, 2011)

In this latter passage, as well as in the previous one, in which I emphasized the importance of the detail, it's possible to outline an affective and value-driven itinerary, which has to do with the field of knowledge and passion, defining a way to know and to 'show', i.e. a way to bring the readers closer to what is shown ('The moments spent on those mountains are some of the dearest memories that I carry in my soul'). This happens through the construction of a gaze that circumscribes a position of meaning and belief to which the reader can decide to join or not. In addition, on the discursive level, on the one hand the thematic–figurative isotopy of gender identity is constituted through the lexemes 'male' and 'female'. Both interact with the having-to-be of the subject ('like I thought others wanted me to be'), where the 'destinant' is other people's judgment: this puts the subject in a certain state of mind, the fear, in opposition to desire, thus the wanting-to-be, where the anti-subject is the inner conflict ('the opposites that animate me').

The relationship between gender identity and ethnic identity is problematic, since it concerns the impact that the first has or may have on the construction of individual and collective identities in the process of mediation between adherence to the culture of origin and to the culture of birth or in which one grows up. In this sense, generation could have an impact in terms of dissonance among adult migrant women and young women born or raised in the country where they live: while the narrations of the first ones are consistent with the female model activated by the culture of origin, the autobiographical and testimonial stories of the latter ones bring to light the traces of the subject's adherence to the values of the culture in which they live, repudiating, sometimes partially, the values of the culture of origin.

There are also cases where these dissonances are developed in a system of oscillation of the tensive states, generated by introducing into the text the modes of the ironic discourse. One of the texts revealing this trend is *La mia casa è dove sono* (2010), a successful autobiographical novel by Igiaba Scego, who was born in Italy from Somali parents who got away from Siad Barre's dictatorship. It's a story based on a memory, which is not only the memory of a young woman who tries to remember her roots, deeply intertwined with her city, Rome, but also the memory of past generations of immigrants up to colonialism. Therefore it's a narration that contributes to the reconstruction of the post-memory.

> The life of my family is a long act of will.
>
> When my mother told her stories I, a girl born and raised in Rome, was shaking like a leaf and more. But I didn't run away, because I always wanted to get to the end. See the bad guy punished and the good one on the throne. A Manichaean world that reassured me. A cruel world, but neat. And like any child worthy of his name I was a little sadistic.
>
> No, don't think badly of me now. I am a sweet and sensitive woman, I'm honey and ginger, I'm cinnamon and cardamom. I know that the words I just said depict me as a *dhiigmiirad*, a drinker of human blood. But in fairy tales we choose a way of life and death. We bind ourselves to the ancestral world of our forefathers.

The recognition of the witness figure ('When my mother told her stories') as the one who narrates the events he saw and lived, helps to create an effect of sense of reality and truth and leads us to talk about a fiduciary contract. In this case, 'the object of persuasive doing is the *veridiction*, that is to say, the truth … of the enunciator, the hope for counter-object is the 'confidence', 'credence' or, simply, 'truth-belief' that the enunciatee places in the uttered discourse' (Greimas, 1988: 180).

It's a strategy that emphasizes the testimony, where the receiver is the simulacrum of the reader inserted in the utterance and where the text creates an effect of involvement in the reader staging a dialogic me–you relationship ('No, don't think badly of me now') and a return effect to the instance of the enunciation, which helps to create an impression of reality and identification.

> That group consisted of me, my brother Abdulcadir, his son Mohamed Deq and our cousin O. We were gathered around a wooden table. In front of us a steaming cup of spiced tea. Around us the threads of our journeys and our new belongings. We were part of the same family, but no one made the same journey of another

> one. Each one of us had in his pocket a different Occidental nationality. Instead, in our heart we had the pain for the same loss. We grieved for our Somalia, lost in a war that we could hardly understand. A war begun in 1991 and of which no one could see the end. We were a bit like those old jokes. There are an Englishman, an Italian, a Finnish and …

The tale of an individual experience becomes a collective one when there's a transition from an 'I' to a 'we'. This shift reduces the distance between an individual pain and a collective trauma by using the term 'war' and lexicalizing the absence, using the term 'lost', characterized by dysphoria, a painful condition. The appearance of the 'pain', the dysphoric status of the subject, caused by the disjunction from the object of value, in this case Somalia, takes place in the transformation of the subject of state into the subject of doing ('We grieved'). The passionate dimension of the trauma, however, is interrupted by a euphoric state, which indicates the emotional discontinuity and the change of the patemic findable throughout the text. This characteristic is often found in narrations in which emerges a sense of respect for traditions, but it takes shapes an ironic-grotesque discourse about the parents' lifestyles. This ironic arrangement produces an overturning of the thought, orientated to the construction of a point of view different from the ordinary. The alternation between dysphoric situations (pain, trauma, war, injustice, cruelty, etc.) and euphoric moments, determined by the introduction of ironic subtexts, has a dual function: on the one hand it establishes a dialogue that only at this level provides a complicity between text and reader, and on the other hand, just by setting the tensive rhythm, it keeps alive the reader's interest.

Conclusions

This research is not concluded, because there are many texts on which it would be interesting to work on, in the direction of a greater perspective regarding the theories and the conceptual framework I highlighted here; I would also like to analyse the socio-cultural impact of certain narrations and direct testimonies, such as interviews and life stories, that it was not possible to include in this context, but that I consider just as much relevant to the put forward hypothesis.

In most cases, we're dealing with writings and artistic expressions that operate a break of the net of stereotypes, grasping a new and conscious way of thinking and imagining the existence. Here, according to a representativeness principle, I choose to give preference to the writing, which arises as a space of creation and at the same time as a place of self-redefinition, of identity reconstruction and as a place of restoration of those 'divisions and pieces of me', which a narrative of this kind helps to sew or sew again.

From the analysis of the autobiographical narrations that constituted the textual corpus of this study emerges the need to rethink traditions and to promote contamination processes. We're dealing with a tension towards the new, where second-generation migrant women represent a model, because they don't conform with a total rejection of their origin, let alone with the uncritical acceptance of the culture in which they live, but they adapt to ways to live and inhabit the cultures adopted both from their families and from the country that they feel their own.

From the narrations emerges a female subject in transformation, who starts from the personal history of who has seen and lived, of who has made the journey, to become, in turn, testimonial.

In the testimony narrations of second-generation migrant women the value of wanting-to-be and knowing-to-be, rather than having-to-do and knowing-to-do, which on the contrary characterizes the stories of the previous generations, is crucial. In fact, their stories focus on being subjects: they don't narrate stages and proofs (like in their mothers and fathers' stories), but the realization of the subject and its expertise, its will and its belief, where the events reflect an inner state. We are dealing with a synthesis dimension, a work of translation that second-generation migrant women daily implement, something that for them is dilemmatic because it has to take into account both the difference and the identity of feeling part of an encompassing subject. That's why this transformation won't be only about an individual disposition but will depend on a collective connection, in which the primary role won't be played by individual elements but by that macro-system called semiosphere.

References

Appadurai, A. (1990). Disjuncture and difference in the global culture economy. *Theory, Culture, and Society*, 7, 295–310.

Arendt, H. (1978). *The Life of the Mind*. McCarthy, M. (ed.) New York: Harcourt Bace Jovanovich.

Barthes, R. (1984). L'effet de réel. In *Le bruissement de la langue. Essais critiques IV*, 167–74. Paris: Éditions du Seuil.

Eco, U. (1975). *Trattato di semiotica generale*. Milano: Bompiani.

Eco, U. (1997). *Kant e l'ornitorinco*, Milano: Bompiani.

Genette, G. (1987). *Seuils*. Paris: Éditions du Seuil.

Greimas, A.J. and Courtés, J. (1982). *Semiotics and Language: An Analytical Dictionary*. Translation by Crist, L., Patte, D. et al. Bloomington: Indiana University Press (French edn 1979. *Sémiotique. Dictionnaire raisonné de la théorie du langage*. Paris: Hachette).

Greimas, A.J. (1987). *On Meaning: Selected Writings in Semiotic Theory*. Translation by Collins, F.H. and Perron, P. Minneapolis: University of Minnesota Press (French edn 1983. *Du sens II. Essais sémiotiques*. Paris: Éditions du Seuil).

Greimas, AJ. (1988). *Maupassant: The Semiotics of Text*. Translation by Perron, P. Amsterdam and Philadelphia: J. Benjamins (French edn 1976. *Maupassant. La sémiotique du texte*. Paris: Éditions du Seuil).

Greimas, A.J. and Fontanille, J. (1993). *The Semiotics of Passions. From States of Affairs to States of Feelings.* Translation by Collins, F.H. and Perron, P. Minneapolis: University of Minnesota Press. (French edn 1991. *Sémiotique des passions: Des états de choses aux états d'âme.* Paris: Éditions du Seuil).

Hall, S. (1992). New Ethnicities. In Donald, J. and Rattansi, A. (eds) *'Race', Culture and Difference*, 252–9. London: Sage.

Hall, S. (1995). Fantasy, Identity, Politics. In Carter, E., Donald, J. and Squires, J. (eds) *Cultural Remix: Theories of Politics and the Popular*, 63–9. London: Lawrence and Winehart.

Kuruvilla, G., Mubiayi, I., Scego, I. and Wadia, L. (2005). *Pecore nere.* Roma-Bari: Laterza.

Lévi-Strauss, C. (1973). Race et histoire. In Lévi-Strauss, C. *Anthropologie structurale deux*, 377–422. Paris: Librairie Plon.

Lévi-Strauss, C. (1977). *L'identité. Séminaire interdisciplinare dirigé par Claude Lévi-Strauss, professeur au Collège de France – 1974–1975.* Paris: Grasset.

Lotman, J.M. (1973). Different cultures, different codes. *Times Literary Supplement*, 12, 1213–15.

Lotman, J.M. and Uspenskij, B.A. (1975). Sul meccanismo semiotico della cultura. In Lotman, J.M. and Uspenskij, B.A. *Tipologia della cultura*, 39–68. Translation by Barbato Faccani, M. Milano: Bompiani (Russian edn 1971. O semioticeskem mechanizme kul'tury. In *Trudy po znakovym sistemam,* v, Tartu, 141–76).

Lotman, J.M. (1985). Una teoria del rapporto reciproco fra le culture (da un punto di vista semiotico). In Lotman, J.M. *La semiosfera. L'asimmetria e il dialogo nelle strutture pensanti*, 113–29. Translation by Salvestroni, S. Venezia: Marsilio (Russian edn 1983. K postroeniju teorii vzaimodejstvija jul'tur (semiotièeskij aspekt)).

Pezzini, I. (2007). *Il testo galeotto. La lettura come pratica efficace.* Roma: Meltemi.

Sassen, S. (1999). *Migranti, coloni, rifugiati. Dall'emigrazione di massa alla fortezza Europa.* Translation by Gregorio, M. Milano: Feltrinelli (German edn 1996. *Migranten, Siedler, Flüchtlinge. Von der Massenauswanderung zur Festung Europa.* Frankfurt am Main: Fischer Verlag.

Scego, I. (2010). *La mia casa è dove sono.* Milano: Rizzoli.

Sharmahd, N. (2011). *Un'italiana non italiana. Le peripezie di una 'straniera' in Italia.* Bologna: Gingko edizioni.

Soysal, Y.N. (1994). *Limits of Citizenship: Migrants and Post-national Membership in Europe.* Chicago: Chicago University Press.

Turner, B.S. (1994). Postmodern culture/modern citizens. In van Steenbergen, B. (ed.) *The Condition of Citizenship.* London: Sage.

Visconti, L.M. and Napolitano, E.M. (2009). *Cross generation marketing.* Milano: Egea.

Index

Adorno, Theodor Wiesengrund 182
Amba Galliano 29
amnesty 2–3, 5–6, 10–11, 39
Andall, Jacqueline 42
Anderson, Bridget 42
Arendt, Hannah 72n13

Benhabib, Seyla 178, 182
Berlusconi, Silvio 182
Biagi, Enzo 43
Bollezzoli, Maria 25n13, 28
Bonomi, Luigi 29
Butler, Judith 23

Caldara, Costanza 29
Campani, Giovanna 42
Canossa, Luigi di 28
capitalism 64–6, 68–73
Capograssi, Giuseppe 67n8
Carrara, Camillo 30
Casanova, José 177, 179
Cattaneo, Celestino 30
Christianity 26, 34, 178–9, 188–90, 208
  Catholic church 31, 185, 187, 189
    Italian exceptionalism 182–5
  Catholicism 27, 34, 122, 187–90
citizenship 14–16, 65, 85–7, 89, 97–9, 102, 104–5, 110, 113, 149, 216–17
  acquisition of citizenship 6, 8, 87, 195–213
    Italian legislation 197–200
    jus culturae/jus domicilii 204–5
    jus sanguinis/jus soli 196, 200, 202, 204, 209, 217
    reform bills 202–5
  constitutional citizenship 85–7
  nationality 33, 82–3, 86–8, 91, 92n21, 129n31, 228
  second generation migrants (G2) 195–213, 215–30
    'deliberative democracy' actions 206–10
civilization 21, 26, 27, 128, 152, 162, 179, 182, 183
clandestinity 2, 6, 150
  aggravating circumstance of clandestinity 6, 150
  crime of clandestinity 6
Comboni, Daniele 21–35
Committee on Economic, Social and Cultural Rights 84
constitutionalism 79–80, 178
Coseghi, Maria Annunziata 24n12
Courtés, Joseph 220n7
criminal law 6, 120, 123, 143–59, 163–5, 170, 173–4
  cultural defence 167–8, 173
  culturally motivated crimes 143–5, 150, 155
    female genital mutilation (FGM) 145, 149–55, 164–6, 171–3, 179
    honour killing 144, 164, 166–8, 173
    male circumcision 153n14, 164, 172–3
  function of punishment 146–8
    symbolic function 6, 150, 152–4

Dalmasso, Francesca 28n28
De Lamenie De Brienne 27n27
Degli Esposti, Gianluigi 43
detention centres for immigrants 4–5
  centri di permanenza temporanea e di assistenza 4n6
  centri di identificazione e di espulsione 4n6
domestic and care work 2, 5, 7, 9, 10–11, 13, 39–59, 63–76, 91, 97, 103
  Acli-Colf 42, 44
  badante 41, 68, 73
  colf 41, 44

Filippina 45
legislation 43, 48–51
live-in/live-out domestic workers 11, 44–5, 47–9, 52
male domestic workers 53
redistribution between men and women 9, 46–7, 51–2, 64
'double burden' thesis 52, 64–5, 70
regularization of domestic workers 40
domestic violence 137n50, 144, 150, 162, 170
femminicidio (femicide/feminicide) 163, 167–8
Durham, Cole 186

Egypt 21n3, 24, 27, 29–30, 34, 128n26, 129–30, 151n10
Engels, Friedrich 68
Eritrea 23, 29–31, 33–5, 45
Ethiopia 30–32, 34
ethnocentrism 152, 217
Europe
European Court of Human Rights 72, 84, 100n13, 169, 177n1, 180–81, 187, 190
European Union (EU) 3, 10–11, 50, 81, 84, 89, 91, 98n5, 99–100, 106, 112–13, 131, 134–5, 199, 206
anti-discrimination law 65, 83, 88, 99–104, 110–14
EU Agency for Fundamental Rights 84, 91, 106n28, 106n29, 106n30
EU Charter of Fundamental Rights 82, 98n5, 112
EU Commission 106n28, 107n36, 209n51
EU Court of Justice 6n12, 82, 89, 112n42
EU Parliament 81
Fortress Europe 1, 10–11
evangelization 21–2, 25, 27, 30, 33–5
Comboni religious orders 21, 25, 29, 33
Mahdi revolt 23, 28–9
missions in Africa 21–37
Nigrizia 21–3, 25, 27–8
Piano per la rigenerazione dell'Africa 22, 24–5, 27
Pious Mothers/Worker Nuns of Nigrizia 21–37
indigenous novitiate 23, 31

family relationships 2, 9, 11, 45, 47, 51, 52, 54, 63–76
children interests 119–21, 125–6, 131, 133–7
family reunification 3, 7–8, 10–12, 119, 121–2, 125, 130–37
marriage 6, 8, 12, 27, 81, 87, 107, 119, 121–40, 170, 174, 179, 190
divorce 45, 119–22, 127–30, 136, 174
heterosexual and monogamous paradigm 81, 87n11, 123, 170, 174
limping marriage 129n29, 129n30
polygamy 122–5, 127, 132–5, 137, 164, 170–71, 174, 179
polygyny, *see* polygamy
repudiation 124–5, 127–30, 132–4
talaq, *see* repudiation
nuclear family 11, 131–2
Fanon, Franz 190
feminism 45, 52, 55, 63–78, 121, 162–3, 167–8, 171, 173–4, 181–3, 188–9
essentialism 66
'Failed Feminist Revolution' theory 63–5, 68–9, 72
private/public sphere 40, 45–6, 52–4, 63–4, 69, 81, 92, 111–12, 114, 121, 177–9, 182–3, 185, 187–90
self-determination 77–81, 144, 217, 219, 221
sexuality 77–8, 81–3, 85, 103, 119, 151, 152, 165–6, 182
sexual orientation 65, 72, 81–3, 87n11, 92, 99
women subordination 78, 84, 87, 111–12, 144, 189–90
anti-subalternity principle 79
anti-subordination principle 79, 97, 111–12
Festa, Andrea 31
Folbre, Nancy 65n3
Foucault, Michel 174
Fraser, Nancy 64n2

Gallino, Luciano 65n3
Gasperini, Jacopo 29
gender relations and migration 9–12, 41, 52–4, 73, 97, 112
agency 123, 127, 131, 137, 169
equality 52–5, 69, 79–83, 86, 88–9, 99, 104–7, 110–14, 119, 122, 124, 126, 130, 132, 134–6, 145–6, 148, 164–4, 169, 171, 180–90, 205, 207, 209
feminization of labour and migration 7–8, 41–2, 85
female migratory flows 7, 42, 45
gender and migration studies 7–8, 42–3, 63–4
male/female breadwinner 9, 53, 65n3, 70, 73, 90, 92
migrant women's working conditions 9–11, 43–53, 72
health conditions 100–102
mobility 8–11, 21–37, 48, 53, 90, 99, 108, 123, 185
patriarchy 45, 64–5, 70, 120–21, 123, 161–76, 182, 189–90
reproduction 8n15, 12, 34, 42, 69, 80–81, 92, 101, 105, 119–20, 172, 190
Genette, Gérard 223
Ginzburg, Natalia 44
Girola, Mariateresa 21n1
globalization 42, 63, 65–6, 69–72, 215
Google 69
Greimas, Algirdas Julien 217, 220n7, 220n8
Gruenbaum, Ellen 172n18

Habermas, Jürgen 206
Hall, Stuart 224
Horkheimer, Max 182

immigration
asylum seekers and refugees 3, 31–2, 48, 91–2, 98n3, 155n15, 166
illegal immigration 2–7, 10, 13, 39–40, 48–53, 82, 85, 87–9, 91, 98, 150
expulsion 3–6, 48, 50, 86, 136n49
refoulement 3–4
regularization 2–3, 5, 7, 8n15, 40–41, 48–51, 53, 91n19
immigration models 1–2
integration models 4n7
Mediterranean immigration model 2
industrialization 41, 43, 66n6, 70–73
intersectionality 63, 77, 82–3, 91–2, 102–4, 106, 137, 164n4, 173
class 44–8, 51–3, 78, 83, 135, 162, 164
diversity 82, 111, 113, 121, 143, 145, 148–9, 152, 155, 162, 178–9, 225
identity 44, 54, 65, 77–8, 82–5, 92, 102, 107, 111, 143–4, 147, 149, 153, 164, 170, 177–9, 182–3, 187, 196, 198, 205–208, 215–30
race 21, 23, 32, 54, 63, 77–8, 82–4, 91–2, 99, 162, 189, 191
Islam 26, 28, 122, 167–9, 172, 174, 178, 180, 182, 187, 189, 208
Hanafi school 126
Islamic Law 122–4, 127–30, 136
khola/khul 127n19, 130
Italy
colonialism 21–37, 45, 78, 164, 189–90, 227
British colonial administration 32, 33–4
constitution 70, 77–84, 86, 98n5, 104, 111–12, 119, 145–7, 150, 161–3
emigration 1, 7, 85
extracomunitari 3
Italian immigration model, *see* immigration models
Italian theory 12
migration policies and legislation 2–7, 48–51
Bossi-Fini Law 4–5, 40, 132
Foschi Law 2, 49
Martelli Law 3, 49
pacchetti sicurezza (security packages) 6, 149–50
Turco-Napolitano Law 3–4, 49
modernization 41, 43, 45, 54
welfare system 2, 5, 7, 9, 11, 29–34, 40, 47, 51, 66n5, 80, 89–91, 98n5, 104n21, 125, 145, 147, 150, 155
health and social services 4–5, 55, 68, 71, 89, 91, 98–117
women's employment rates 1n1, 8n15, 9, 45–6, 65n3

Judaism 189
Jewish circumcision 172

Kandiyoti, Deniz 173
Kimlicka, Will 143n1, 144
Kuruvilla, Gabriella 221

La Russa, Ignazio 51
Lévi-Strauss, Claude 217
Lonzi, Carla 162
Lotman, Jurij M. 215, 217n3, 218
Lotti, Vittoria 44

Mancini, Susanna 174
Marani, Pia 29n31
market 63, 64–5, 66, 70–72
labour market 5n8, 7–9, 42, 46, 49, 53n29, 91, 99, 104
Marx, Carl 161, 166
Mazza, Nicola 24, 27
Morocco 8, 126, 133
Morokvasic, Mirjana 8
Mubiayi Kakese, Ingy 220
multiculturalism 4n7, 120–23, 111, 143, 145–6, 148–9, 161–4, 166, 171, 196, 206, 216
assimilationist model 4n7, 145–6, 148, 150
multicultural conflicts 120, 149, 156n17, 161, 166, 179
Muonwe, Michael 190

Napolitano, Giorgio 200n17
National Bioethics Committee 172–3

Okin, Susan Moller 163
Organisation for Economic Co-operation and Development (OECD) 1n1
orientalism 121, 127, 182

Parreñas, Rhacel 42
Pearson, Allison 65n3
Pezzini, Barbara 111–12
Phizacklea, Annie 8
Plaskow, Judith 189
Polanyi, Karl 64
Pope Pious IX 24
postmodernism 161
Praetorius, Ina 66–7
private international law 121–3, 126, 130
international public order 122, 124–9, 132–3, 136, 183–4
Puglisi, Giuseppe 33

Quascé, Fortunata 22, 23n7, 27–8

Rawls, John 206
religious symbols 177–192
Christian symbols 180n6
crucifix 177–8, 182, 185, 187–8, 190
Islamic veil 169–70, 177–85, 187, 190
burqa 164, 169–70, 173–4, 183
Jewish symbols 177, 180n3
Roma women 91, 106–7
Roveggio, Antonio Maria 28

Salvago Raggi, Giuseppe 34
Sandel, Michael 60
Sassen, Saskia 42
Scebo, Igiaba 227
Scharffs, Brett 186
Schüssler Fiorenza, Elisabeth 188–9
secularism/secularity 146, 148, 170, 178–80, 185–90, 208
semiotics 215–17, 219–20
migrant women narrations 216–29
belonging 216, 219–21, 224, 227
semiosphere 215, 217
Sharmahd, Nima 222
Siad Barre, Mohammed 227
Sudan 22–4, 29, 34

tolerance 10, 26, 145, 147, 152, 155, 179, 188
Tomellieri, Germano 26n21
Troenzi, Carla 33

UN Refugee Agency 92

Vanzan, Anna 223
Vanzon, Carlo Antonio 22n3
Vernadskij, Vladimir Ivanovič 217n3
Vidale, Maria 21n1
Villa, Pietro 30
Vittorio Emanuele III 30

Weil, Simone 66n6, 67
World Health Organization (WHO)
106n30, 150n9, 165

Zoli, Corrado 30

Kolibri 360 GmbH
Ferdinand-Jühlke-Straße 7
99095 Erfurt, Deutschland
produktsicherheit@kolibri360.de